BALTICS TO BEIRUT

You will not lose your way in the forest of life
The mother of beasts
Will lead you through the warm brambles
Along gentle moaning valleys
(Kornelijus Platelis, Lithuanian poet)

BALTICS TO BEIRUT

A Memoir of Travel, Work, Rest and Play

by

Carole Bell

The Memoir Club

© Carole Bell 2011

First published in 2011 by
The Memoir Club
Arya House
Langley Park
Durham
DH7 9XE
Tel: 0191 373 5660
Email: memoirclub@msn.com

All rights reserved.
Unauthorised duplication
contravenes existing laws.
British Library Cataloguing in
Publication Data.
A catalogue record for this book
is available from the
British Library

ISBN: 978-1-84104-529-0

Typeset by dna graphic design, Morpeth, Northumberland
Printed by Xpresslitho, Washington, Tyne and Wear
Illustrations by Keith Robson, Hartlepool

For Alan, Alison, Carolyn and Hannah, without whose love and support I would not have had the courage to venture along the Baltic Road.

In memory of my parents Arthur and Dorothy Wharton, who are greatly missed. I hope I have inherited the commitment, duty and strength of purpose of my mother and a relaxed easy going attitude to life from my father. I have felt his invisible hand guiding me whilst writing this book.

CONTENTS

List of illustrations		ix
Foreword		xiii
Prologue		xv
Chapter 1	A Glimpse Behind the Iron Curtain	1
Chapter 2	'But It's My Right'	4
Chapter 3	Friends in the North	10
Chapter 4	Big Thoughts, Small Island	18
Chapter 5	A Safe Haven and No Rain	22
Chapter 6	Easter Celebrations in Malta	35
Chapter 7	Lithuania: In From the Cold	37
Chapter 8	First Steps Along the Baltic Road	40
Chapter 9	Lietuva – a Brief History	51
Chapter 10	Life as a 'Twinner'	56
Chapter 11	Standing at the Centre of Europe	74
Chapter 12	Hot Baths in a Cold Forest	80
Chapter 13	Communicating in Croatia	84
Chapter 14	Better Regulation in Zagreb	96
Chapter 15	A Turkish Escapade	99
Chapter 16	Further Travels Along the Baltic Road	103
Chapter 17	Warsaw and Krakow – A Tale of Two Cities	110
Chapter 18	A Middle Eastern Sojourn	114
Chapter 19	Four Excursions to Riga and a Day in Belfast	120
Chapter 20	Sveiki! Latvia	127
Chapter 21	Living in Old Riga	137
Chapter 22	The Travails of Travel	142
Chapter 23	A Balkan Assignment	146
Chapter 24	Bucharest – a Spoilt City?	156
Chapter 25	The European Debate	163
Chapter 26	In the Footsteps of Dracula	168
Chapter 27	Full Circle	176
Chapter 28	Reflections of a Traveller	179
End Notes		181
The Working Week of a Resident Twinning Advisor		182
A-Z of the European Union		185
TEN CONSUMER ADVICE TIPS		187
TEN TRAVEL TIPS		188

List of Illustrations

Maps

Map 1 A voyage from the North Sea xviii
Map 2 To the Mediterranean xix

Photographs

Between pages 44-45

1. 1966: My first car – I wish I had kept it!
2. National Egg Week 1967
3. Romania 1970: On holiday at the Black Sea
4. On the Dingli cliffs with Grace and Frank Farrugia, waiting for the sun to set
5. Vilnius 2004: Launch of the Consumer Protection Twinning Project
6. The Angel of Uzupis
7. Trakai Castle in Summer
8. Trakai Castle in Winter
9. Taking consumer protection to the regions in Lithuania in Rokiskes
10. Training at a Business Incubator in Kaunas
11. Relaxing on the regional tour
12. The Hill of Crosses, Siauliai – a place of pilgrimage
13. Vilnius skyline with its Baroque, Gothic, Renaissance buildings
14. Gedimino Prospektus – premier shopping street in Vilnius
15. Old Town, Vilnius
16. 2005: 'Last Supper' at La Provence restaurant, Vilnius

Between pages 108-109

17. Beirut 2007: Train-the-trainers group
18. A meze in Beirut with Market Surveillance Inspectors
19. Sitting on Lenin's foot – Grutas Park, Lithuania
20. Pula 2005: Enjoying a drink
21. Poland 2006: Paddling in the Baltic Sea
22. Riga opera house in the pink
23. Vela Luka – a lunar landscape
24. Beautiful Rovinj
25. 2008: Training Latvian staff in Customer Care skills
26. Nick Riordan checking out the yachts
27. Showing off my 'Soviet' cast
28. With Alan and Lelde at the office Christmas Party
29. Robin Croft in a wintry Riga
30. Bridge over the river Daugava, Riga
31. One of many bridges in Riga that are covered in locks
32. Lovers' locks

Between pages 172-173

33. Jurmala 2008: Alison, Hannah and Carolyn on the Beach, Latvia
34. Alison and Hannah Borthwick with a grumpy statue in Riga
35. Latvians celebrating Jani Day – the summer solstice
36. The family
37. 2009: On my way to work across Revolution Square, Bucharest
38. The Atheneum – my favourite building in Bucharest
39. The car park in Bucharest, now a fragrant garden for the music festival
40. Monument of Revolution commemorating those who died in the Romanian Revolution in December 1989
41. Palace of Parliament, Bucharest
42. The former Bucharest secret police building, now occupied by the Architects' Union
43. Silviu and his new wife – a Romanian Orthodox wedding in Bucharest
44. With Mike Hanson and Malcolm Adams on the office balcony in Bucharest
45. The project team in Bucharest
46. 1970: CB on the beach in Mamaia, where this journey began
47. 2011: Hannah, aged 7, at Lake Windermere
48. *'I must go down to the sea again'* – back home in Hartlepool

Foreword

The early years of this millennium were a time of great change for many countries as they relentlessly pursued their goal of becoming full members of the European Union. The people in those countries had suffered huge challenges for several decades whilst being governed by others not of their choosing. Their hopes and desires for themselves and their countries had been stifled and they were ready to seize and enjoy a different future.

Carole Bell bravely took the challenge of playing a part in those changes, and fortunately recorded her experiences and the experiences of those around her. The result is this book, a unique time-capsule of that period.

One might expect a simple travelogue – but that would be wrong. Yes, there are lots of interesting and useful facts about places which are only now becoming more regular fixtures on a traveller's itinerary – but these are greatly enhanced by Carole's personal experiences as she moved around some of those less familiar pockets of Europe. Local people add their own personal experiences and views. Their optimism and enthusiasm is heart-warming.

Since I first came into contact with Carole, some 12 years ago when we first worked together on a major UK consumer project, I have admired her energy, tenacity and eagerness to tackle difficult and diverse tasks through to successful conclusions. I believe that this book is testament to those views.

Jim Spinks

Jim Spinks is an independent adviser on consumer issues and a Trustee/Director of the UK National Consumer Federation. He was head of a trading standards and consumer service organisation for many years before developing systems to share the UK expertise in this field at home and overseas.

Prologue

'An iron curtain has descended across the Continent. Behind that line lie all the capitals of the ancient states of Central and Eastern Europe'. (Winston Churchill)

Churchill was addressing an American audience when he made his 'Sinews of Peace' speech in 1946. In it he coined the term 'Iron Curtain' to describe the line in Europe between the self-governing nations of the west and those in Eastern Europe that had recently come under Soviet communist control. The division between east and west was reinforced in 1961 when the Berlin Wall was erected, dividing half of Europe from the west for nearly three decades. When the wall came down in 1989 it took everyone by surprise, though there had been anti-Soviet protests in Eastern Europe earlier that year. In June, the Solidarity movement in Poland won seats in Parliament, resulting in a non-communist government, and this was followed by similar demands by other former soviet satellite states. Hungarian citizens demanded democratic and free elections; there was a 'Velvet Revolution' in Prague; Estonia, Lithuania and Latvia jointly staged a peaceful protest. This widespread dissent had a common aim – the restoration of independence and democratic Government. Previous protests against Soviet rule had been crushed but this time they led to the end of communism and the Cold War, though not without significant loss of life for many of those citizens fighting for freedom and democracy. Watching the amazing events unfolding in Berlin in November 1989, when thousands of East German citizens breached the wall and walked through to the west, I could not possibly have predicted that it would impact on my own future life and career.

Although I use the term 'Eastern Europe' throughout this book, I should issue a caveat because there are different views of what is meant by 'Eastern'. I once worked with Hungarians who insisted their country was in Western Europe, and many of the countries described in this book might be more correctly termed Central European. Nor do the Balkan countries fit this description. Eastern Europe is a general term, loosely referring to the European countries that broke away from Soviet-style communism and the Russian sphere of influence after the fall of the Berlin Wall, when a historical period came to an end. It includes East Germany, Czech Republic, Estonia, Hungary, Latvia, Lithuania, Poland, Slovakia and Slovenia - former communist states that became full members of the European Union on 1 May 2004, along with Malta and Cyprus. Romania and Bulgaria were admitted four years later. The region is now referred to as 'New Europe'. Far from being new, however, these are the *ancient states* referred to by Churchill that disappeared behind the Iron Curtain for so long. 'Newness' refers to the fact that they have recently acquired the status of democracy and have greater civil and economic freedoms, freedom of movement and labour. I visited these countries in a professional capacity at a unique time in their history, after the restoration of independence when they were seeking membership of the EU and NATO to become part of an expanded Europe.

I had never imagined that my work in Trading Standards would take me overseas but in 2003 I was unexpectedly offered an extraordinary opportunity: to live and work in the new democracies of Europe. It was an amazing journey. Along the way I discovered fascinating towns and cities, was beguiled by beautiful buildings and charmed by people who had suffered so much at the hands of occupying forces yet were always ready to offer a stranger friendship and hospitality. This book chronicles my work as a Consumer Protection expert in Europe and beyond and is based on diaries I kept during that time. It has been said that keeping a diary is about dealing with loneliness because it becomes your companion, and there is some truth in that. But I didn't keep a diary because I was lonely; I have always recorded episodes in my life and look upon a diary as having a conversation with a silent friend. I have written about events in my life - key moments, fears and feelings - into several hard backed notebooks, some written in shorthand (a very private business), and family and working life recorded in annual diaries, laboriously written in longhand. Latterly I have kept an electronic diary of overseas projects. It can be a chore but during the last decade when I lived alone and worked among foreigners, not having anyone to discuss the day's events with after work, it was cathartic. Written only for myself, they have inadvertently provided the source material for this book. The journey has taken me from northern England to the Mediterranean, Eastern Europe and the Middle East, from Citizens Advice - a uniquely British institution - to that of consultant working on projects for the European Commission. It is a personal memoir of some lesser known towns and cities where I have lived and worked, people I have met and places I have visited. The common link is that they were all aspiring or working toward bringing their consumer laws and enforcement regimes up to the standard of the European Union. Some, like Malta and the Baltic States, are now full Member States; others like Lebanon never will be, but with EU support they are in a better position to trade with it.

I have been privileged to live and work in this New Europe, made possible by the fall of the Berlin Wall and the enlargement of the European Union. I hope this book will encourage others to discover the beautiful towns and cities contained within that region, learn something of their history and culture and gain an insight of their struggle for independence.

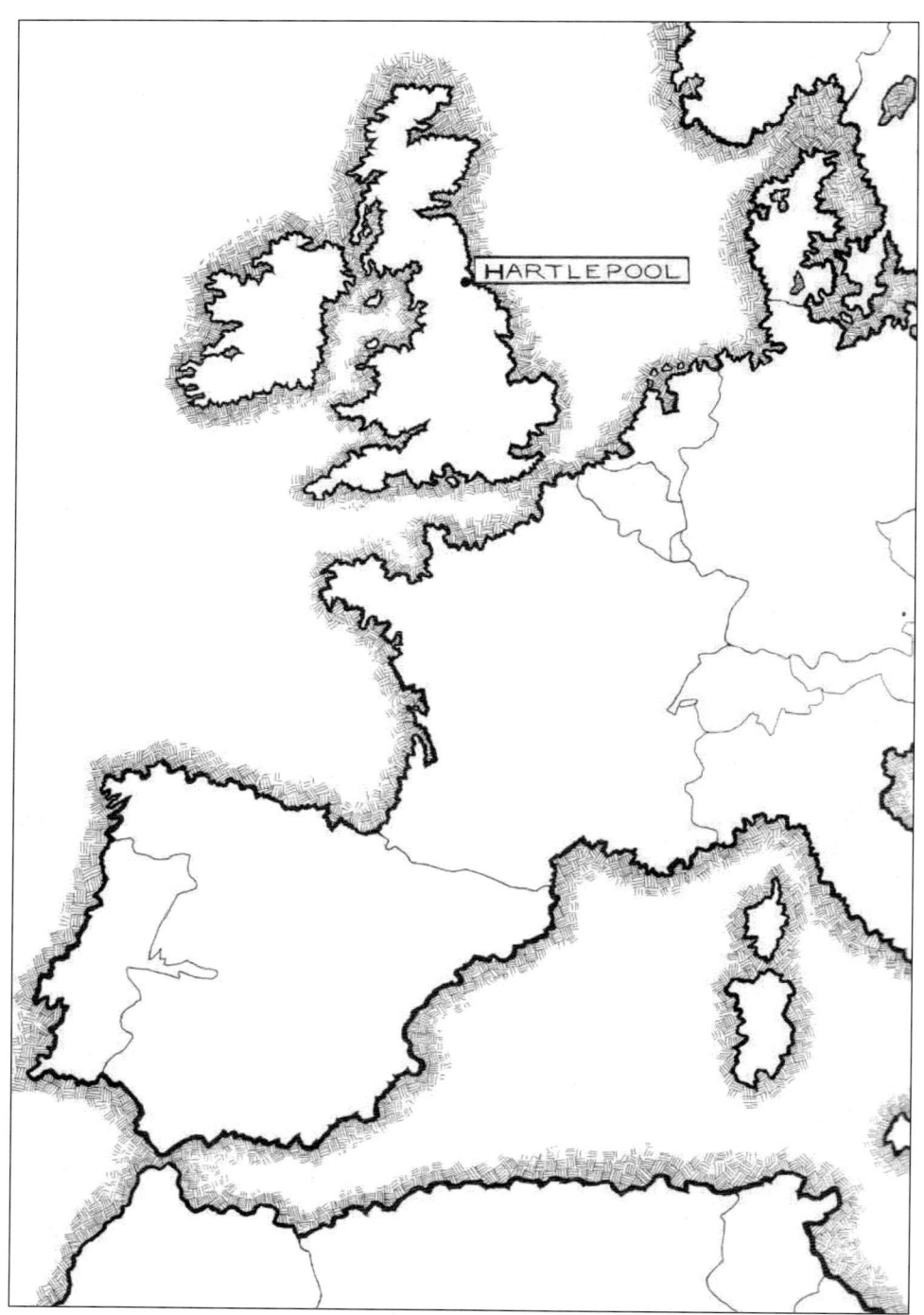

1. *A journey from the North Sea*

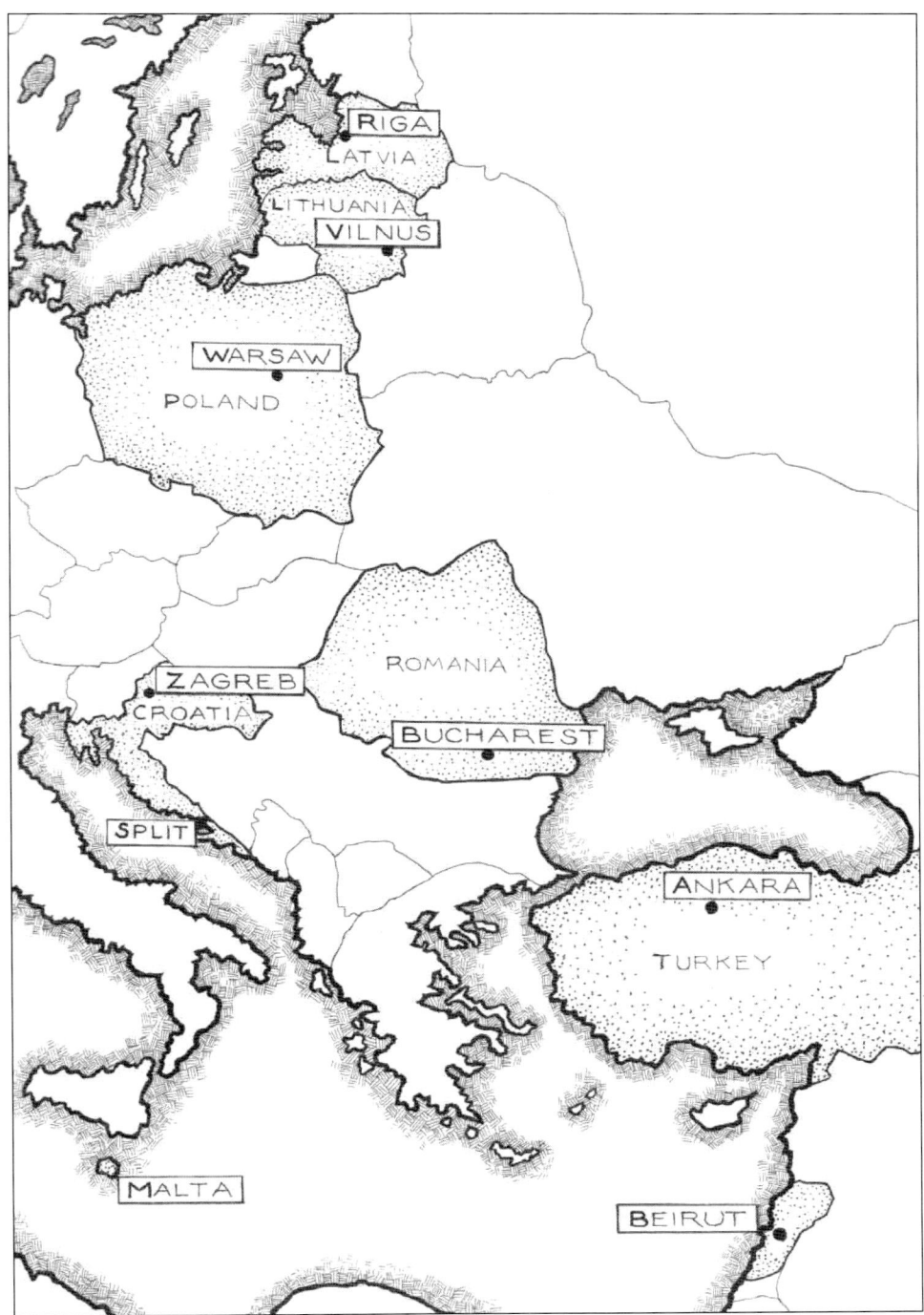

1. *To the Mediterranean*

CHAPTER ONE

A Glimpse Behind the Iron Curtain

THE EVENING IS hot and sultry. We are walking along the beach; there are sand dunes to our left, fragrant with the odour of honeysuckle. It is dark and peaceful, but far from quiet. We can hear the lapping of the waves to our right; the crickets, hiding in the sand dunes, pierce the night-time air with their noise and from a nearby café comes the sound of numerous voices, but none in a language we can comprehend. Soon we will join them, but for now prefer to savour the dusk that has temporarily shadowed the ugly buildings behind us. We dodge the old ladies brushing the streets; larger teams of women are weeding the flowerbeds with makeshift tools and they offer a gentle smile. They and we are alert to the ever-present eyes of the authorities – civil and military – who maintain a careful watch for the slightest hint of disobedience. This is Romania in 1970 and never for a moment do we forget that we have travelled behind the Iron Curtain.

A sense of chill engulfs the air and we make our way to a bar, our purpose is to watch an important football game. England and West Germany, long-standing rivals, are facing each other in the quarter-finals of the World Cup. A small black and white television is mounted high on a wall, enforcing a stiff neck upon me when I try to watch. We are the only English visitors in this bar in Mamaia on the Black Sea and, neither of us being tall, there is little hope of getting a good view. Germans and Romanians are already crowded round the television and have no intention of giving way. The café is crowded and clouded with smoke, the atmosphere tense. Suddenly there is jubilation as West Germany win 4 – 2. It is a matter beyond pride to the Germans, who have never forgotten what happened in London four years earlier, when England beat West Germany at Wembley and a victorious nation rejoiced. The cards have turned and the German supporters celebrated victory as we quietly crept out of the bar.

Winning the cup was one of many highlights in the late Sixties. It was a heady time in the West. The Beatles were still making music, though not for much longer; America had put a man on the moon; Concorde flew supersonic; Woodstock epitomized the idealistic hopes of a generation. I suspect most of this had passed Romania by. In 1970 the country was in the yoke of a strict communist regime, ruled by Ceaușescu. Our hotel, in true communist tradition, was cheerless with no plugs in the bathroom and a hard iron bed. We could only buy souvenirs at one government-owned shop and the taking of photographs was discouraged, if not forbidden. We were warned tourists could be imprisoned for changing money in the street (the demand for foreign currency was strong) and not to sell our clothes to locals, though we were offered high prices for our jeans and T-shirts. When armed soldiers circled our plane on landing we were in no doubt of the risk.

But there was another side to this country. We met a young couple in the café, Romanians who, like ourselves, were recently married. Huddled close together, we strained our ears to listen as they told us, in whispers, about their life under communism, even though they were forbidden to talk to western foreigners and feared the secret police might be listening. We reflected on the contrast in our upbringings and the freedoms we enjoyed in the West. The only possibility for us to venture outside Mamaia was to take a government-sponsored bus tour, accompanied at all times by a guard. Passing a military-looking installation en route, he shouted to tell us not to look and that the taking of photographs was not permitted. We stopped at a beach famous for its Black Sea mud where we watched a group of middle-aged and older people, who seemed to be amusing themselves scooping up mud onto their naked bodies before running into the sea. They waved their arms wildly, shouting for us to strip off and join them. Apparently the mud has healing and rejuvenating powers, but we were young and felt our bodies needed no help. That night we attended our first opera, *Die Fledermaus,* performed in an open-air theatre. It educated me on different levels: ordinary people are the same everywhere; not all citizens in a communist state are as stern and forbidding as we had been taught to expect; they are not prudish, and people of all ages and classes have a deep appreciation of classical music and opera. It also made me glad to live in a free democracy, until then something I had taken for granted.

When Alan, my husband, had spotted this holiday in a travel brochure it awakened an interest to take a peek behind the infamous Iron Curtain. Most of our friends were holidaying in Spain that year but we had wanted a different experience. It would, I thought, be my one and only foray into Eastern Europe. As it happened I was wrong, though four decades would pass before I returned to Romania.

CHAPTER TWO

'But It's My Right'

JUST BEFORE SHE DIED my mother came to visit us in our new home in Hartlepool. She was recovering from an operation and I had persuaded her to stay with us for a week while she convalesced. During her stay she had wanted to take her granddaughters, then only three and six years old, into town to purchase new winter coats. It was a welcome gesture because at this time we solely relied on my husband's income and kitting them out for the winter was always a major expense. We had also recently moved house and taken on a larger mortgage. This was the Seventies, a decade of raging inflation, strikes, the three-day week and fuel cuts. Sadly Mum was too ill to venture out of the house but on leaving to return home to Derbyshire she pushed some notes into my hand, making me promise I would buy the coats immediately. Sadly she did not see her granddaughters wear them; this was to be her final visit and she died two weeks later.

I didn't see as much of my parents as I would have liked because they still lived in Derbyshire, where I had lived for the first nineteen years of my life. Born a few years after the Second World War I was part of the 'baby boom' generation. Raised in 1950s suburbia our family life ran on traditional lines – husbands worked, wives stayed at home to shop, clean and cook and I have no recollection of my father ever preparing a meal or undertaking any domestic duties. His job was to grow the raw ingredients; in this we were quite self-sufficient. I was always by his side in our large garden, helping him to plant and harvest vegetables and fruit and tend to our chickens. My father worked at Aristoc, a local factory making fully-fashioned stockings. A clever man, he had won a scholarship to Heanor Grammar School but had to leave at sixteen because his parents needed another wage in the house, and he became an apprentice knitter of silk stockings. He told me he was glad to escape when called up for service in 1939 and seems to have enjoyed his time in the RAF. He worked huge machines that made a continuous noise night and day. I was very close to my father and as a child he sometimes allowed me to observe him at work, showing me how all the bobbins of nylon had to be wound into the machine to produce the stockings. The heat, pungent stench of grease and the roar of the machines have stayed with me. When tights were invented (essential after Mary Quant launched the mini skirt) he left and enjoyed a new career in the Civil Service, where he remained until retirement.

Toward the end of his life I asked him to write down some of his memories of growing up in the pre-war period.

'Memories tend to fade with the passing of years but some linger on,' he wrote.
> 'My school days are still very clear and I enjoyed them, I was captain of the football and cricket teams and very sad to be taken away at sixteen. One frightening aspect of my teenage years was an incident with a gun. With a friend we were roaming the fields on his uncle's farm a couple or so miles from where we lived. Suddenly the gun went off. George gave a cry, grabbed his arm and said he had been shot. The guns were both hair trigger and neither of us were experienced with guns at that time but the horrible fact was it was my gun that had discharged and shot poor old George in the arm! After a week or so in hospital he was discharged, seemingly no worse for this bad experience. We were both well known at the local billiard halls and after this whenever I appeared in the doorway all the other lads dived under the tables for cover! There were no hard feelings on the part of George or his parents, who could have been upset to say the least as he lost a week or two off work without any income.'

Growing up in the 1950s my sister and I were free to play in the streets or at the 'rec', where the poor state of the swings and slide would horrify today's parents. Such freedom was not without incident. An energetic child, I frequently came running into the house with a gashed knee, blood everywhere, and a couple of times a broken limb, but it failed to curb my appetite for adventure. There were weekend trips to walk in the Peak District, where I once fell off the stepping-stones into the river Dove and had to be carried to the local hotel to be dried out. On bank holiday weekends we drove with friends, in a convoy of vehicles, the hundred miles to the coast to play cricket and rounders on the beach, followed by a dip in the freezing sea. On the way home there was always a stop at a pub so the men could have a beer – no children allowed inside then. We stayed in the car with our mothers and were brought Tizer and crisps. It was a time when patriotism was taken for granted (we had to stand when the National Anthem was played at the theatre and cinema) and conformity was unquestioned - a difficult concept for me, as I have a habit of questioning authority.

During our childhood my older sister Heather and I had a full-time mother but in our teens she followed the example of her father and brothers and bought a business – a general dealers' shop. She was successful in business, working tirelessly until illness forced her to sell up in her late fifties. She was a well-known and popular woman, much mourned by her customers, friends and family. An obituary in the local newspaper praised her entrepreneurial skills. After her death my father found it increasingly difficult to remain in the family home and for the last eighteen years of his life he lived in the highlands of Scotland.

My mother had always dressed my sister and me in matching clothes with a sense of pride, especially on Sundays when we all went to Church. She insisted on the same standards for her granddaughters and, following her wishes, I bought two tailored wool coats from a quality children's clothing shop in Hartlepool. They were quite expensive but the girls looked exceptionally smart and I thought how proud my mother would have been. A week or two later I noticed the seams on one were beginning to give way and felt it incumbent on me to do something about it, especially as it had been my mother's last gift. I returned to the shop but the sales assistant refused to admit the complaint, suggesting my young daughter must have caused the damage, which I knew not to be the case. 'But surely I have rights?' I asked. 'No, there's nothing I can do for you,' she replied curtly, dismissing me with a wave of her hand. Leaving the shop I felt rather humiliated, but with a sense of injustice and unwillingness to leave it there. A friend suggested I call in at the newly opened Consumer Advice Centre in Victoria Road. An adviser sympathetically listened to my complaint, wrote it all down on a printed form, and examined the coat. 'This is clearly in breach of the Sale of Goods Act 1893,' she said, adding, 'Goods sold by a trader must be of merchantable quality, comply with any description and be fit for their purpose. This clearly does not meet that requirement. You are entitled to a refund and I suggest you go back to the shop and ask for your money back'.

I didn't think I would be able to remember all that legal advice, nor did I possess the confidence to return to the shop, recalling my previous dismissal. Noticing my unease, the adviser picked up the phone and spoke to the trader, who immediately capitulated and agreed to return my money in exchange for the coat. I went back to the shop, only to be offered a different coat. I declined, insisting on a refund. We did not then have the wide range of retailers now taken for granted, but consumer choice is an inalienable right. It meant going up to Newcastle, but I was able to buy a coat from another shop. I returned to the advice centre to thank the adviser for her help. This was my first introduction to consumer protection. I hadn't thought very much about consumer rights before this - that there was a large body of legislation protecting consumers from unfair trading practices or the existence of government-funded advice centres - and told her I thought she had an interesting job. She acknowledged this and told me more about her work. I felt envious, both of her job, the knowledge of consumer rights she clearly displayed and the pleasant working environment. 'It must be wonderful to work in such a place as this,' I thought, little knowing I would do just that one day. At this time I was a full-time mother and it was to be several years before I had the opportunity to return to work, but my mother's untimely death was a turning point in many ways. Not only had it alerted me to consumer rights and advice work, it awakened a latent ambition to have a worthwhile career, at least parallel her own success in the business she ran in later life and to find a rewarding and challenging occupation that would fit in with my home responsibilities and hopefully lay the foundations of a career.

This was the first time I had ever felt drawn to any particular occupation, not having shared the preferred career route of my contemporaries, rejecting all suggestions of university or training to be a teacher or nurse. It was a mistake of course. From an early age I enjoyed learning and was an avid reader, and although I did well at school it had failed to stimulate or challenge me and I was not keen on several more years of study. Self-motivation and scholarly study came much later. I have always thought that consequently I left very little mark on Aldercar School, yet when my school friend Heather Mills persuaded me to go to a school reunion with her a few years ago, I was surprised how many people remembered me. I was called up to the stage to receive a present for being the former student who had travelled furthest to get there. I was working in Lithuania at the time. In the Sixties I was impatient to get a job, be independent and earn money to buy Mary Quant clothes and to have my hair styled by Vidal Sassoon. I wanted to work in London, but my parents put their foot down and I was sent to a local college to take further qualifications and train as a secretary. Two years later, equipped with good speeds at shorthand and typing, I applied to the House of Commons as a Hansard writer. They sent me a polite letter of rejection saying I was too young and suggested I try again in a few years' time. Instead, I went to work at the Shire Hall in Nottingham as a stenographer, where the criminal Assize Court and Quarter Sessions were held. My job was to take down the trial evidence of defended cases. It was a fascinating place to work. Situated on High Pavement in the Lace Market area, the Shire Hall was built in Georgian times but had been the site of a court and prison long before that. I was once taken down to the cells and dungeons underneath the building to search for the transcript of an old case now being appealed. The ledgers into which shorthand writers over the years had written down trial evidence were stored there, covered in dust, in cells hewn into the rock face of the building. The ledger would then be taken to the writer, providing they could be traced, for transcription. If he or she could not be found I was given the task of interpreting another writer's shorthand – not easy because we all create our own short forms. It sounds rather archaic now but in those days there was no recording equipment; instead the evidence in a defended criminal hearing was taken down verbatim using a special ink shorthand pen. My speeds were fast and I had no problem recording the evidence of witnesses for the prosecution, defence and the Judge's summing up, transcribing it into typewritten documents only if the defence appealed the decision. I wrote shorthand evidence for dozens of trials and for years expected a call to transcribe one. Thankfully it didn't happen.

My first job in the morning was to step across the road in the Lace Market to an old pub opposite the Shire Hall and collect a pile of bacon buns made by the landlord for the judges and lawyers' breakfast. The pub is still there, now a gastro-pub and unlikely to make bacon buns in the early morning. The Shire Hall is now a museum called the Galleries of Justice, and a few years ago I had the strange experience of sitting at the desk where I wrote shorthand all those years ago. The office banter with barristers and judges and the cases I heard day after day furthered my education, shocking my parents when I recounted the day's trials at the dinner table. My mother always said it was the first time the word 'buggery' had been spoken in her house and admitted she still didn't know what it meant.

This was the 'Swinging Sixties'. They say that if you can remember anything about this iconic decade, you were not really there. I was part of it and remember it clearly. New clubs opened in Nottingham in the style of Liverpool's Cavern Club and on Saturday we hitchhiked to Manchester for all-nighters at the Twisted Wheel. I saw most of the Sixties groups play live: the Beatles early in their career, George and Paul excitedly jumping up and down, John Lennon's brooding presence on stage, all shaking their hair, driving us young girls wild; the Rolling Stones when they were still an R & B group; Cream and a young Rod Stewart at the start of his career - I remain a fan of his. Before the Beatles I was listening to single records on a Dansette record player, listening to the Everley Brothers, Eddie Cochran and Bobby Vee. There was one song on the A side, another on the flipside. We couldn't afford LPs (long playing records) containing several songs. Other memories are: watching, on black and white television, the first astronaut to orbit the earth and later Neil Armstrong landing on the moon; England winning the World Cup; the *Lady Chatterley's Lover* trial at the Old Bailey. But there was a dark side to the Sixties: the civil rights movement in America; assassination of a popular President and his brother; the Cold War; the Hungarian Uprising; student riots in Paris; the Cuban missile crisis; the start of the Vietnam War; African Independence; the threat of the nuclear bomb.

I remained in Derbyshire until my late teens, moving to Newcastle-upon-Tyne in 1967. I had met Alan - my future husband - at Loughborough College the previous year at a football match. He was playing centre half and halfway through the game I found a football boot winging its way toward me, managing to catch it before it knocked me out. His boot had torn away at the toecap whilst executing a tricky move and he threw it to me deliberately, having previously failed to attract my attention by traditional means. He played on with just one boot and a sock on the other foot for the rest of the game. Our fate was sealed! After graduating he returned home to Hartlepool and, feeling in need of a change, I decided to give the north a try.

CHAPTER THREE

Friends in the North

AGED NINETEEN, I had never been further north than the Peak District, but Newcastle-upon-Tyne seemed a good place to base myself. It was a vibrant city in the late Sixties (still is) with a marvellous music scene and an abundance of shops. I found the dialect difficult to understand, not realizing until much later that people exaggerated it in order to tease this young girl from the Midlands. I enjoyed living in a large city, away from the confines of a small town where everyone knew my family. The only sadness was selling my car, a 1953 Ford Popular, complete with leather seats, running boards and pop-out indicators. Black of course. At the time it was built Henry Ford made his famous statement that customers could buy a car in any colour as long as it was black.

It was always breaking down but I was working at a college where the majority of the students were young men so there was no shortage of willing hands to come to my rescue. In Newcastle I booked into the YWCA in Saville Place just off Northumberland Street for a month but found their rules and regulations more stifling than living at home and soon found a flat to rent in Buston Terrace, Jesmond with two girls from Tynemouth. We stayed up all night reflecting on the meaning of life, threw some wild parties and frequented the local music clubs. I started out doing temporary secretarial jobs for an agency, which proved a good way to navigate my way around this new city, and got used to being called 'pet' and 'bonny lass' instead of the Derbyshire 'me duck'. My first job was at the office of a large boatbuilding company on Scotswood Road. Coming from the Midlands it was the first time I had seen huge ships at close quarters. Another job was at a small office developing underfloor heating, unheard of then, located on the Newcastle Quayside - at that time a place no respectable girl frequented, though I always enjoyed telling people I worked down on the Quayside just to see their baffled expression. We stepped across the road for lunch at the Red House, an ancient inn, still popular today.

After a few more temporary jobs I settled down to work at Newcastle General Hospital as secretary to Professor Jackson, a Consultant Cardiologist. He was quite terrifying, in the way of all consultants back then, and I had to buy a medical dictionary in order to spell the words he dictated to me (it would have been far too embarrassing to ask) but the junior doctors were much more approachable and fun. I would like to have remained in Newcastle but in 1968, with flowers in my hair and the elderly organist in our small country church trying his best to play Procol Harum's 'Whiter Shade of Pale' in tune, I walked down the aisle with Alan and after a honeymoon in Paris we began our married life in Hartlepool, where we brought up our two wonderful daughters. We still live nearby in Hart Village, though I don't think I will ever get used to living on the North Sea coast and should have listened to Eric Burdon, lead singer of my favourite Geordie group *The Animals,* who said Newcastle was *'where the rain comes at you sideways'.*

Interviewed for a job as Medical Secretary at Hartlepool general hospital the only question the doctor who was seeking a new secretary asked was: 'What book are you reading at the moment?' After we had discussed my reading preferences and his advice on other books I should read, I found myself secretary to Dr Michael Lidgate, a Consultant Psychiatrist. Unlike my previous employer, informality was the key with him and he treated all his staff as equals, insisting everyone in our unit assemble in the kitchen twice a day for coffee, cigarettes (he was a chain smoker with yellow, nicotine stained fingers) and conversation. He told everyone that I was a superb secretary whilst constantly imploring me to leave and go to university. He gave me a library of books to read, eager to discuss them later - once managing to get hold of an unexpurgated copy of *Fanny Hill.* Every day he would ask if I had finished it, eager to have my views, whilst

I had mounting embarrassment discussing such an explicitly sexual book with my boss. After he finished his surgery I would go into his office, sit across the desk clutching a shorthand notebook and with pen poised, to take dictation. The psychiatric assessment and compilation of a case history of the patients he had seen that day had to be produced and sent to the referral doctor and social workers; sometimes a patient might have to the 'sectioned' under the Mental Health Act. Dictation took a long time and I needed no dictionary because Dr Lidgate constantly stopped to explain his diagnosis and the causes of mental illness, as well as dispensing advice such as, 'The way to avoid mental illness is to inherit good genes', and 'Avoid hospitals at all cost, they are full of sick people'. He would also digress into discussions ranging from religion, politics, sociology, history and culture. Today such a relationship between two people, especially with a large disparity in ages and status, would be looked upon as inappropriate, but it never felt like that. He was a wonderfully eccentric character, clever and witty, and one of the most intelligent men I have ever encountered. Most importantly he was a mentor and I learned so much from him. When I told him I was leaving to have a baby he attempted to persuade me to stay and work part-time like his registrars, but it simply was not possible. However we continued to work together for a few years on a voluntary basis for the local branch of MIND (then the Mental Health Association) he had set up and for which I was secretary.

As with most women in the Seventies I gave up work when pregnant, this being before the days of organized childcare when only those well off could afford the luxury of a nanny. It was the norm for women to be questioned at job interviews about their home life and whether or when they intended to start a family. We were well aware that admitting to having children or even the likelihood of becoming pregnant could hinder our hopes of being employed. Of course the same questions were never directed at men —despite the nascent 'Women's Liberation' movement equality was still a distant hope. I still had the optimism of youth and the confidence of my generation that all things were possible and anything could be achieved if you really wanted it, but the reality was that without full-time child care, a mother of young children would find it almost impossible to forge a career. I'm pleased this has changed, but I have to say I would not have wanted to miss out on the years I stayed at home bringing up my daughters.

In 1981, after a few part-time jobs, I saw an advertisement for Manager of a Citizens Advice Bureau (CAB) in the Durham new town of Peterlee. It was not a full-time position so I would be able to fit it in around the school run. The job specification matched my qualifications and skills, thus I applied, was offered the job and suddenly found myself delivering advice services to the people of East Durham. Sent to London for a week's training course, it was the first time I had been separated from my children, but they survived. One or two of the delegates were already CAB volunteers and knew what the job entailed; others like me were new to it. The service I was setting up - taking a fully equipped mobile advice bureau to a different location each day - had not previously been attempted. A new minivan was purchased, which I was allowed to utilise for my own purposes, and it carried the information system used by all CAB advice centres. A trolley was specially made to hold three steel boxes that contained the files. They were quite heavy to lift in and out of the van every day and hook onto the trolley, but fortunately I was fit and strong. Having no typewriter or telephone at the advice sessions, I had to call in to the local CAB office in Peterlee to do the administration work. At this time, of course, there were no computers, Internet or mobile phones. In 1984 a young man came up from the head office in London to demonstrate a microfiche system then being developed. It would have revolutionized my work - no more dragging the heavy trolley and boxes as the information could be held in a compact format. I felt the white heat of technology but disappointingly heard no more about it.

With the aid of two volunteers we took the mobile CAB every day to an East Durham village using a variety of locations, mainly libraries or community centres. In Seaham we used the Registrar's office, occasionally halting the advice while a marriage service was conducted. Most of the complaints were about welfare benefits or housing problems but as a generalist service CAB will take on any problem. I liked the fact that when opening the door you never knew the type of problem to be resolved. It might be an appeal against a Social Security decision, lack of housing, a family dispute, consumer or legal issues. The cases that particularly distressed me were abused women. In the early 1980s the Women's Aid Movement was gaining momentum and in Peterlee, as in most areas, there was a safe house for victims of abuse and their children. The address was kept secret to ensure the safety of the women who lived there and of course male visitors were not permitted to enter. They gave shelter to abused women but sadly too often victims would return to the abusive husband or boyfriend. Visiting the elderly and disabled in their homes was another part of the job and I always received a warm welcome. Quite a few had small dogs to keep them company - usually Yorkshire Terriers that sat on their own cushion. Many housebound people were lonely but at least they were able to live in their own home. Visiting a sheltered housing complex for the elderly in Sedgefield one day I met the new Member of Parliament – an incredibly young looking Tony Blair. He was a popular and respected figure in the constituency and praised by local people for helping to resolve their problems.

The mobile bureau was always busy but advice services became even more necessary in 1984, when the Miners' Strike began. It came after a government announcement to close twenty coalmines with a loss of twenty thousand jobs, and the National Union of Miners responded by calling a national strike. There was sympathy for the miners but it didn't have the same impact as the previous strike action of the Seventies, when the country was plunged into darkness with power cuts and a three-day week. Fewer people now relied on coal - gas and oil had become popular sources of fuel and the railways had switched to diesel and electricity. Significantly the Government was ready for a strike this time, having stockpiled coal before the strike was announced and able to keep the electricity generators running. Standing firm they were determined to win, resulting in violent demonstrations and the dispute divided public opinion. All of my advice sessions were deep in the heart of the mining community and I saw at first hand the deprivation the strike caused. Union members received no money while on strike, causing severe hardship to themselves and their families, though outside the mining community the strike had less impact. Durham County Council gave CAB additional funding to run more advice sessions, recognizing miners were falling into debt. Most of their enquiries were related to lack of money and I heard some heartbreaking stories from the miners' wives. I tried to do what I could to help, not just on the advice side but also by leaving bags of clothing for them and their children at the community centres. They retained their pride, families looked after each other and didn't want handouts, but as the strike dragged on they were glad of any assistance. The dispute did have one unexpected outcome in that it made women in the mining communities stronger.

The strike lasted a year and the coal mining industry never recovered. When the dispute ended in March 1985 there were few pits left in the northeast, and the coal industry was privatized in 1994. I am not qualified to comment on the rights or wrongs of the miners' strike but when I now drive through the tight-knit communities of East Durham I feel sorrow for the loss of the mines and the employment the industry had given to entire families. My grandfather had been a coalminer in Nottingham and as a child I heard grim tales of life underground. He made sure none of his sons followed him down the mines. Growing up, his novels had a profound influence on me, particularly the largely autobiographical *Sons and Lovers*. Few of us would chose to do this job but the miners I met displayed huge dignity of labour and the mutual support they gave each other was heroic. Sitting in my office waiting to dispense help and advice, trying desperately to obtain some income for people who had none and who largely relied on charitable payments, or for CAB to challenge a refusal for benefit from Social Security, I felt a privileged outsider. At the end of a day's session I returned to my nice village and comfortable home with two incomes. CAB advisers are trained to be non-political and non-judgmental at all times, but it was impossible not to be affected by this very bitter dispute. Mining communities are traditionally close-knit but the dispute tore families apart. I began to feel that I was not making a difference.

This had been a worthwhile and interesting job with a variety of tasks: advice giving, recruitment and training of volunteer staff, writing newspaper articles, putting on displays at summer shows and visiting Women's Institutes to talk about the history and aims of CAB. It had given me a good grounding in management and legal knowledge and I knew that the advice sector was where I wanted to work and make my career. Best of all, I had been able to fit the job in with taking and collecting my daughters to the village school, so the guilt all working mothers feel was lessened. My next job was unlikely to provide the same variety or flexibility, nor would I be provided with transport, but it was time to move on.

After leaving Citizens Advice in 1985 I joined Cleveland Trading Standards as a Consumer Adviser at Hartlepool Consumer Centre, where I remained for the next eighteen years. The advice centre had not changed much since my earlier visit and I sat at the same desk as the adviser who had helped me a decade ago. Citizens Advice is a non-governmental organization and sets a high standard for the operation and performance of its paid and volunteer staff, but as long as its branches follow the rules set down by head office, a local bureau and its manager have a large degree of autonomy. Working for Local Government was very different and it took me a long time to adapt. It also meant working full-time, something I had not done for years, and I felt my energy level drop after mid afternoon, my body telling me it was time to call it a day. It was another steep learning curve in order to equip myself with the knowledge required not only to answer a myriad of enquiries every day, and to understand and be able to apply the law, but also to master the skills of mediation. The Council sent me to Manchester University for a crash course in consumer legislation and it reawakened my thirst for knowledge. I continued to study for several years, first for the Diploma in Consumer Affairs and then the degree Dr Lidgate had so urged me to take.

    As at Citizens Advice, we never knew when opening the Consumer Advice Centre each day the problems we would be required to help with, and this was why I enjoyed the job so much. Most people had genuine complaints and it was a joy to resolve them and get refunds or monetary compensation, but there were some who would demand 'But it's my right' or 'it's not the money, it's the principle that counts', becoming infuriated if they were told they had no rights. We were also able to prevent people from falling victim to scams and losing money – home-working schemes, lotteries and prize draws that promise reward but rarely deliver – in addition to money advice and debt management. Consumer education was a big part of the job and I went to local schools to tell teenagers about their rights and spoke to organizations such as the WI and the Rotary Club. I wrote endless articles for the *Hartlepool Mail*, the local newspaper, warning consumers about rogue trading practices and explaining consumer rights. In the Centre we not only gave advice, but also mediated with traders on consumer disputes (like my coat complaint years ago) and attended the County Court with clients who sometimes had to sue a trader to obtain redress for defective goods or services. Consumers find this difficult to do alone, many will avoid it even if it means giving up their claim, but my experience working at the Shire Hall courts in Nottingham came in useful and I was accepted by the District Judge as a lay advocate, able to speak for a consumer in a small claims action. The civil court is informal, unlike the criminal court, but prospective litigants still worry about the legal process.

    The job of a consumer adviser is to apply the civil law, give advice and mediate where necessary. A successful solution requires goodwill and compromise on the part of buyer and seller. Employed within the Trading Standards department, civil advisers are also trained in the criminal law - for example weights and measures, false trade descriptions, the complexities of consumer credit and clocked or 'stitched' cars. It was our duty to report any possible criminal implications to our Trading Standards colleagues even if the consumer did not want their complaint being taken to the criminal court, and we sometimes accompanied enforcement staff on visits to catch the crooks. I enjoyed this part of the job but have always been most interested in the civil law, where a case depended upon a 'balance of probabilities' rather than strict legal doctrines. It meant absorbing a myriad of legislation. The 19th century Sale of Goods Act that gave me the right to obtain redress for the coat many years ago had now been succeeded by the 1979 Sale of Goods Act. Like its predecessor it regulated contracts for the purchase and sale of goods and defined the rights of the parties. The test was no longer one of 'merchantable quality', but replaced with 'satisfactory quality'. Consumer rights were further strengthened by the Unfair Terms in Consumer Contract Act, Trade Descriptions Act, Unsolicited Goods and Services Act, Supply of Goods and Services Act, Consumer Credit Act and many more. I soaked this up, reading law books and Court of Appeal decisions for enjoyment. At this time I rarely gave a thought to European legislation – the supremacy of EU law over national law, the aims of the Single Market, free movement of goods. I knew even less about the assistance given by the European Commission to countries outside the European Union. As we entered the twenty-first century, this was all about to change.

CHAPTER FOUR

Big Thoughts, Small Island

I AM SITTING AT a small outdoor café near the Barrakka Gardens, alone, sipping a chilled glass of white wine. It is early evening but the warmth remains, and I am peering across the Grand Harbour to the 'Three Cities'. It is a relatively new café and was not here on my previous visit, but it has one of the best views in the city, on a terrace jutting out into the harbour. I discovered it recently and have taken to calling in for a drink after work to unwind from the difficulties of the day, my thoughts turning to my family back home in England whom I am missing. I am aware that I probably give the impression of a lonely middle-aged woman sitting alone in a bar with nowhere else to go, though this is far from being the truth. The owner of the café strikes up a conversation, telling me something of the history of this island, that there was some excitement today when Brad Pitt and other actors sailed ancient boats through the harbour - the film *Troy* was being filmed in Valletta. He points to a boat tethered to the quayside at Vittoriosa opposite; it is his pride and joy and when he can escape from his new business he hoists the sail and puts to sea. 'It is my dream to sail my little boat around the world,' he told me with some passion. I felt quite sorry for him; it must have been a torment to gaze on his boat all day, unable to set sail because he needed to make a success of his business. But few of us have free will, and we are most of us tethered to something one way or another.

He enquires whether it is my first visit, assuming I am a tourist. No, I respond, though I was here on holiday some years ago with my sister, when we spent a wonderful week at the Fortina Spa hotel in nearby Sliema, enjoying daily thermal baths and seaweed wraps. We speak of the changes taking place in his country and what membership of the European Union is expected to bring. As I finish my drink and prepare to head back to my hotel he says he hopes to see me at his bar again. He would – the Festa season began the next day with, I had been told, an amazing firework display in the Grand Harbour, and this bar had the best view in Malta.

Far from being a tourist, I was in Malta to work on a consumer protection project for the European Commission; plucked, it seemed, from obscurity in northern England and transported to the sunnier climes of the Mediterranean. It may sound like a dream posting but in fact the work was far from easy and initially things were not going as well as I would have liked in the Consumer and Competition department where I was based, hence the need for a period of quiet reflection after work. It was 2003 and Malta, currently a 'pre-accession' country, was poised to become a member of the European Union the following year. The process of harmonizing legislation in line with the EU and strengthening administrative structures had been going on for some time. The purpose of my project was to support a new consumer information and education campaign, ensuring consumers and businesses were aware of their new European rights and obligations. I was also to write a strategy, deliver training and workshops for Ministry officials and consumer associations and launch a public awareness campaign. It seemed rather a lot to fit into nine weeks, but I was up for the challenge and where better to do it than a sunny island in the Mediterranean?

As Malta prepared to change its history and join a brave new world I too was plotting a further change of direction, one that would take me to an unknown country. It would require a permanent break from my job of eighteen years and temporary absence from family and friends. I had received a further offer of overseas work and my decision was awaited. It would have to be made soon but for the moment I decided place it at the back of my mind. Sitting on the terrace finishing my drink, the sun dipping toward the horizon, I reflected on what had brought me to this small island. How had a former secretary become a self-employed consultant taking British expertise in consumer protection to Europe and beyond? It had all started when, sitting at my desk in Hartlepool on a grey rainy day in January, I received a telephone call from someone I then hardly knew – Jim Spinks calling from London. 'Would you like to go and work in Malta?' he asked.

I had met Jim at a meeting in London a few years earlier when he was developing the Consumer Support Network (CSN), a new initiative overseen and funded by the Department of Trade and Industry (now Business Innovation and Skills). A Labour Government elected in 1997 had stated their intention to improve consumer protection, both for consumers and businesses, and CSN was one of several ideas designed to further this aim. I joined a team of thirty Facilitators who came from diverse backgrounds – Trading Standards, CAB, consumer specialists working in the area of media and academia. I enjoyed this work and combined it with my full time job by using annual leave. My portfolio was broadly the North East of England and the first task was to sell the project to Trading Standards departments - without their participation, forming a local CSN was unlikely to happen. After this it was a case of persuading other key stakeholders, such as the Citizens Advice Bureau and businesses, of the merits of forming a network. The project was successful and within five years Consumer Support Networks covered 98% of the country, with organisations that previously had little contact with each other now willingly sharing information and working together.

Shortly after setting up CSN, Jim moved on to work as a consultant scoping and setting up projects overseas, and I hadn't seen or heard from him for a year or two, so it was a surprise when he called with the offer of working in Malta. 'It's only a short project, it wouldn't be worth leaving your current employment, perhaps you can take unpaid leave of absence,' he suggested, going on to outline the work and remuneration I would receive. It almost sounded too good to be true and I didn't have to think too long before replying, 'Yes, I'll do it.'

A year or two earlier I might have refused, but at this time the job I had enjoyed for almost two decades was at risk. Cleveland County Council had been abolished in 1996 and I was transferred to Hartlepool Council, a small unitary authority. My new managers never seemed to be convinced of the importance of consumer and money advice, frequently reminding me that consumer advice was a non-statutory service – unlike Trading Standards, which is mandatory. I told them about the offer I had received and applied for unpaid leave of absence. Initially it was denied but I persisted, reminding them that they had approved unpaid leave for a male colleague to take an extended holiday. I was determined to take up this unique opportunity even if it meant leaving a full-time job of eighteen years. It was a risk - there would be no going back as it had been obvious for some time that the Council was looking for services to cut. I was saved from making this decision when my application to take unpaid leave was approved. As it happened they did close the advice service the following year.

Working overseas was not something I had ever contemplated doing but it was an exciting prospect. Although it was only for two months I sensed that it might be just the change of direction I needed. I was in my fifties when this new career began – a time when many people are thinking about retirement and looking after grandchildren. The decision was made easier by the fact that my daughters had by this time completed university, had good careers and husbands and no longer lived in the northeast. We are a close-knit family but they would manage without me, though I would not have gone without their support. I think they looked upon this work in Malta as a single opportunity, certainly not life-changing. Accepting the CSN work years earlier had been one of those turning points in life, not knowing what it would lead to. This was another – had I not seized the challenge of the project in Malta I'm sure I would have continued working for Hartlepool Council until retirement.

The work in Malta had hardly got off the ground when Jim Spinks rang again to ask if I was interested in another project, this time in a less familiar country. I had a difficult decision to make, but sitting in this pleasant bar on a warm evening, I tried to displace it from my mind and concentrate on the current work to be done in Malta, knowing that very soon I would have to give Jim my answer.

CHAPTER FIVE

A Safe Haven and No Rain

MALTA: THE SMALLEST of the ten countries to join the European Union in 2004, achieved independence from Britain in 1964. Romans called this small island *Melita*, the Phoenicians *Malet*, meaning a haven or place of shelter, in reference to its many bays and coves.

I like the Phoenicians' name for Malta. The idea of working overseas was quite daunting back in 2003 but this was a good starting point and provided a temporary haven in many ways, assisted by several factors. I knew the Maltese people to be friendly and welcoming, English is widely spoken and they even drive on the left. It was quite easy to feel at home, though the climate was very different. The skies and sea were an eternal blue, quite unlike the weather I was accustomed to in Hartlepool, where the grey North Sea comes crashing over the promenade and a summer picnic can be ruined when a 'sea fret' rolls in. That Malta was one of ten states now preparing to join the European Union was not surprising given its historic connection to Britain, though in fact the referendum held just before my first visit was bitterly fought, with the opposition arguing that membership of the EU would jeopardize Malta's independence. There was a high turnout with 53.6 voting for membership with 46.4 opposing.

Jim suggested we make a short visit to Malta in the spring of 2003 to meet departmental heads in the Consumer and Competition Division (CCD) of the Office for Fair Trading to assess their requirements. It wasn't exactly convenient as I was due to deliver a two-day training course for the Money Advice Trust in Leeds. It was too late to cancel so I went ahead with the training and after it finished took the train to Manchester for a direct flight to Malta. As I stepped out into Valletta at midnight into a warm balmy evening, it struck me as a stark contrast to the dark and drenched northern city I had left only a few hours earlier. It was an early start the next day to meet Jim for a breakfast briefing served on an outdoor terrace at the Phoenicia hotel, bathed in sunshine. Here I met Robin Croft from Liverpool for the first time; he was working on a consumer protection project in the same department and therefore a good source of information. A Ministry car arrived to drive us to meetings with the beneficiaries, after which they took us to lunch in Valletta. Looking back to this first working visit to Malta I can still recall that moment of feeling slightly out of my depth, but Jim was supportive and if he sensed my unease he refused to show it and always treated me with respect. It is completely different working with people from another culture and for whom English is a second, sometimes third, language and it can be difficult trying to work out what it is they actually want to achieve, but Jim was experienced at this and knew the right questions to ask.

The following month I returned to Malta, this time on my own, to begin work on the project, staying at the Phoenicia hotel again as it was close to the bus station. I was pleased to find Robin Croft there and we took the bumpy bus to work each day. The offices of the Consumer and Competition Division (CCD), who have the main operational responsibility for market surveillance activities in Malta, were based out at St Venera. On arrival I met Marcel Pizzuto, the Director General of the Office for Fair Trading, a quiet and polite man. We discussed the project and what he hoped to achieve, before I was passed over to Mr. Schembri, head of the Consumer Department in whose office I would be based. He reminded me of the fiery former Prime Minister of Malta Dom Mintoff, liable to ride roughshod over other people's feelings but at the same time bringing progress. I particularly disliked his aggressive approach to some of his staff and lack of sympathy to consumers' needs. His ace card was being the only member of staff at that time to have received training in Britain as a Trading Standards Officer, and he consequently knew he was more qualified than many of his colleagues. However his department did a good job in protecting consumer rights in Malta, with a free telephone service and consumer education and programmes. I worked from a table in Mr. Schembri's office, a dark room with no natural light, finding it increasingly difficult to concentrate as he shouted and argued with his staff and anyone else who crossed his path. He liked to remind me of his time in London whilst studying for the Diploma in Trading Standards, proudly pointing to the twenty-year old training files he still kept on his desk, covered in dust, convinced that he knew more about consumer protection than anyone else in Malta. As it happened, there was an efficient market surveillance department downstairs where Robin Croft was based, and they got on with their enforcement work quietly and effectively.

Mr. Schembri seemed reluctant for me to meet anyone in the department or outside of it, but gradually I began to explore the other offices, introducing myself to staff. They all had bright sunny rooms and there was laughter you seldom heard in our part of the building. I became a regular visitor to the lawyers' office to talk to the bright and astute young women who worked there to ask questions about Maltese consumer law, and they were very helpful. They also had lots of questions for me about how Britain regulated and enforced consumer protection. The Maltese have high respect for British institutions and traditions and there was so much goodwill towards my country. Notwithstanding the difficulties I faced, I found that almost twenty years in Trading Standards had equipped me with sufficient knowledge and skills to be able get on with the job and establish my own contacts with consumer groups and trade organizations. They were the key to meeting the project objectives.

Joyce Borg, who carried out similar duties to my own in Trading Standards at home, did the main work in the consumer department. She told me that like me she was a member of the Institute of Consumer Affairs, a British organization that represents personnel working within the area of consumer protection, and so we had a fair bit in common. She was a regular guest on radio and television, and on my second day in the office invited me to accompany her to the television studio of *Super One* where she was talking about consumer rights on their live lunchtime show. I was also interviewed about the project and what we hoped to achieve. After the interview we drove to Kalkira where Joyce was giving a talk to a pensioners' group about their consumer rights. Although English is widely used, these people only spoke Maltese. Joyce was a member of the Council of Women and took me along to their meeting one evening. These professional women all spoke English fluently, were well informed and asked lots of questions about the

British model of fair trading schemes designed to improve customer service. 'Shops here have a terrible attitude to their customers,' I was told. Another young lawyer said 'There is so much apathy; people just give up when they have a consumer problem and don't pursue it'. I was drafting a consumer survey, to be conducted throughout Malta in the summer, in order to provide data on the level of consumer awareness. I 'road tested' it on the group and they suggested some additional questions. Grace Attard, a gracious and elegant woman who was President of the Council, impressed me and we continued to communicate for a number of years. The group had a good overview of the various consumer bodies but not how it all fitted together. Grace asked, 'If I have a consumer problem do I go to the Office for Fair Trading, a consumer association, or the newspaper?' I explained it by way of a jigsaw puzzle. Each has a role to play: the Consumer Directorate deals with consumer rights, arbitrates with traders and is involved in consumer education in schools. The non-governmental Consumer Association gives advice to their members but also has an important role in lobbying and commenting on new legislation. Another part of the jigsaw is the media, who can highlight consumer issues. The *Maltese Times* published a weekly consumer column and was not afraid to 'name and shame' bad traders and issues of concern. All have a role to play and by working together are able to achieve so much more. I was surprised how much I already knew about consumer protection in Malta!

Consumer associations may be an essential part of consumer protection, but I found the CCD reluctant to liaise with them. This is not unusual. In most countries, including my own, there can be a difficult relationship between the statutory and voluntary sector and I have experience of this at first hand, having worked in both sectors. In Britain we have gone a long way to improve it, notably through the Consumer Support Networks initiative. Wanting to establish contacts with the Maltese Consumer Association, I arranged to meet Paul Micalleff one evening in Valletta. In addition to his voluntary work Paul is a well-known lawyer who previously worked in the Consumer Directorate, but at this time was employed by the Telecom regulator. He lived with his mother in a charming little house round the corner from the famous St John's church and suggested we have our meeting there so that he could introduce me to his mother. Coming from anyone else, I might have been worried about being invited to the house of a man who was merely a stranger to me, but it felt right and my instincts are usually good. A clever, intense and serious man, Paul was extremely helpful and knowledgeable about consumer law and in fact was the author of much of the consumer legislation in Malta. He gave me a paper he had delivered to an international conference on consumer access to justice, which I still have. After the first mission he wrote to me, setting down his thoughts about what needed to be done in Malta and how I could assist the process. The letter began, 'You are someone from the outside who can view things more objectively and suggest ideas from a different perspective.' He admitted that, 'There is competition between the Division and consumer associations but as an outsider you will be able to encourage better co-ordination.' His ideas and advice helped to form the basis of my work during the second mission. Paul enhanced my view of consumer protection, not just in connection with Malta but also in a European context, having delivered many papers to conferences in Brussels. He also introduced me to Dr David Fabri, another lawyer, who worked at the Malta Financial Services Authority and lectured in consumer law at the university. He and Paul had strong ideas about what needed to be done, much of it based on the British model.

Consumer education work was also being carried out at the university, where I spoke to members of a consumer education focus group. They were writing the material to be taught in schools in readiness for when consumer advice was to become part of the school curriculum in September 2004. I was given a copy of their report *Creating the Future Together*. Not for the first time I wondered why Malta felt they needed the help of a EU expert when they already seemed to be making a good job of it themselves. At the university I met Carmen Delia. She lectured in economics at the university but my interest in meeting her was in her role as Chair of the Consumer Affairs Council. The Council vets and advises on new laws proposed by Parliament. We discussed Carmen's three-year business plan, I made some suggestions to strengthen the Council and she urged me to press her cause at the Ministry. She had a clear idea of what needed to be done, particularly for disadvantaged groups, but recognized they would benefit from working in co-operation with other organizations in the state and voluntary sectors. We also spoke about European Consumer Centres, as Malta would be required to establish one once they became members of the European Union. There is a network of European Consumer Centres throughout the EU for consumers to seek help on problems with goods and services purchased in any member state. The centres offer mediation and alternative dispute resolution, a particular interest of mine. Carmen showed me the entries for a Young Consumer Competition she was judging, held annually, with a very high standard of entries from schools. Picking up on my interest in dispute resolution, she suggested I visit the Consumer Arbiter.

The Consumer Claims Tribunal was housed in an adjacent office and Carmen introduced me to the Arbiter who hears and deliberates upon consumer disputes two days a week. He allowed me to sit in on his hearings. The tribunal is part of the justice system and the Arbiter is legally qualified. It is an inexpensive and effective way of resolving disputes but consequently there is always a large backlog of cases. I was impressed with Malta's method of resolving consumer disputes. There are a few simple rules, such as a minimum/maximum amount of the claim and the consumer must first lodge the claim with the Office of Fair Trading who then has fifteen days to resolve the case before it goes to arbitration. The Arbiter was fair, giving both parties to the dispute the opportunity to present their sides of the argument. One of the cases that day involved a set of saucepans. The consumer said they burnt food and wanted a refund, the seller accused the consumer of using too high heat. After their arguments flew back and forth, when it seemed they might come to blows, the Arbiter decided that the seller must go out to the consumer's home to witness how they were being used before making a decision. The trader said 'Forget it, I'd rather give the consumer her money back now,' and proceeded to take a bundle of notes from his pocket. The Arbiter replied, 'No, you had the opportunity to do that when the consumer first complained to you. Having allowed the case to come this far you must abide by my decision'.

Consumer redress is helped by the fact that Tribunal cases are reported in the newspaper, including the names of shops that have not paid fines imposed on them. Malta is a small island where everyone seems to know each other; therefore a shop that treats its customers badly is unlikely to survive. It was time to meet the journalist who wrote a consumer page in the *Maltese Sunday Times* and who clearly was not afraid to expose issues of consumer detriment or name the bad traders. I was warned that he was a notorious ladies' man, a flirt and a charmer. Adrian Muscat-Inglott turned out to fulfil all of these categories - a tall charismatic and charming man who bowed to kiss my hand on every occasion. We arranged to meet at my hotel for coffee – a safe environment I thought. I found him to be very knowledgeable about consumer issues and he clearly enjoyed irritating the Office for Fair Trading, who he felt did not protect Maltese consumers sufficiently. He insisted I meet a friend of his, the president of the Maltese Consumer Association and a lecturer at the university, suddenly announcing, 'we will go there immediately and talk to him.' Driving across the island to the university, he told me to expect a man who looked exactly like Albert Einstein. His description was accurate. Benny Borg Bonnello, Einstein's double, was Assistant Registrar at the university and had a longstanding interest in consumer affairs. He and a small group of volunteers ran the Malta Consumer Association with dedication on a shoestring. After our meeting Adrian suggested we drive to his house to look at his press cuttings - the second invitation from an unknown man that week! I tried to decline but he had already started the car and was telling me about his family. It still seemed a bit dubious but in fact he had a beautiful home – and an English wife. They had met when Adrian was working in London and after marriage returned to Malta where they had brought up their teenage sons. True to his word, Adrian took me to his study to see the famous press cuttings and his wife brought us a sandwich lunch.

Paul Micalleff, Benny Bonnello and Adrian Muscat Inglott were all members of the Consumers' Association and invited me to sit in on the consumer advice surgeries they held twice a week. Only members of the association are entitled to receive free advice and mediation, for which they pay a nominal sum annually, but the Association has a small membership that it needs to increase and to access additional funding. Working out of a tiny office with few resources, I could only admire their dedication to the cause of consumer advice, such a contrast to my consumer advice centre back home – a double fronted high street office, well equipped with three trained advisers providing advice on all consumer matters. We discussed different ways they could increase their membership, raise awareness and access funds. Paul came up with the idea of holding a public meeting at which I would talk about consumer protection. 'The local priest owes me a favour and will give us a meeting room,' he said. The meeting on 27 October 2003 was held in the crypt of St Augustine Church in Old Bakery Street, Valletta. Marcel Pizzuto gave an opening speech about his work and my presentation was entitled *Helping Consumers by Working Together*. We had a good audience and it certainly was a most unusual venue.

Businesses are another essential element of consumer protection. Improve their relationship with consumers, encourage them to abide by legislation on product safety, labelling, advertising and consumer rights and shoppers will be better protected. I found the Chamber of Commerce in a beautiful historic building in the heart of Valletta. I hadn't made an appointment but took a deep breath and proceeded to enter into an imposing hall, faced with a grand sweeping staircase. It was very quiet and motionless and there was no one about. After unanswered knocks on a few doors, I spotted a woman looking down from the top of the staircase and introduced myself. She took me to meet Simon Barberi, the Chamber's EU Affairs Coordinator. He was receptive to my suggestion of a seminar for retail businesses and in fact had already made attempts to liaise with CCD, receiving no encouragement. We agreed that I would speak at a seminar and the Malta Business Bureau would provide accommodation, refreshments and send invitations to members. It went ahead on 21 October under the title of *Consumer Protection Legislation – Rights and Responsibilities for Traders*. Simon designed the programme and flyer, describing me (rather too grandly I thought) as a 'UK Consumer Consultant seasoned with many years experience in this field'. The meeting was well attended and ran on longer than anticipated because the delegates had so many questions and ideas. Business representatives also had criticisms of the Consumer Directorate. It was becoming a familiar refrain.

Visiting the imposing Federation of Industry, I was graciously received by the Director Edwin Calleja, who immediately called for their in-house photographer to record the event. We discussed Malta's problem with labelling of goods. 'Importers are dumping foodstuffs on to the Maltese market with best-before dates about to expire and it distorts the market' Mr Calleja told me. 'Consumers need to be better educated and encouraged to read labels; we also need a campaign to persuade consumers to buy only Maltese products'. As Malta was about to become a member of the EU this would, of course, be difficult. As this was a courtesy call I decided not to mention this however. We also discussed another matter causing controversy in Malta at this time. A ship was anchored at sea selling books at discounted prices. They had been refused permission to bring the ship into the harbour and allow people on board to purchase the books. The captain responded by shuttling customers to the ship in small boats. The Federation of Industry and other supporters of Maltese traders were determined to stamp out this practice. Malta was not yet a member of the European Union so effectively they could do this if it did not conflict with national law, but it would be a different matter after they joined.

Knowing travel and tourism to be an important part of the Maltese economy, I paid a visit the Malta Tourism Authority (MTA) at their offices in Valletta. This was another beautiful building – I envied the working conditions here, very unlike our bland civic centres at home. Noel Furzon told me they not only receive requests for advice about travel from Maltese consumers. 'There are five cruise ships in the harbour today, bringing tourists into the city. We want them to shop and be satisfied with the products they buy. They complain about many things, from timeshare, car hire and taxi charges to faulty goods'. He was also keen to improve customer service and the Authority had paid for taxi drivers to go to Britain to take the taxicab examination. He hopes to repeat this with bus drivers. 'An excellent idea' I said, 'but they will need an intensive training course from what I have seen.' The Tourist Authority offered to distribute consumer advice brochures through their information centres and at the airport. I was shown a prototype of an interactive information point soon to be placed around Malta. Consumers will be able to obtain all kinds of information on a touch screen and it might be possible to include a link to the CCD free phone. I made a note to pay them another visit when I returned in October.

Part of my work in the Consumer Department was to draft the text for a set of consumer brochures and these would be printed using EU project funds. There was insufficient time to do this in office hours, so I found myself spending weekends in the hotel's business centre writing the text whilst tourists were outside enjoying the sunshine. I completed the leaflets, leaving them for the beneficiaries to check and approve before my return. They would be published in both languages, Maltese and English, as required by Maltese law. I also designed a consumer survey, to be carried out by departmental staff over the summer. An independent survey is important to establish a baseline, from which the department could measure future success and track consumer needs. It's always useful to have a gap between missions and allow beneficiaries to take the work forward, but there was another reason in this case. From the end of May to the beginning of October civil service staff only work during the mornings due to high temperatures and humidity after lunchtime. I was assured that they work longer during the winter months so their total working hours are similar to other countries. I couldn't help thinking they had the work/life balance right.

At the end of the first mission I had a constructive meeting with the Director General. He said he was aware of tensions in his office, that they affected the department's relationship with other stakeholders and was working to change this. 'I understand the opposition to new ideas that you will face by some of my staff but I want you to go beyond the terms of the project terms if necessary,' he said. 'Be bold in your recommendations, identify areas that can be improved even if they will be unpopular with existing staff, and don't be unduly influenced by different factions.' This was good advice and I have followed it on other projects. We discussed the work I would continue in the second mission and the structure of the training courses I would deliver. He apologized for not having had time to offer hospitality, but made me a promise: 'When you return to Malta I will take you out to dinner; also I will make sure you have your own office and no resistance from any of my staff.'

I returned to Malta to complete the project in the autumn. I was travelling out from Gatwick with Jim Spinks, who had access to a business lounge and signed me in, and I was surprised how quiet and peaceful it was, whilst down in the noisy departure area holidaymakers were fighting for uncomfortable seats. It was a long journey; for some reason we first had to fly to Dublin, land and take on more passengers, before heading south to Malta, but we made good use of the time by planning our strategy for the next few days. At a meeting with the Director the following morning, Marcel made good on the promises he had made on my departure in May, assuring me, 'You will have no problems with any of my staff.' He was right: I didn't and he gave me an office of my own. That evening Marcel collected Jim and me, driving us to a superb fish restaurant in St Julians, going into the kitchen to speak to the chef and to select the freshest fish.

One of the tasks in the second mission was to organize media training for staff. Ann Kaye, ex BBC producer and a media trainer I had previously worked with, came out for a week to assist. Over three sessions we trained staff in media and communication techniques and had a keen and receptive audience. After learning about media techniques from Ann, participants had to design and deliver a short training session to colleagues. All of them gave confident presentations and one young woman showed us how to make the famous Maltese lace, which was very interesting.

Grace Attard from the Women's Council heard about the training and pleaded for us to train members of her group. Ann prefers to train only a small number of people at a time, but wanting to include everyone, I persuaded her we should give a lecture to the whole group and then select one or two for the radio and television interviews. It had to be done in the evening and became a bit chaotic toward the end, but everyone was very appreciative of the training and we were glad to do it. We returned to the hotel exhausted and opened the bottle of gin Ann had bought in duty-free.

During the previous visit several people had told me I should meet Frank Farrugia, from the Tourist Authority, but we always seemed to miss each other, despite leaving messages at his office. We eventually met during this second visit. As I was sitting in my hotel room on the first Saturday evening, preparing to have an early night, the hotel manager rang my room. 'Mr Farrugia is in reception and asking to see you.' I told the manager I could be down in fifteen minutes, but he seemed to be in something of a panic. 'No you really must come immediately,' and with his voice rising added, 'It is Mr Farrugia from the Malta Tourist Authority.' After throwing on some clothes, I found the normally calm and cool manager and his staff rushing around in reception, very concerned at receiving a visit from the Director of Tourism on a Saturday night. What worried them even more was he had gone wandering around the hotel and when I arrived they couldn't locate him. The Tourist Authority had recently closed down a hotel in Sliema for not being up to scratch, and they were obviously worried. In fact Frank and his wife Grace were taking a walk down memory lane, having held their wedding reception in the hotel many years previously. We finally made the introductions and they explained that they had been on their way to an art gallery reception in Valletta when Frank had spontaneously decided to call at the hotel to ask if I would like to accompany them. I was more than happy to abandon my plans for an early night. The reception was interesting; I met his colleagues and was introduced to the young woman artist exhibiting her paintings. Frank suggested a drive up to Sliema where we all walked along the promenade until late evening. The next morning they collected me from the hotel to spend the day at a wonderful festival being held in Vittoriosa, one of the three old cities across the Grand Harbour. Everyone was dressed in medieval costume, there were parades and concerts and they introduced me to many of their friends.

After meeting Frank and Grace, my social life improved greatly and they were excellent hosts. Alan met them when he came out for a visit and they took us to their favourite restaurants and on excursions around the island to places not generally known to tourists. We went to a special cliff top by the sea, near the Megalithic temples, where Frank and Grace regularly went to watch the sunrise. At the Dingli cliffs we ran into members of their family and joined in their picnic. We also visited their home in Zejtun, met their three teenage children and walked to their local church, where the Sunday evening service was flooded with worshippers, young and old. They had always wanted to visit the Lake District and the following year we invited them to spend a week's holiday at our apartment in Windermere. They also visited me in Vilnius just before Christmas and we have remained friends.

Weekends can be difficult when you are working away from home, but it helped that Malta is a popular tourist destination, and I tried to make the most of my time there. On Saturdays I took the small ferryboat over to Sliema to walk along the sea front and look at the shops. On Sunday I often took a bus to the former citadel of Mdina (meaning *walled city*). The Phoenicians had built a protective wall around the city and it is also known as *Silent City*. I visited at quiet times, wandering around the narrow streets before stopping to eat at one of the small restaurants. I found it to be a most peaceful and restful place, but with more and more cruise ships docking in Valletta ferrying busloads of tourists Mdina runs the risk of losing its special atmosphere. One Sunday I took the ferry across to the island of Gozo to look at the Citadel. The Upper Barrakka Gardens in Valletta, particularly at sunset, provided calm after work. I spent a musical Saturday evening at the Manoel Theatre watching a live production of *The Sound of Music*. Another Saturday Barbara, a Maltese lady from the office, invited me out with her friends. We drove up to Sliema to a beach restaurant where Sharon Stone was also dining with friends. The actress was in Malta making a film, as was Brad Pitt, but I didn't run into him. We watched the colourful little fishing boats – the *luzzu* and the *kajjik* - bobbing about in the sea, with their watchful eyes painted on the prow. They were dwarfed by a cruise ship sailing out of Grand Harbour, covered in lights, everyone on deck taking a last look at Valletta. It was a hot sultry night; I felt a long way from home.

I have many good memories of my time in Malta but an abiding one will always be a hot Sunday in October 2003. Whilst relaxing at the swimming pool at the Le Meridian Phoenicia hotel I heard I had become a grandmother. It had been an anxious two days since my daughter Alison had gone into hospital and a great relief when the phone call came through to say that Hannah had been born safe and well. Having no one immediately to share this marvellous news with, I went to my room to write Hannah a long letter welcoming her into the world and describing her family, to be opened at some time in the future. I was dining with Robin that night and he ordered a good bottle of wine to celebrate. The next day when colleagues asked if I had enjoyed my weekend I was able to reply, with pride and great delight, that something very special indeed had happened.

The project ended in October 2003 with a high-profile closing conference. Jim invited Jacqui King over to give a presentation and she amused us with a witty history of consumer protection. Summing up, Marcel announced that the project had met the objectives and advanced the work of consumer protection in Malta, then took us all out for lunch. The night before I flew home Frank and Grace collected me at the hotel and we drove to Sliema for the evening. There was to be no walk along the promenade this time as the weather had changed and it was cold and windy. Over coffee they presented me with a lovely silver necklace. 'It's to make amends for the poor hospitality you received during your first visit,' Frank said. Grace told me that her husband had made the purchase and when asked by the sales assistant if the recipient was young he had replied, 'Yes, she is young at heart'. I was touched by this compliment and their hospitality. It did not end there. They insisted on collecting me from the hotel early the next morning to drive me to the airport, where Frank helped me check in. When I arrived at Heathrow I had a six-hour wait before my connecting flight to Newcastle and was surprised to be told that I had access to the BA business lounge. It does help being accompanied by the Director of Tourism when checking in.

This new experience of working overseas was the first time I had ventured abroad alone, so it was a challenge both professionally and personally. Before embarking on it I had asked myself: *would I be able to deliver the results of the project? Could I adapt to living on my own in another country and working alone?* In fact I had found the skills needed to meet the project objectives. There had been some minor difficulties, as there are in any project, but they had been overcome and the work was enjoyable. I now felt ready to take on the new challenge of a larger project in unknown country. It seemed I would not be returning to my job at Hartlepool Council.

CHAPTER SIX

Easter Celebrations in Malta

WE HAD ALWAYS INTENDED to return to Malta and in 2010 Alan and I finally found time to make a short visit, this time as tourists. I wanted to see if the island had changed after joining the European Union. About 180 million Euros, most of it from the EU, have been spent on regeneration, bringing much needed improvements. It is now possible to walk around Valletta and admire the ancient merchants' streets without stepping over rubbish, and many of the fine old buildings have been restored. We sat in the newly-smartened Upper Barrakka Gardens; took lunch at the Phoenicia hotel swimming pool; visited the ancient church where I had held the consumer seminar; took the ferry over to Sliema to walk along the smart promenade and felt the warmth of the sun in Palace Square, splashed by spray from the new fountains. The pretty *Karrozzin* horse-drawn carriages that transport tourists around the city used to stand in this square and in the summer heat the smell was unbearable. Charming as they are, I was pleased to see they have been moved away to the City Gate. We also called at the bar overlooking the Grand Harbour, which was doing good business, its owner having even less time to sail his boat. The improvements in Valletta were impressive and the renovations are not yet completed. I reflected on my good fortune to have had the opportunity to work on this beautiful and friendly island. The department where I worked in 2003 is renamed the Malta Competition and Consumer Affairs Authority and Joyce Borg is now Director of the Consumer Division. Mr. Schembri and Mr. Pizzuto have retired.

    A priority on arrival was to call in at the headquarters of the Malta Tourism Authority in Valletta to look up Frank Farrugia. We had arranged the trip at the last minute with no time to contact him, so he was surprised when I walked into his office. The next morning, a public holiday to celebrate Freedom Day, he and Grace were at our hotel at 9 a.m. to take the ferry for a day in Gozo and for a wonderful tour of this small island, first stopping at the Ggantija temples at Xaghra. This awe-inspiring megalithic complex was erected in stages over a period of several hundred years from c3600 BC. Grace showed me a map of the complex with an outline drawing of the temples, pointing out that the two main temples inexplicably follow the female shape. We stopped at a charming seaside hamlet called Zledin, for lunch at a restaurant run by friends of Frank and Grace. Although closed, being out of season, they opened it especially for us and brought the chef in to cook us fantastic fresh fish. The next morning Frank and Grace collected us again at our hotel for another tour, this time to take part in the celebrations on Maundy Thursday, where tradition dictates that families must visit several churches during the day and night to pray together. There were impressive tableaux on display in every church. On Easter Sunday local men run through the streets carrying these heavy tableaux to celebrate the resurrection. Every church was full of fragrant flowers. This Catholic tradition is in marked contrast to English Protestant churches, where no flowers are allowed during Lent. That evening Frank and Grace took us to village markets where stalls sold all kinds of bread and sweets, only baked at Easter. At midnight the streets were packed with people and many remain in the church overnight until the bells ring out early the next morning to announce Good Friday. They took us to visit the historic Mosta Church the next day, Good Friday, followed by lunch at one of the restaurants at the newly restored quayside – built for the many cruise ships now docking in Valletta. I don't like to visit the past too much but this was a wonderful few days and it will not be our last visit to Malta.

CHAPTER SEVEN

Lithuania: In From the Cold

I AWAKE FEELING COLD, chilled further by the knowledge of being alone in an unknown city and a new region of Europe. The echoing sound of church bells is very close and they soothe my soul. As I open my eyes I seem to be surrounded by images of Romeo and Juliet acting out their famous balcony scene. It takes a few moments to realize that facing me on the opposite wall, and dominating the room, is a large oil painting of the lovers. On another wall are smaller portraits of the couple, this time in black and white. Books of Shakespeare's plays and poetry line the shelves, along with other references to our most esteemed poet. I get out of bed, nervously open a curtain and smile. Facing me is a splendid gothic church (source of the bells) and there is a small courtyard below the window. How appropriate. I have spent my first night in Vilnius at the Shakespeare Hotel (or 'boutique' hotel as the manager likes to points out), allocated their Romeo and Juliet room. All rooms are in fact named after a Shakespeare play or a philosopher, though why this room is not reserved for couples I don't know. I am the sole occupant and the romance and tragedy of the couple in the painting add to the feeling of loneliness I am trying to suppress, begging the question *what am I doing here?*

There was an absence of light when I arrived last night, and very late. There had been no time to explore the city or even the hotel and a lot to take in. I landed at an airport very different from any other I knew, small with ornate Soviet imagery on the ceilings.

When I presented myself at passport control, the severe expressions on the guard's face inflicted an intense feeling of guilt upon me similar to the one you have when driving and, seeing a police car, assume you have been speeding and are about to be pulled over, even though you know you are innocent of any crime. The guard looked from passport to my face several times, seemingly about to announce he would refuse to let me into his country. I was reminded of my first visit to America years before when on arrival I was threatened with immediate deportation. I had felt so excited arriving at Kennedy airport, eager to get through passport control and into a yellow cab to the Big Apple. I waited patiently in the queue, placing my bag on the floor. A small beagle wearing a smart green coat placed a paw on top of the bag. I patted him - big mistake. Far from being a pet, he was on duty and promptly alerted Homeland Security to a banned substance in my luggage. I was whisked off, the entire contents of the bag removed and the contraband placed on the table by a mean looking guard. We both stared at it, then each other. It was an apple – and not even a big one at that. An apple, the guard told me, meant I could be sent back to England on the next flight, such was the seriousness of this offence. He waved a document in front of me that I had signed confirming I had no contraband in my possession. Did I now admit this was an untrue statement? I admitted it was - what else could I say? On this occasion the guard said he would be generous and allow me to stay. He didn't look at all generous – and neither did this passport officer now standing in front of me, deliberating whether to let me in. Lithuania may have come in from the cold, but not long ago it was part of the mighty USSR, regarded by my government as an enemy of the West. When the Cold War had come to an abrupt end at the end of the 1980s, Lithuania grasped at freedom and was one of the first Eastern Bloc countries to declare independence. It was now a candidate country, soon to join the European Union. Did the passport control officer, whose serious face was reminiscent of the Cold War, not know this?

I collected my luggage from the small carousel and walked through automatic doors to an arrivals hall packed with TV cameras and excitable people clutching elaborate bouquets of flowers.. There were loud cheers from the crowd. The contrast from passport control was surreal. Is this the way Lithuanians greet all visitors, I wondered? Yes and no. Following behind me was a group of impossibly tall young men who had arrived on another flight. The television crew and audience were here to greet members of the Lithuanian basketball team, who were returning jubilant from a foreign match. Greeting people with flowers, however, is normal. You never met anyone, man woman or child, at the airport without flowers and it was a custom I subsequently followed. I must have looked bewildered, and I suppose very English, because a man came forward and introduced himself as Andy Calvert, First Secretary at the British Embassy. He had been watching a football match with friends but interrupted it to meet me at the airport with the embassy car and take me to the hotel. It was dark but on the way into the city I peered out of the window, eager to see as much of the environs as possible, which mostly seemed to consist of huge slabs of ugly Soviet-style apartment blocks, interspersed with small wooden kiosks selling cigarettes, newspapers and sweets and flowers. Crossing the river Neris, I guessed we had reached the city when I saw the Cathedral and castle sitting above it, both blazed in light. Andy abruptly swerved left down winding cobbled streets, coming to a halt at a warm charming hotel.

Finding myself in Eastern Europe felt strange. For most of my life half of Europe had been hidden behind an Iron Curtain; as a child I was very aware of the Cold War and the threat posed by the Soviet Union, with its spies and atom bombs. After a good night's sleep and breakfast I ventured out into a bright but cold Sunday morning. I felt a frisson of excitement leaving the shelter of the hotel to venture along the cobbles on Bernadinu Street that led on to Pilies (Castle) Street, the main thoroughfare through Vilnius old town. It felt different from anywhere else in Europe I had visited, but before long I was enchanted by this lovely city, hidden from the west for so long. This was Jim's proposed new venture and I was here to look around, meet the officials at the Ministry of Justice where the project was to be based and consider if I could spend the next year and a half here, helping them prepare for their accession to the EU. Was I mad to even consider this?

CHAPTER EIGHT

First Steps Along the Baltic Road

I ALWAYS LOOK upon my journey to the Baltics having its source in the Mediterranean. The first project in familiar Malta was a good initiation into European work, preparing me for the larger task ahead in a colder climate and unknown country. Politicians like to talk of 'road maps' these days, but I had no such plan of action. In fact there was no reason to think that when I accepted the two-months' work in Malta it would lead to my leaving a full-time job I had carried out with enthusiasm and dedication for eighteen years; even less that I would go on to work in the Balkans or the middle-east. It's good that we cannot see into the future, otherwise I may have found the idea too overwhelming and opted for the safe option of staying at home.

    The opportunity to work in Lithuania had again been suggested by Jim Spinks before we even started the work in Malta. 'Take a look at the project terms of reference,' he said, 'it's similar to the one in Malta. You may not be interested but let me know what you think anyway.' Assuming by this description it was another short-term project in a country already familiar to me, I eagerly opened his attachment. I hoped that it was in Cyprus, maybe even Prague, both pre-accession countries. In fact, the only similarity seemed to be the subject - consumer protection. It was a long-term commitment and I would be required to live in Vilnius, capital of Lithuania, for eighteen months. I knew very little about the Baltic States, other than they had been part of the Soviet Union since the war, and must confess I had to look Vilnius up on a map. Only later did I discover Lithuania's fascinating history and the role it had played in the uprisings that swept across Eastern Europe in the late 1980s. Like everyone else I had been amazed by television pictures of the fall of the Berlin Wall, the West holding its breath waiting to see if Russia would take retaliatory action. The world's media was focused on Berlin but it is worth mentioning here that another unique protest was also taking place that summer in the Baltic

States. Lithuania, Latvia and Estonia had organized a peaceful protest to demand independence and democracy for their countries and it played an important part in the fall of communism. *The Baltic Way*, as this protest became known, was a unique form of resistance against Soviet oppression. Ordinary people joined hands in a human chain that stretched for 650 kilometres that started in Vilnius and continued without a break through Latvia up to Tallinn in Estonia. The chain was made up of two million people - young and old, men, women and children, all holding hands. What made this protest unique was that those taking part agreed to refrain from using any form of violence. Not a single shot was fired; no one was killed, although there were attempts by the Soviet authorities to provoke such a reaction in order to have an excuse of using military force. It was described as the 'The Singing Revolution' because in moments of danger people began to sing folk songs that had been banned during Soviet times and now took on a political significance. For the Soviet forces it seemed that these songs, and the flowers thrown down from the sky by international television stations broadcasting the event sparked more fear than guns. The movement had no leader or leading party, it was a demonstration of solidarity among three nations and ordinary citizens saying they wanted their independence. One wonders now how it was all put together when they had no Internet. Within six months of the protest Lithuania declared independence, followed by Estonia and Latvia. Fifteen years later I met Lithuanians who had participated in the Baltic Way protest and they told me that Soviet soldiers simply did not know how to respond. In Vilnius there is a memorial plaque near Gediminus Tower, with the words *stebuklas* (meaning miracle) marking the spot where the Baltic Way started. It is on Cathedral Square near the bell tower, and tradition dictates that you must stand on the circle, turn clockwise three times and make a wish. I can't tell you what I wished for, or it wouldn't come true, but I often reflect on the two million people who had the courage to take on the might of the Soviet Union by simply holding hands and singing.

Once I had located Lithuania on the map and registered an interest, Jim told me more about the work. I would be proposed as the Resident Twinning Adviser (RTA), an odd title for a job that encompasses a variety of tasks and many different skills. Some explanation of EU jargon is required. *'Twinning'* is the term given to European Union projects that transfer personnel from an existing Member State to a country working towards bringing their government institutions in line with those of the EU (referred to as the 'Beneficiary Country'). The RTA, usually a senior civil servant, is seconded from the Member State to work in a similar institution in the beneficiary country and is responsible for the day-to-day running of the project. He or she is required to be resident in that country for a minimum of a year and must have the required qualifications, such as a degree, length of service in the subject of the project and fluent in English as all written reports, presentations and training must be written in English. How lucky we are! The word *'Adviser'* is a misnomer, giving the impression that the RTA simply gives advice, whereas the tasks required of the holder of this post include 'Overall management co-ordination, implementation development of the Strategy, co-ordination of short-term experts and all reports associated with the project' – according to the Twinning Manual published by the EU. I would not be working alone, however. A project leader oversees the project from the UK, visiting Lithuania every quarter to chair the project steering committee. I have been fortunate to have Jim Spinks as project leader on three projects - with his expertise and good contacts in consumer protection he never failed to answer any problem I had and provided strong support.

With a better understanding of European twinning projects and the work involved in being a Resident Twinning Adviser, I still had little idea of what the job actually entailed when I agreed to Jim's proposal. At the time I had only just started working in Malta, which represented a challenge even though it was only for nine weeks. This new proposal was potentially life changing. The outline of the work was familiar enough - I had worked in consumer protection for many years and knew I was qualified to do the job - but it was a huge commitment and would take me away from home and family for what seemed like a long time. Did I want to do this? It also seemed to me that a more senior person was required, though I sensibly kept this thought to myself. I was due to meet Jim in London to discuss the schedule of work in Malta, and after our meeting I decided to raise the matter of Lithuania. When I told him I might be interested he seemed surprised. It's never a problem to recruit short-term experts for overseas projects, but few will sign up for a full-time lengthy commitment. It just felt right at this point in my life to take a risk and leave my job in Trading Standards. Northern Ireland Co-operation Overseas (NI-CO), a not-for-profit public body based in Belfast that specializes in managing development projects, would take on the overall management of the project and I would negotiate my contract with them. NI-CO had been actively involved in supporting Lithuania's accession since 1997 but this would be their first consumer protection project in the country.

Jim went on to tell me about Beth Baker, a Trading Standards Officer from Suffolk who had just begun work as a Resident Twinning Adviser in Latvia, hoping to give me reassurance. He spoke in glowing terms of her professional ability and of setting up a home and office in Riga. I experienced a crisis of confidence. 'Could I do the same and was I really up to the job?' I answered my own question – I was sufficiently qualified and relished the challenge. 'Go out to Vilnius and see if you like it,' suggested Jim. Ah, a reprieve, I thought; if I don't I can turn it down. Also, our bid would be competing with other European countries and we might not even win the tender. Breaking a large task into small chunks makes it seem more manageable and less daunting. I decided to look upon this opportunity as an expenses paid trip to a city I would otherwise be unlikely to visit.

A visit to Vilnius was arranged, where I met Oonagh McAliskey, one of NI-CO's young executives. The only document we had at that time was a broad outline of the expected results of the project (called a Fiche), which was to strengthen the Consumer Rights Board, develop consumer protection legislation, introduce consumer education, and improve the institutional system of consumer protection and that of consumer NGOs. Training was to be provided in unfair contract terms, advertising, E-commerce, product safety and other consumer related issues. A special programme for the training of Judges was also expected. We sketched out a strategy to convince our hosts that the United Kingdom was best placed to deliver the improvements they wanted. Oonagh and I got along very well from the start and although still in her twenties, she had plenty of experience and nothing seemed to faze her. It was also her first visit to Lithuania so neither of us really knew what to expect and we excitedly explored the city together.

Early the next day Oonagh and I presented ourselves at the National Consumer Rights Protection Board (CRPB), the beneficiaries of the project and where I would be based, accompanied by Andy Calvert. The Foreign Office, through their embassies, give support to UK projects overseas, as well as supporting British nationals. Our meeting was with three senior members of staff: Marius, Edita and Augusta. The two young women were tall and willowy and spoke good English, Marius was even taller –a dark Slav-looking man with razor sharp cheekbones who sat silently and looked extremely serious and formal. He broke out into big smiles however when Oonagh distributed presents of Bushmills whiskey and Irish chocolates. I later learned that Marius had written the application for the project and like me was interested in consumer education. His face and manner at this first meeting, however, gave nothing away and he spoke little. In fact once I got to know him I found he was an exceptionally warm and benevolent man, just unsure about his ability to speak English.

After the meeting Oonagh and I continued our exploration of Vilnius. I sought out a bookshop. When visiting a new country I try to buy a book that is either written by a local author or set in the place I am visiting. Vilnius is full of bookshops and I found a small book of Lithuanian poetry, translated into English, *Snare for the Wind* by Kronelijus Platelis, which I still find inspiring. In his introduction the author contemplates where poetry comes from, who perceives it:

> Poetry is like wind: it's not clear where it comes from.
> It's not clear where it goes. And it's not
> Clear what it means.
> What a strange, naïve thing – a snare for the wind!

For me the poem encapsulates the lyrical and poetical nature of Lithuanians. I was snared by the essence of Lithuania; it had me in its trap straight away. Later I read a book review in the *Baltic Times* about a British author, Stephen Collishaw from my hometown of Nottingham, who had lived in Vilnius for some years, and I tracked down his novel *The Last Girl,* inspired during the time he lived there. The story is set at the end of the 20th century with flashbacks to World War Two, about a poet who is haunted by a terrible secret and is fearful of resuming his writing, thereby fanning the embers of his memories. Much of the action takes place in the old part of Vilnius, in the streets and courtyards I came to know so well. It is a story of memory, love and the heartbreaking choices made in times of war.

On our first night in Vilnius Oonagh arranged for us to have dinner with an RTA who had lived in Vilnius for two years whilst working for NI-CO on an agricultural project in the three Baltic States. Gerry suggested we meet outside Amatininkai, a popular pub in Old Town, telling us to look out for a 'Man on a Barrel'. We were doubtful we would be able to locate the area, but lo and behold opposite Town Hall Square we spotted an inn that above the sign had the required man sitting astride a barrel of beer. It's a popular venue and there are few people who have been to Vilnius and not visited – Jeremy Irons and Helen Mirren were spotted having a drink there two years later; they were filming in the area. On this

1. 1966: My first car – I wish I had kept it!

2. National Egg Week 1967 - I am the 'Egg Chick' on the right

3. Romania 1970: On holiday at the Black Sea

4. On the Dingli cliffs with Grace and Frank Farrugia, waiting for the sun to set

5. Vilnius 2004: Launch of Consumer Protection Twinning Project Jim Spinks, CB, Feliksas Petrauskas

6. The Angel of Uzupis – calling me to Vilnius

7. Trakai Castle in Summer

8. Trakai Castle in Winter – with my friend Myrna Wilson, sliding on the ice

9. Taking consumer protection to the regions in Lithuania in Rokiskes with Jim Spinks, Robin Croft, local dignitary, CB, Neringa Ulbaite, Mike Kitson, Greta (translator)

10. Training at a Business Incubator in Kaunas

11. Relaxing on the regional tour – it's not all work!
Greta, Neringa, Dainus (musician and poet), CB, Jim, Robin, Mike

12. The Hill of Crosses, Siauliai - a place of pilgrimage

13. Vilnius skyline with its Baroque, Gothic, Renaissance buildings

14. Gedimino Prospektus – premier shopping street in Vilnius

15. Old Town, Vilnius: Oonagh at the Gates of Dawn, the only surviving gate in the city wall with the sacred Chapel of the Blessed Virgin Mary above.

16. 2005: 'Last Supper' at La Provence restaurant, Vilnius,

occasion we didn't go inside. Sensing Oonagh would be paying on the NI-CO credit card, Gerry suggested a better restaurant and took us round the corner to the Markus Bar. Over dinner he explained all about life as an RTA in Vilnius. Mentoring prospective RTAs was a role I was also to perform many times over the next few years.

I was back in Malta when the call came to attend a formal interview in Vilnius where the tenders for our project would be considered. The timing was not good – Alan had flown over for a short visit and I had to leave the day before he was due to return home. It involved flying from Valletta to Heathrow, then take a coach to Gatwick for a flight to Vilnius. Jim asked me to go a day early and represent Britain at an interview for a food safety project they were also bidding for, but gave little information about it. The proposed RTA was Cecil, a wonderfully eccentric Professor at Queen's University and a great raconteur with an abundance of interesting anecdotes. I spoke during the introductions, then sat back and hoped they wouldn't ask me any questions on food safety. They didn't, in fact the spotlight was predominantly on the proposed RTA. It did prepare me for my own interview the next day however; up to then I had no idea what to expect. It was also Oonagh's first project interview and she was even more nervous than me; being a good Catholic girl, she went to a chapel at the Cathedral to pray. Andy, representing the Foreign Office, accompanied us to both interviews - their support is important in the selection process and we were joined by Joanne Lenzi from NI-CO. We faced an interview panel of twelve people from different nationalities, representing the beneficiaries, the EU Delegation and European Commission. A Spanish woman from the Commission fired questions at me and seemed quite hostile, though over coffee and cakes later she was very friendly. I realized then, and many times since, that if people of other nationalities appear to be aloof or uncommunicative it's because they are not conversing with us in their own language, whereas I am always speaking in my first language of English.

We were competing with the German bid. They were well prepared and had brought with them a large delegation from the State National Consumer Protection Agency. They were staying in the same hotel as us and we wished each other the best of luck after the interviews. I was quite sanguine about the process; having now had this unique opportunity to visit Vilnius twice, with flights paid by NI-CO, was reward itself. If we didn't win the project I still had a job back home. There was also a third UK bid up for selection that day, for a veterinary project. The proposed

RTA was Archie Hunter, accompanied by his project leader Gareth, both from Scotland. That night they joined our NI-CO group, plus Andy, who recommended a Georgian restaurant - a cosmopolitan group of English, Irish and Scots, being served by Russians in a Georgian restaurant in Lithuania! It had been a stressful two days and we were all ready to relax and indulge in some amusement. After several courses and plenty of wine, we were presented with the bill, only to be told they did not accept credit cards, something we take for granted in UK restaurants. We had to visit cash machines to settle the bill.

Two weeks later Oonagh's prayers were answered —the news came through from Brussels that our bid had been selected. Initially I was more shocked than pleased. For months I had assured friends and family it was unlikely that our bid would be chosen to run the project - the Germans had seemed so confident. Now I had to face up to a radical change of direction. Archie's bid was also selected though Cecil was unsuccessful. His project had been awarded to Germany and he was bitterly disappointed. Two years later, near the end of my project, Edina, a Director of the Board and one of the beneficiaries, told me that from our first scoping visit they had already decided to choose our bid, helped by the fact that I reminded her of her English mother-in-law, of whom she was very fond.

Oonagh began to draft the Twinning Contract, a comprehensive document that sets out exactly the terms of the twinning, the activities, outputs and results to be achieved, potential risks, the names and CVs of all short-term experts. Once we had completed this task we made another brief visit to Vilnius to meet the newly appointed director of the Consumer Rights Board, Feliksas Petrauskas. I liked him —physically he resembled former President Brezhnev. He could be difficult however and some members of his staff did not always find him easy to work for, though he had a charming side and could be flirtatious. Oonagh brought out presents of whiskey and chocolates again and he succumbed to her Irish charm. On this occasion I decided to take a trip out of town to visit Trakai, a magical place set in the middle of five large lakes with an enchanting castle. The town was once Lithuania's ancient capital, thirty kilometres west of Vilnius and easily accessible by train. It is home to the Karaite, a small religious group who came to Lithuania from the Crimea as bodyguards of Grand Duke Vytautas in the fifteenth century. There is still a community of their descendants and I ate delicious Turkish cuisine in one of their restaurants by the lake. They keep their culture and religion alive and have a small ethnographic museum. Trakai castle is set in the middle of several lakes with access by boat or the medieval footbridge, looking like something out of a fairytale with a moat and turrets. I was to visit this town many times over the next two years. Idyllic in summertime, the lake and town are transformed in winter by deep snow and ice and once when Myrna Wilson, my friend from Hart, was visiting, we walked across the frozen water. We reckoned it was safe enough when a motorbike rode across the lake at some speed. We stopped to watch the fishermen drill a circle in the ice, sit on a small stool and dip their fishing rods into the icy water.

Back in Vilnius I took the opportunity to view some apartments and get a feel of where I would like to live. At the time I still could hardly believe that this city would be my home for the next eighteen months, but during subsequent visits my first impression of Vilnius never changed. The city had captured my heart and now I couldn't wait to start the project. There were, however, some matters to arrange back home. I had to complete my work in Malta, leave Trading Standards, give up my CSN work, complete the PGCE course I had embarked on the previous year, cancel teaching commitments with the Money Advice Trust and, most importantly, spend time with my family. My life was about to change dramatically.

At this time I was still employed by Hartlepool Council, having returned there after completing the first mission in Malta. I was greeted with the news that the consumer advice centre was to be closed and I was transferred to work from the Civic Centre. Heather and Darren, my two assistant advisers, had already seen what was happening and left to take up jobs elsewhere. A freeze on recruitment meant they could not be replaced, leaving me as the only adviser. I asked for a meeting with the Council chiefs to discuss the future of the service, knowing that if they agreed to resource it properly again I might turn down the offer of work in Lithuania. Instead they told me they intended to close the service and direct consumer complaints to the Citizens Advice Bureau. It was time to leave. It saddened me that a service that had been so strong for thirty years and served the needs of disadvantaged people in Hartlepool could be dismissed so lightly.

The part of my life that gave concern and caused a lot of soul searching was leaving my family. I now had a grandchild in addition to a husband and two daughters, all of whom I would miss terribly. I could not have made the decision without their full support, but they insisted I must seize this opportunity, reminding me that the expenses included a flight home every month. They promised to come out to visit, and after all Hannah would be less than two years old when I returned. It still felt unreal - I had never foreseen that I would reside anywhere other than in England, especially not take up work overseas. Several months passed before we had the go ahead to start the project. The process to agree the terms of the Twinning Contract and obtain all signatures and approval from the beneficiaries and the European Commission is a lengthy process and although I had been told to be ready to fly out in October 2003, it was not until the following March that I did. I was impatient to get started as I had by then left Hartlepool Council, but at least the delay afforded me time to spend in the Lake District, our second home.

Resident Twinning Advisers are required to attend a training course in Brussels and I looked forward to this, not having visited the city before. Staying at the same hotel was another new RTA, Brendan from Belfast, a data protection expert also working for NI-CO. He had recently completed a project in Lithuania and by coincidence was due to go to Malta on a twinning project and was already making plans for his family to visit. We exchanged tips about these two cities and from him I learned more about Vilnius. Later I was surprised to hear that he had been rejected as RTA. Both new to Brussels, we managed to find our way to the Commission building and were directed to a large conference room with flags on the tables. There were about thirty people of various nationalities on the course who were being posted to the ten new Member States set to join the EU in 2004, and delegates sat at the table flying the flag of the country we would be working in. Under the flag of Lithuania— yellow (golden fields) green (the countryside) and red (the blood that was shed for the new Republic) - I was introduced to three other RTAs, all male, in fact there were only one or two women RTAs. It was reassuring to meet those who would be working in the same country; these are the people who can help and support you once the project starts. They included Frederic from France working in the Ministry of Interior, an energy specialist from Denmark whose name I have forgotten, and Friedrich from Germany, a professor in food safety whom I had met at the interviews in Vilnius some months earlier. Frederic was a charming French man, married with a teenage family at this time. I lost contact with him after a few months in Vilnius and heard later that his wife had died of cancer and he had returned to France to be with his two teenage children. I was later surprised to hear he was back in Vilnius to complete his project. He called one day to tell me he had married a Lithuanian woman and they now had a baby, inviting me to tea. He seemed very happy, but I have often wondered whether he stayed in Vilnius, separated from his older children, or if he returned to France with his new wife and child. Although at this time I found the other Friedrich, a professor in food safety, to be rather brusque and opinionated, I later changed my view and surprisingly ended up seeing more of him than the other Resident Twinning Advisers.

A number of speakers inducted us in the ways of twinning, including a former RTA from Prague, a jolly lady who made it sound hard work but fun, and the director of the EU's enlargement process and neighbourhood policy. It was all a revelation to me and I realized I had huge gaps in my knowledge of the workings of the European Union. At lunch all the Brits on the course were invited to lunch courtesy of the British Embassy. Brendan and I got talking to some of the other delegates and we all went into the city that evening to visit the Christmas markets and sample the mulled wine. The next day we regrouped to visit the relevant area of the Commission, for me this was the Consumer Protection Directorate. Here I learned more about the policy and strategy of the Consumer Directorate at the European Commission. There were only two of us on this occasion, my companion being Javier, a Spanish consumer expert who was being posted to Bulgaria. He was part of a larger group from Spain (they must have won several projects) and I joined them later for coffee. The next day we shared a train to the airport. They were very lively and I regret not keeping in touch with my Spanish counterpart.

The meeting at the Consumer Protection Directorate opened my eyes to new possibilities. I had been working in this area for almost two decades but the new millennium did not auger well for consumer protection in Britain. The first term of New Labour in 1997 had seen many new initiatives such as the White Paper, *Modern Markets, and Confident Consumers* and Consumer Support Networks that set the agenda for an improved consumer protection regime but at the turn of the century the services delivered at local level faced reduced funding. It was refreshing to be introduced to EU policy that was fertile with new legislation and strategies intended to put consumers at the heart of all European policy.

After Brussels I flew to Belfast to sign my contract at NI-CO and meet the back-up team. It was my first visit to Northern Ireland and Oonagh drove me around Belfast, taking me to Stormont (grand but deserted as politicians could not agree to form a government) and East and West Belfast. We stopped to walk along the Falls Road in the nationalist area, with its mural of Bobby Sands as well as other republicans, and on to the loyalist Shankill Road, separated by the Peace Lines. Until then I had not understood the enormity of the barriers that separated Catholic and Protestant neighbourhoods, nor the painted kerbs that divided the area: red white and blue in the loyalist area, Irish Republican colours to indicate nationalist sympathies.

In 2004 I was still slightly unsure of what I was signing up to, other than eighteen months away from home. If everything comes with a price, what would I have to pay in terms of sacrificing family life? How would I adapt to this new adventure offered to me in late middle age? There was only one way to find out.

CHAPTER NINE

Lietuva – a Brief History

LIETUVA (LITHUANIA): A COUNTRY located in Northern Europe on the shores of the Baltic Sea. The largest of the Baltic States, it borders Latvia in the north, Belarus in the east and Poland and Russia (Kaliningrad) in the southwest. The country is covered with forests, lakes and rivers and people have a deep attachment to the countryside and their traditions.

I knew little of Lithuania's history when I accepted the position as Resident Twinning Adviser working in the Ministry of Justice in the capital city of Vilnius. It has a proud history riddled with troubles along the way: a Grand Duchy in the 13th century, the Baroque period during the 17th and 18th centuries left a legacy of beautiful buildings; it was annexed by Russia in the 18th century and occupied by the German army in 1915. After the Great War the country proclaimed itself as an independent state, restoring statehood and the right to self-determination. Over the next two decades Lithuania began to create democratic and modern institutions but this was brought to an abrupt end in 1939 when the country was first annexed by the Soviet Union and then Nazi Germany. At the end of the Second World War Lithuania became a Soviet satellite state. Thousands of Lithuanian partisans took to the streets and forests to fight for their country's freedom, but dissent was crushed.

During Soviet occupation the flame of independence was kept alive by the Sajudis freedom movement. In Kaunas, where the resistance movement to Soviet occupation was strong, my assistant Neringa pointed out a memorial in what she called Freedom Alley dedicated to Romas Kalanta, a young man who had set himself on fire in 1972 to protest against Soviet oppression. A decade later change was in the air in Russia and Gorbachev's *perestroika* was to have an unexpected impact on events in many countries in Eastern Europe, including Lithuania. Challenges to the ruling communist party continued to be crushed but Lithuania declared independence in 1989, recognized by the international community though not, of course, by Russia. Two years later the Soviet authorities attempted to overthrow the government by force, storming Seimas, the seat of parliament. Fourteen demonstrators were shot before the Russians finally departed; their memories are kept alive by photographs and poems, as a shrine to brave citizens. You can still see the barricades, left near Seimas as witness to these events. There are more memorials at the Television Tower, marking the spot where unarmed civilians were killed whilst trying to regain control of the tower.

Walking up Gedimino Prospektus, the main shopping street in Vilnius that connects the Cathedral with Parliament, I noticed names and dates carved on stone slabs at the base of the court building facing Lukiskiu Square. There was no explanation as to their significance but I discovered they were the names of freedom fighters, tortured and killed in the basement of this neo-classical building. It had been the headquarters of the former KGB in Soviet times when a huge statue of Lenin, his right hand outstretched, stood in the square opposite. Hundreds of citizens, including two Bishops, were imprisoned in the basement of this building; many more were shipped off to Siberia. It is now open to the public as the Museum of Lithuanian Genocide Victims and visitors can walk into the cold cells and listen through headphones as a former prisoner describes the dreadful function of each cell. I took the tour. Two cells were padded; one had a stained straightjacket pinned to the wall. But it was the ice-pool cell that was the most disturbing. A lowered concrete floor was filled with cold water and the prisoner, wearing only underwear, would be forced to stand for hours, sometimes even days at a time, in temperatures of minus 30 degrees on a small raised circular block. The frozen water, I was told, turned red with the blood of the prisoner. Another cell contained a mountain of shredded paper. Apparently in the last days of communism the Soviets tried to destroy all the evidence of what had happened in this building, but were forced to leave before the task was accomplished. There was an execution yard; the adjoining room has a glass floor where the heart-rending possessions of victims are displayed. It is a grim place, more so for being located in what is now a modern part of the city. Around the corner on Auku (Victims' Street) is a small brick memorial to those who died, where a flame always burns. Despite this, there is humour. Local people ask, 'Do you know where you had the clearest view in Vilnius in Soviet times?' The obvious answer is from the highest point, the television tower. The Lithuanian answer is, 'It's from the KGB building on Lukises Square opposite the statue of Lenin. From there', I was told, 'you can see all the way to Siberia'.

There is no humour to be found in the fate of Lithuania's Jewish community. Before 1939 Vilnius had one of the largest Jewish populations in Europe and a thriving culture. By the end of the Second World War ninety-four per cent had perished in the Holocaust. One weekend Archie Hunter, who had his car in Vilnius – having driven it from his home in Scotland – invited Isabelle who worked at the EU Delegation and me to visit Panerai forest, ten kilometres from Vilnius, scene of the mass murder of 100,000 people, mostly Jews from the Vilnius Ghetto. It was difficult to find and there are no signs to help, though Archie seemed to know where it was and the terrible things that had happened there. He remembered it was close to a railway line (used to bring in victims) and we followed that into the forest and came upon two modest monuments, one Jewish and marked with the Star of David, the other Soviet, plus a small museum that was closed. We saw a series of circular pits, now grassed over. In 1941 the Nazis occupied this area and decided to take advantage of these large pits (previously dug for oil warehouses) to dispose of bodies. Victims were lined upon the edge of each pit and shot in the back of the head. When Soviet troops advanced in 1944 the Nazis tried to cover up their crimes by forcing workers to dig up the corpses, which were then burnt in trenches, the ashes ground up, mixed with sand and buried. Eleven of these workers survived and gave testimony to the terrible crimes. Archie is a vet and during the foot and mouth crisis in Britain he was sent to Cumbria to oversee the burning of diseased cattle. These trenches reminded him of that time. He told me that the air would carry the odour for miles and that people living in the vicinity of Panerai must have suspected what was taking place.

In this dark silent forest, where no birds sing and there is still evidence of the pits and a trench, the atmosphere is oppressing. As I stood to say a silent prayer for the victims I was startled when a goods train suddenly rattled through the forest; it didn't stop, but I couldn't help thinking of those thousands of people for whom the train did stop at Panerai. Were they aware of their fate?

When my friend Ann Kaye came to visit we tried to seek out some of the Jewish culture. She had been told some of her ancestors came from Lithuania, but it proved a disappointing quest. The one remaining synagogue (there were a hundred in Lithuania before the War) was closed for repair but we located a small archive of historical documents in an office on Pylimo Street, run by an elderly man. We had the impression he received very few visitors but he made us most welcome. I also showed Ann a map carved on a wall in Rudninku Street in Old Town, on the site of the former gate to the Vilnius Ghetto, illustrating where the Jewish population was held before being sent to the camps. These memorials are important to remind future generations of the past. As Santayana remarked: *Those who cannot remember history are bound to repeat it.*

Vilnius boasts a Cathedral and Castle among its many fine buildings. The Cathedral, built in the French-classicist style, has a portico with six columns and statues of Three Saints and a fabulous Baroque chapel. This beautiful church was used as a grain warehouse and later an art gallery in Soviet times, returned to the Catholic Church in 1990. The separate bell tower is on Cathedral Square near the statue of Grand Duke Gediminas, the city's founder. On a hill above the Cathedral stands the Castle, giving a breathtaking view of the city. On my first visit to Vilnius I was surprised to see a large gaping hole in the ground behind the Cathedral, all that remained of a 16th century Royal Palace. Over the years I have watched the rebuilding of the Palace and witnessed its completion in 2009 when Vilnius was European Capital of Culture. Between the Cathedral and river is the Lower Castle area that includes a collection of preserved buildings: the National Museum, Museum of Applied Art (formerly the arsenal) and the Museum of Archaeology. Moving south along Pilies and Didzioji streets is the Old Town, originating from the early middle ages. A walled city in the 16th century, only one gate remains – Ausros Vartu (Gates of Dawn), also known as the Medininkai Gate with a chapel above the arch.

All the statues of Lenin and his friends had been pulled down in 1989 when the country turned to the west, so it is surprising to find a Soviet-style bridge in the centre of Vilnius, dividing the north and south bank of the river. This is the Zallasis Tiltas, commonly known as the Green Bridge, that spans the river Neris, named after a Red Army general and built in 1952. At each corner is a pair of heroic figures representing Agriculture, Industry, Construction and Education. After the fall of communism it was expected the statues would be demolished but they are still there – a further example of not forgetting the past.

On a lighter note, Vilnius is full of amusing places and monuments. Not long after I arrived I discovered an interesting part of the city not far from Cathedral Square. Crossing a bridge you are greeted by a *Welcome to Uzupis* sign, declaring itself a republic independent of Vilnius. Nearby is another - *Every dog has the right to be a dog.* No, I don't know what it means either. Up the hill is a tall column topped by a golden angel blowing a horn. On a visit in 2001 the Dalai Lama blessed the 'Angel of Uzupis', saying the angel's horn would sound throughout the world. Unsurprisingly Independence Day is celebrated on 1 April. It is a charming district peopled by artists, with one or two good restaurants. Frank Zappa's music did sound throughout the world and a little known fact is that the only statue of this musician is to be found in Vilnius, though it is tucked away in a courtyard and hard to find.

There is plenty to see and do in Vilnius. Ballet and opera are performed at the National Theatre and classical music at Congress Hall and the Philharmonic. None will break the bank. Eating out is also inexpensive and there are lots of good restaurants catering for all tastes. We were never short of a good place to eat and in Old Town there were many choices. Just after I arrived a reasonably priced French bistro called Les Amis opened and it became a regular haunt. Other favourites were Lokys, a Lithuanian hostelry with a full sized stuffed bear outside; Avilys with its own microbrewery and where all the food, including ice cream, is cooked in beer; Literati, a Swedish up-market restaurant (now closed); the superb La Provence; and Da Antonio for the best oven-baked pizza. Torres with its outdoor terrace has the best view and the Markus Bar in Old Town serves the best steaks, with music from a saxophonist or pianist playing most nights.

The Old Town can easily be covered on foot but beyond its limits are trams and the trolleybus. I mainly used the privately owned microbus, once I got the hang of the routes. You don't need to be at a bus stop to get one, but simply stand on any street corner and wave. Once aboard they speed away before you have chance to find a seat and it's normal to pass your fare to the person sitting in front and it will be passed down to the driver, with any change similarly making its way back to you. They will stop anywhere en route but you have to shout to tell the driver to stop —*Stotelė!* in Lithuanian.

When I arrived in 2003 and friends and family started to visit, my colleagues at the Board were amused at the idea of tourists visiting their city. It was a new concept for them, and even now Vilnius does not receive the numbers of tourists of, say, Prague. It is all the better for that, but I'm sure it will change as more people discover this corner of Europe.

CHAPTER TEN

Life as a 'Twinner'

THE EUROPEAN UNION developed the Twinning Programme as a pre-accession tool, designed to help candidate countries seeking to join the EU develop modern and efficient administrations. The input from an existing member state administration includes a Resident Twinning Adviser (RTA) who works full time in the corresponding ministry to implement the project, a project leader and specialist short-term experts. A local project assistant, fluent in English, completes the team.

After a lengthy delay, when I began to think this new career would never get off the ground, we suddenly received the green light to start and I flew out to Vilnius on Sunday 7th March. My younger daughter Carolyn and her husband came home for the weekend to say goodbye and Carolyn came up to Newcastle airport with me the following day for my early morning flight. As she and Alan waved me through security she thrust a carrier bag into my hand containing magazines, sweets and biscuits for the journey. It was a touching gesture and a complete role reversal from when I used to send her off to Guide camp with a 'goody bag'. The magazine had a free wash bag and I have carried it with me on every project since then. For some reason, when you work away from home you cling to certain objects and traditions; they seem to give comfort. This time flying over Lithuania I looked down on a winter wonderland, the trees white with snow. Deep snow also covered the city streets, blessing Vilnius with a sense of enchantment.

I checked in at the Shakespeare Hotel and again was allocated the Romeo and Juliet room, where I stayed until I found an apartment. Setting off to walk to work the next morning I felt both excited and apprehensive. It was impossible to predict whether I would succeed in this new career, or settle into a foreign city, knowing so little about either. I walked slowly, absorbing my new surroundings. It was a pleasant walk and I never tired of it: along the narrow and winding Bernadinu Gatve to Pilies Street, glancing up to the castle on the hill and the Three Crosses standing proud, across Cathedral Square past the imposing statue of Grand Duke Gediminus, the bell tower and Cathedral, finally up Gediminus Prospektus, the main thoroughfare. I noted with interest that a new French boutique had opened here since my last visit and there were some smart new shoe shops. An electronic sign at the Post Office building reminded me it was 8 March 2006, Carolyn's birthday. As I arrived at the Consumer Rights Protection Board (NCRPB) I was greeted by a group of men, led by the Director carrying armfuls of flowers. I was handed tulips. It was International Woman's Day, celebrated throughout Eastern Europe and would be celebrated in Britain if I had my way. Unlike Valentine's Day, when half the female population remains disappointed, all women can enjoy this day, whether in a relationship or not. It is customary for men to give the women they know a flower – traditionally a single stemmed tulip. The Chairman of the Board, Feliksas Petrauskas, a man very fond of the ladies, led his male colleagues around the offices giving out flowers, heart shaped chocolates and of course planting a gentle kiss upon his female staff. Once settled into the office Augusta, a tall, slim and confident young woman who was appointed my counterpart at the Board, put the kettle on and presented me with a delicate cup and saucer. 'We know that English women always drink their tea from china cups,' she said. It was a nice gesture and I decided it was not wise to mention that I was more used to drinking out of a mug at work. I still drink tea from Augusta's cup.

One of the first tasks for any Resident Twinning Adviser is to appoint a project assistant, but as the procedure must follow EU rules and be open, fair and transparent; it can take a few weeks to get someone in place. I interviewed several capable applicants but Neringa Ulbaite stood out. Of similar age to Augusta, she was mature for her years, a lawyer, superb assistant and translator. The Board's offices were housed in an ageing building that had previously been a music school. The reception and directors' offices were on the ground floor but our project office was at the top, up five flights of stairs – there was no lift so we avoided going downstairs unless it was absolutely necessary, but it kept us fit. Four desks were pushed against each other and it was a squeeze to get in, but it was a happy office and we achieved a lot of work in it and there was always laughter.

At this time Lithuania was a pre-accession country and still had a European Delegation Office. I was expected to report to them within a couple of days of arriving in Vilnius and was immediately greeted 'You must be the new Twinner,' a strange term. I also had to register my details at the British Embassy in Vilnius and introduce myself to the Ministry of Finance officials who would scrutinize our spending against the objectives and outputs of the project. I was fortunate in that the government agency in Lithuania that dealt with twinning projects was extremely helpful, headed by a polite man called Gintarus (which is Lithuanian for amber), whose advice and support was invaluable. Personnel in other projects I worked on were not always so helpful, frequently causing more problems than they solved. I also had to apply for an identity card, and this process proved challenging, entailing multiple visits to the relevant government office – a rundown building on the edge of the city. I persisted, having been told I could be asked for this at the airport, but Neringa and I almost lost the will to live trying to find a way through the maze of bureaucracy.

I had arrived just before World Consumer Rights Day (15 March) and Feliksas, who was organizing a conference to celebrate this event, invited me to speak. This is an important day in consumer protection, celebrated all over the world, except in the one country that probably has one of the best consumer regimes – Britain. I only had a couple of days to design a presentation outlining the project objectives and decided to begin with some famous words. World Consumer Rights Day has its origins in a speech President John Kennedy made to Congress in 1962. In this speech he outlined four basic rights: the right to safety, to be informed, to choose and the right to be heard:

'Consumers, by definition, include us all. They are the largest economic group in the economy, affecting and affected by almost every public and private economic decision.'

I wonder if the Chief Officers at Hartlepool Council had heard these words perhaps they might have been persuaded to retain the consumer and money advice service. It was very different in Lithuania - there was a large audience of people from State institutions and NGOs interested in hearing about consumer protection. Britain is unique in that consumer protection and market surveillance is carried out by Trading Standards Authorities based at local level, whereas in the countries I have worked in it has always been at Ministry level and my colleagues were career civil servants, not local government employees.

The conference provided me with a good opportunity to find out the current state of play in Lithuania as far as consumer protection was concerned, and to meet stakeholders. For the first time I had to make a speech using a microphone and headphones for simultaneous translation. On other occasions I had consecutive translation with a translator standing next to me repeating my words into their language. The following year Feliksas decided to put on an even better show and impress the newly appointed Minister of Justice. He hired a conference room at Seimas – the home of the Lithuanian government - and brought out a British speaker, Theresa Perchard from Citizens Advice, intended to inspire consumer NGOs in Lithuania. At the mid morning coffee break he took us to a VIP area, where in addition to coffee, glasses of brandy and whisky were lined up. The guests seemed to find this quite normal, though I did not partake myself.

Once in post Neringa worked tirelessly to set up our project office and we drew up a work plan to bring out the short-term experts. In all we had thirty experts and most came for multiple missions so we got to know them well and of course had our favourites. Some of them I recognized from Trading Standards or CSN, others I met for the first time when I collected them from their hotel early on Monday morning. The best experts were those prepared to adapt their knowledge and skills to that of a very different regime in Eastern Europe. A few found this difficult, producing the same work or delivering training as if they were working at home, but with encouragement adapted their style and language to a foreign audience.

It was only after I was settled into Vilnius that I fully appreciated what a huge project I had taken on. The budget was 1.29 million Euros.

Some of this was ring fenced for a supply contract to procure equipment for market surveillance institutions and a new European Consumer Centre and Consumer Education Centre that we were to set up. Detailed specifications for the tenders had to be written and this was the task of Phil Weston, the first UK expert to come out. It all took a long time, due to the bureaucratic process, but the Lithuanians were delighted when all the new computers, printers and other equipment began to arrive. Project objectives to be carried out by UK short-term experts included bringing Lithuanian legislation in line with the EU consumer Acquis (body of law) according to the best practices of European member states; improving the administrative capacity of the Board and other market surveillance institutions; developing and implementing national strategies on consumer protection, establishing a European Consumer Centre and consumer education. There was also a lot of specialized training to organize, including the training of judges. Another huge task was to develop new curriculum and modules to introduce consumer education into the State system and I enjoyed working with consumer education experts from Britain, whose names were familiar from my own work in this area. Robin Croft was tasked with establishing a system for the implementation of an Injury Prevention Programme. He had recently introduced a similar system in Malta. The benefits speak for themselves. It is a valuable EU initiative with the potential to save lives by Member States contributing to a European database that records injuries sustained from goods and services. Also to be introduced was the RAPEX system, another European system for the rapid exchange of information on dangerous goods and services so that they can be immediately withdrawn from the market. We had just the right expert for this technical work – Phil Weston again, an IT expert from Surrey whom I knew from CSN, who also delighted in updating the Board's computer systems. Other CSN colleagues included Malcolm Adams, Jacqui King, Sue Payne and Ann Kaye.

In addition Feliksas had his own list of activities that he wanted to include, one being support to the regional directors he was in the process of recruiting. The title of the project included the words '*and Promotion of local Non Governmental Organisations (NGO)*'. There is not always a meeting of minds between a government department and an NGO and a way has to be found to encourage joint working. In Lithuania there were about fifteen consumer NGOs in 2004, all demanding government funding whilst fiercely guarding their independence. A large amount of my time was spent with them and I acknowledge the important part they play, usually with inadequate funding. Jacqui King came for a few missions to work with consumer associations, eventually persuading them to join together in a network to give them a united voice. I always welcomed her visits because she is such good fun both at work and socially. Ultimately we were able to bring NGOs together into a network and organize training sessions for their members. It met the project objective but at the end of the project I was never sure if we had advanced their cause sufficiently.

All projects are required to have a 'kick-off' meeting. They are usually low-key, attended only by the main beneficiaries, but Jim and I thought it should be a high profile conference so as to build contacts with consumer NGOs and businesses that would be important to the success of the project. It is customary to extend an invitation to the British Embassy. His Excellency Colin Roberts, British Ambassador to Lithuania, had recently taken up his posting and I invited him to be the keynote speaker. He told me it was his first public engagement in Vilnius yet he amazed everyone by delivering most of it in Lithuanian with Neringa standing at his side, ready to provide additional interpretation if required. Our paths crossed several times after this - he was an informal friendly man, not at all what I had imagined an Ambassador to be like. I also opened my speech in Lithuanian, thanks to a private tutor I saw once a week. It was only brief but included the words 'welcome to the European Union', which drew claps and cheers. Two days previously, on 1 May 2004, twelve countries had been admitted to the European Union and it was a proud moment for Lithuania. I had prepared a PowerPoint presentation for the conference and was surprised when I saw my name had been 'Lithuanian-ized'. Instead of Carole I had become Carolina. Female names in Eastern Europe end with 'a' which is always pronounced (unlike the 'e' on Carole) whereas male names usually end in 's'. There is an interesting tradition regarding surnames. When a woman marries she takes her husband's surname and adds 'iene'. I therefore became Carolina Belliene – much more exotic than Carole Bell I thought. It will be interesting to see if this tradition persists or if women fight against taking an extended version of their husband's name.

To celebrate Lithuania's accession to Europe the EU delegation took over Torres restaurant in Uzipis for a party and there was copious food and drink. The terrace at Torres is set on a hill, overlooking the castle and Cathedral, giving a grandstand view of the fireworks. Cathedral Square was crowded with people celebrating this historic occasion and their singing and music wafted across to us. The celebrations continued and a week later I was invited to a cocktail party to celebrate Europe

Day which was held at the Museum of Applied Art, attended by all the European Ambassadors and those of us working on projects funded by the European Union.

Once these events were out of the way it was time to bring out the short-term experts from Britain who would work on the various elements of the project. Part of my enjoyment was working with UK experts and learning more about their own area of work. I already knew or had worked with most of them. Bob Imrie and John Whisson were former colleagues at Cleveland Trading Standards in the Eighties, both having left to take up new positions elsewhere and I don't suppose any of us imagined we would work together again in Eastern Europe. John, now a lecturer at Teesside University, came to deliver training and was popular with Board staff and we had some good nights out. Bob's expertise is in the area of credit and his job was to harmonize Lithuania's credit legislation with EU Directives. Richard Ferry, another Trading Standards Officer from Gateshead, came to train Judges and we paired him with County Court Judge Jolly from Hampshire – a man who lived up to his name.

I thought that living alone in a strange country might be an ordeal of boredom and wondered how I would spend time outside of work. I need not have worried - my social life got off to a good start without delay and although I did occasionally suffer from bouts of homesickness I found plenty to do. Archie Hunter was already settled in Vilnius with his wife Cynthia when I arrived and they introduced me to people they knew. During my first week Andy from the British Embassy arranged a party in a local pub for us to meet the other British experts working in Vilnius and we enjoyed a traditional Lithuanian meal courtesy of the Embassy. A few nights later Augusta invited me to join her at Torres accompanied by her boyfriend and teenage sister and we had a wonderful evening listening to live music. It became a favourite venue. I also met foreign RTAs working on various projects. Francesca Davoli from Rome made contact and suggested a meeting. She was an energy expert and the only other female RTA. She suggested we meet at *Sconis Ir Kvpas* (taste and smell) teashop – it was my first visit but I became a regular visitor after that, sampling their impressive range of leaf tea that was presented in an unusual teapot. When brought to the table it is upright and the waiter tells you how many minutes to allow it to brew, depending on the tea you have chosen. You then turn it on its feet and pour. I bought one for myself and it really does improve the flavour of the tea. Later that year Francesca invited me to her closing conference and evening dinner, a swish affair held at Literati, an elegant restaurant opposite the Cathedral. I was seated next to her partner Tom, who is English, whilst the other guests on our table all came from different countries. I had a long conversation with a young woman from East Germany who enlightened me about growing up communist GDR and the many restrictions and deprivations she experienced before unification with West Germany. She was a similar age to my own daughters but their respective upbringings were very different. At the same event I met Violetta, a lawyer with her own law firm, who had studied in Vilnius and St Petersburg. She explained to me about the deprivations in her home city whilst growing up; food supplies in the shops were scarce and people had to queue all day for a loaf of bread or meat. On returning from visits to Russia she would fill her suitcase with toilet rolls, as they could not be bought in Lithuania, and remembers queuing several hours to buy bread or meat.

A priority for any RTA during the first weeks of a project is to find an apartment to rent. Some don't go into their office until the search is over and the apartment made ready, but from the first day I was too busy to take time out of my working day and did the majority of the viewings in the evenings. Actually it's not such a bad plan because you soon realize that apartments that may look perfectly all right in the daylight or summer months present concerns when it is dark and snowing. I quickly found the perfect place, a luxury apartment between Ausros Vartu (Gate of Dawn), the most historic part of Old Town, and Rotuse, the Town Hall. It was in an old building beautifully restored with exposed ancient frescoes in the hall, housing six apartments and a penthouse. The apartment was spacious, with a balcony and wood-burning stove. However, it was over budget and I continued the search. I found another, in a converted convent (guaranteed to have amused my friends), and was on the point of taking it when the agent said there might be a chance of negotiating on the rent for the other one. I met the owner, Remigijus Andriunas, a glamorous and respectable man with long curly hair. He called at my office one day and the girls thought he must be Italian - he certainly displayed some of their glamour, with his fashionable clothes. We bartered over the rent, eventually agreeing 1,200 Euro (4140 litas) a month and a contract was drawn up. The lawyers at the Board offered to look over the document and found many flaws. In fact they practically re-wrote it and I was worried that Remigijus might back out of our agreement. We had another negotiation over the fittings. Being a flamboyant character he had furnished the apartment with a modern white leather suite, strange looking chrome and glass tables, heavy ornate drapes at the windows and huge beds. When I gave him a list of essential items such as pans, crockery, cutlery, iron etc. he hurled it back at me, growling 'I'm a very busy man, I don't have time to go shopping for all this'. 'Perhaps your wife could do so,' I suggested. 'No, she is also too busy.' In the end he agreed that if I bought what was needed he would reimburse. The problem was that I was living in Old Town where the shops sell fashion, amber and linen, not basic household equipment. Indre, a girl at the office, came to the rescue and one Saturday she and her boyfriend took me to an out of town shopping mall to buy everything I needed. The boyfriend loaded everything into his car and unpacked it all back at the apartment, checking everything worked. Initially I had little confidence of being repaid by Remigijus but he surprised me by calling at the office one day and drew a thick wad of notes from his pocket. I had typed out all the items and their price, along with receipts, but he waved them away and just handed over the money. The young receptionist watching us looked aghast.

In addition to rent I had to pay for utilities and opened a bank account to make direct payments. On entering a bank you took a ticket from the machine, indicated the nature of your business, and waited for your number to come up on one of the electronic signs. Previously in Soviet times people had to queue for everything, so at least this system was fair. In Lithuania, and elsewhere in Eastern Europe, the government-owned supplier operated utilities centrally and it decided when the electric heating would be switched on or off, determined by the temperature over a period of a few days in the spring and autumn. Consequently, after a warmish spell in the spring you would return home from work to find the heating switched off. In the autumn there was always a period of two or three weeks when the apartment was freezing cold, though once it came on, it stayed on every hour of every day and public and private buildings were a constant temperature. My apartment also benefitted from underfloor heating. During the first spring I was there the heating had been switched off just before we had snow and the apartment was cold. I mentioned it to Feliksas and knowing I had a stove he said surely that would keep me warm. The problem was, I had no logs and no way of transporting them up to the apartment. He immediately called for his driver, instructing him to take me out of Vilnius to find logs. We drove to the outskirts of the city and the driver flagged down the first lorry that came along loaded with logs, asking how much it would cost to fill the car. After agreeing a price the logs were transferred from the lorry to the car, and he carried them up to my apartment making a neat pile. There were so many, I never needed to buy more logs.

This was the first time I had lived alone in an apartment and whilst missing my English house and garden, I enjoyed the contrast. It was in a perfect location. Ausros Vartu refers to the 16th century gate, which is the only surviving fortification. The chapel above the entrance to Old Town houses a holy image of the Virgin Mary, reputed to have miracle-working powers. It is impossible not to be moved by this image and the sheer number of people who come to worship the icon, many prostrating themselves on the cobbled street in front of it. I watched old women crawl up the stone stairs to the chapel on their knees, saying a prayer with their rosary beads on each step, worn down by generations of worshippers doing the same. Pope John Paul II had visited the city after independence and here and at many other locations around Vilnius a candle is lit and flowers left at the commemorative plaque.

The state recognizes several religious groups that enjoy legal status, though there is no state religion as such. The predominant religion is Roman Catholicism – banned of course in Soviet times. I can attest to the fact that most churches are full on Sunday and weekday services, by the young and old alike. Their popularity would be the envy of churches in my own country, but Lithuanians tell me of the Soviet years - when religious worship was banned and had to take place in secret, always with the worry that someone would report you to the KGB. Living in Old Town, I was surrounded by churches and it was soporific to be woken up on Sunday morning to the bells of St Casmir's, the oldest Baroque church in Vilnius. Beauty and history are lost on some people though. Passing by this church one day I heard an American couple say 'Well that place has seen better times.' I wanted to tell them it has also seen worse times, when the Soviets used it as a museum of atheism. Further up the road are two other churches - Holy Trinity, also Baroque, and the beautiful pink Russian Orthodox Church of the Holy Spirit with its stunning icons and decorations. In this church the preserved bodies of three martyred Saints are displayed in an open coffin. At Christmas they are clothed in white, black during Lent and red on other occasions, apart from one day when they are naked and worshippers are said to feel a healing presence. I made sure not to enter the church on that day! When Pope John Paul died I woke up to find Vilnius covered in black ribbons – on buildings and wrapped around every lamppost. I decided to walk down to the cathedral and found it packed with people, many sobbing loudly. It was very moving.

Photographs can tell you as much about a country as words in history books. Violetta invited me to attend an exhibition of the Lithuanian Press Photography Competition in 2004, only in its third year, this being a new genre in their burgeoning culture. Photographers representing different Lithuanian newspapers, magazines and news agencies presented their works created over the past year, capturing the real life image of the country. The photographs were included in a book, *Lithuania in Action,* that provides a photographic record of events in 2003 as diverse as a manacled French pop star charged with killing his actress wife, (in an apartment opposite my own), the national basketball team receiving the Grand Cross of the Order of Merit, a cow galloping against the motorway traffic in Panevezys - making a brave escape from the slaughterhouse - to women wrestling in honey. This book never ceases to put a smile upon my face; it is a wonderful reminder of the unique nature of Lithuania and its people, and the photographer kindly signed my copy. I found the exhibition particularly uplifting since by this time I knew something of the grim history of Lithuania, yet despite over four decades of forced Soviet assimilation, people have retained their sense of humour. Many a time I have reflected upon how fortunate I had been to live my whole life in a democratic and open society, something I have always taken for granted. In Lithuania I found a population who didn't dwell on this, preferring to look to the future rather than the past whilst retaining their traditions. They are a special people, polite, charming, generous, delightfully eccentric and quirky in their fashion, art and ceramics.

In 2004 there was quite a large 'ex pat' community in Vilnius, of different nationalities, who were working on a range of European projects designed to bring Lithuanian institutions in line with the standard required by the EU. Through Archie I got to know other RTAs and his colleagues from the Food and Veterinary Service. I also met up with the men I had met on the training course in Brussels. I often ran into Friedrich Johannson at conferences and one weekend he invited me to a party in his apartment, where I met his friends and colleagues. I had previously found Friedrich quite overbearing and nearly didn't go, but as a host he was completely different and it was a good evening. He brought in the chef of a local restaurant to cook for us and insisted I taste his homemade wine. Friedrich organized a monthly RTA get-together at the bar of the Hacienda hotel, where the owner played the piano for us and provided snacks, and anyone working on a project was welcome. There was also a weekly pub quiz loosely run by the Embassy and two English businessmen, long-term residents in Vilnius. They had persuaded a local bar to give them a free room, no doubt with the promise of selling large amounts of beer. I went to the first quiz with Archie and Cynthia and most Monday nights after that, accompanied by any experts or visitors I had at the time. At first only British people went, but later more and more Lithuanians joined us and they were always good nights.

In need of some exercise I heard about a walking/running group called the Hash House Harriers and turned up one Sunday morning to join them for a walk. There was an eclectic mix of people – ex-pats and locals. They had unusual rituals, like throwing flour (or worse) over the heads of newcomers. To start things off the lead Harrier blew a horn and we had to follow a trail set by him earlier in the day. He continued to blow the horn throughout the walk; to what purpose I'm not sure. It was different, but not for me and I didn't go again.

After Francesca returned to Italy I was the only female RTA for a while. Andy told me that another British RTA, Janice Ramsey from UK Customs and Excise, would be starting a project. After she arrived I called to invite her to dinner and we met regularly after that. Janice was a capable and confident woman, very good at her job yet she seemed to have more problems than me with her beneficiaries. They once insisted she sack one of her short-term experts, saying his work was not good enough. We had some nights out together and in December flew to Vienna for a weekend for the Christmas markets. Another RTA I met was Wolf from the Netherlands, veteran of several projects and always fun. He could be found every Saturday morning doing his paperwork at Ida Bassar, a coffee bar opposite the Philharmonic. He proclaimed that if any of his friends or colleagues wished to talk to him they would always know where to find him and I imagine he set up a similar arrangement wherever he was working.

Not wanting to be confined to the city at weekends, I bought a bike to explore the countryside. Neringa found one for sale on the Internet and it turned out that the seller lived in her apartment block. He put the bike on his car roof rack, driving bike and myself to the centre, as I couldn't have found the way back. The bike made a big difference, as I was able to cycle out in the summer evenings and further afield at weekends. I became very adventurous, riding out at the weekend to Belmontas, to rivers and forests on the edge of the city, making my weekends more interesting. Too adventurous in fact, I fell off a couple of times, once on the cobbles of old town, resulting in a damaged knee yet again, along with a swollen hand, which lasted a while. As I was then nearing the end of the project I wisely came to the conclusion of handing it over to another colleague and avoiding further injuries.

I joined the British Chamber of Commerce in Vilnius, mainly in order to make contacts with the business community, and attended monthly breakfast meetings at the Shakespeare Hotel, where there was always an interesting speaker. They also organized social activities. In January 2005 they put on a splendid celebration to honour Burns' night at Rotuksus, the town hall. Alan flew over to join me, very appropriate as he shares a birthday with Burns. Many of the guests, including the British Ambassador, wore tartan (Lithuanians as well as Scots); we ate a traditional haggis meal and danced reels. It was bizarre to be in Vilnius listening to the address to the haggis, traditional toasts and the poetry of Robbie Burns read by a Lithuanian wearing the kilt. It reminded me of another Burns Night dinner, in 1967, when aged twenty, I was asked to give the 'reply to the Lassies' toast. How long ago that seems, and how young and naïve I then was. In Vilnius pipers and a band had been flown in from Scotland and the Embassy supplied the Irish guards who were then based in Lithuania. They wore the tartan uniform, assumed by the Lithuanians to be Scottish. As we left the party it was snowing heavily giving the Town Hall a magical appearance.

I was fortunate to be invited to the Embassy many times, and once to the Ambassador's home. That came about early in the project when I received an official invitation to bring senior colleagues from work, Lithuanians and English, to a dinner at the Ambassador's residence. He lived in a beautiful wooded area in the heart of a forest and we enjoyed a warm evening in the garden and house, his children running around whilst his wife played the piano. The Ambassador made a speech welcoming the presence of British projects and then introduced me to one of his guests, Kim Howells the Consumer Minister from the Department of Trade and Industry who was in the Baltics seeking to gain support for the proposed EU Working Time Directive. He asked if he could visit my office the next day to see the work we were doing and I offered to set up a meeting with Feliksas. He came bearing gifts from Britain, no doubt supplied by Andy who had driven him to the office, and Feliksas presented him with a glossy book about Lithuania, making sure he had his photograph taken with the British Minister. I enjoyed Embassy hospitality on many other occasions; usually cocktail parties when a trade delegation was in town, where good wine and canapés were served and there were always interesting people to talk to. Best of all was the Queen's Birthday party celebration in summer, held under gazebos in the Embassy garden. Hot and cold food was cooked by a series of chefs and included different food from around the Commonwealth. The Irish Guards piped in the Ambassador who delivered the toast to Queen Elizabeth and we all sang the National Anthem. A variety of bands entertained us late into the evening.

During the first summer in Vilnius I met Isabelle, a young French woman from Versailles. I thought it must be wonderful to be able to say, when asked where you lived, 'Actually I live in Versailles'. I doubt you would be asked where it was, as often happens when I reply 'Hartlepool'. Isabelle worked at the EU Delegation office and took me to meet Vijole, a young Lithuanian dressmaker who was making lots of linen outfits for Isabelle's next posting in Africa. We took a taxi to the outskirts of the city and were faced with the usual concrete towers of housing. A short walk took us to Vijole's block and Isabelle pressed a button on the door. It opened and we entered a dark hall, climbed up an echoing concrete stairwell and came to a scratched brown door that had seen better times. There was another bell to ring and we could hear on the other side bolts being drawn across and finally a key unlocking first the outer then the inner door. I felt glad I was not alone, disliking the atmosphere. Once inside the apartment it was very different. The rooms, though small, were neat and tidy and lit with rays of sunshine. Vijole had found space in the sitting room to create a small workshop with a sewing machine, rail for finished clothes and shelves containing many fashion books and magazines. I immediately gelled with Vijole, a warm friendly girl who had been to college to study design and had a passion for making clothes. After this introduction I also began to visit Vijole regularly and she made me several dresses that I still wear. On Saturday afternoons I would source fabrics – there were many good fabric shops - then take a tram to her apartment where we would look at Vogue magazine and pictures from the latest fashion shows. She was a good designer and dressmaker, sketching outlines of different styles for me. I would return for at least three fittings before she was satisfied and I doubt I will ever again have the opportunity to have clothes designed and made for me.

I had many visitors curious to see a part of Europe previously off limits and without exception everyone liked Vilnius and I did my best to show them all the main attractions, but I hadn't reckoned with hospitals being on the list. Two hours after my husband Alan arrived on his first visit he began to complain of stomach pains and went to bed expecting to sleep it off. At 3 a.m. he woke me demanding a doctor and ambulance to take him to hospital. Coming from a man who had never set foot in hospital and kept away from doctors, I knew this must be serious. When the ambulance came the first thing they did was escort me to the ATM so I could withdraw the money to pay them. Looking for something cold to place on his stomach, their eyes lit up when they spotted a bottle of champagne in the fridge - brought out to celebrate my birthday that week - and insisted we place it upon his stomach. We then sped off at high speed to the Santariski hospital with the sirens screaming and ignoring red lights. After a worrying couple of hours in the emergency department Alan was wheeled around to various consultations on a creaking ancient trolley, along dimly lit corridors, still clutching the champagne to his stomach, although it must have been quite warm by this time. The paramedics and hospital staff were quite amused, and I was tempted to donate it, but I still had a birthday to celebrate and it was promised to my colleagues. You couldn't buy Verve Clicquot, or any other good champagne, in Vilnius at that time.

In the early hours of Sunday morning the hospital seemed grim and I had no idea where we were. Lifts were ancient, walls a dingy brown and everywhere in the dead of night looked neglected. Alan kept saying, 'I can't stay here, please get me out of here and on a flight home'. 'Of course,' I assured him, whilst knowing he could go nowhere in such pain. I was contemplating what to do when we were wheeled into yet another consulting room where I recognized ultrasound equipment. It revealed an appendix about to burst; he was taken to a private room and prepared for surgery, still protesting he wanted to go home. They took him down to theatre and I hopped on the bed and slept until they brought him back. I rang Neringa and she and Augusta arrived later that morning bearing strawberries and grapes and went off to talk to the doctors. In daylight the hospital looked better and being a private patient he had a nice room overlooking fields. He was in hospital for a week and although few of the doctors or nurses spoke English he managed to make himself understood. He got talking to another patient whilst walking up and down the corridors - Lithuania's Ambassador in Georgia who had returned home for an operation. After he had mentioned my work, she insisted on meeting me, inviting me to Georgia, where, she said consumer protection was badly needed. I think the country may have other more serious problems to sort out first though, particularly after events in 2008. Alan didn't make my birthday celebration; after visiting him in the evening I invited the girls from work round to drink Pimms. They had never heard of this drink and liked it very much, though I warned them it was high in alcohol content. The next day they all had hangovers and Indre's boyfriend, who had collected them from my apartment, said they were drunk and staggering along the street. Even so, they always expected Pimms at future parties. We drank the Verve Clicquot when Alan came out of hospital.

It was not to be my only experience of a Lithuanian hospital. When Isabelle left to work in Africa she had a party in her apartment and invited me, along with about fifty other people. It's never easy going to a function alone but although I had only been in Vilnius a few months I knew quite a few guests. It was an excellent party but a good walk from where I lived, so when Wolf, an RTA I then hardly knew, said he lived not far from me I decided it was safer to walk back with him. As we descended three flights of stairs from Isabelle's apartment and into the courtyard I stumbled. Most of the concrete had fallen away and whereas Wolf, being over six foot tall, simply strode across them, I fell. Feeling somewhat embarrassed, I insisted I was OK, not wanting any fuss, but on arriving home I was shocked to see a gaping wound across the kneecap pouring with blood. I couldn't clean it properly because it was too painful and I didn't have any antiseptic. The next day was Saturday and I lay with the leg elevated until late in the day I realized it would need stitching and called a taxi to take me to the Baltic-American clinic. The doctor and nurse were very good but the procedure of injecting anesthetic into the knee, cutting out the grit and dirt and stitching it up was extremely painful. I was given potent painkillers and told to call the doctor on his mobile day or night, especially if I had pains in the leg as it could be infected. I returned to the hospital the next day and a few times after this to have the dressing changed, once accompanied by Pat Walker, a friend from home and former nurse who was interested to check out the private clinic. Fortunately it all healed very well. Wolf was shocked when he found out the extent of the injury and felt responsible in some way, but of course it wasn't his fault at all. I promised to be more careful in future.

Another good party, this time without incident, was in Andy's spacious apartment to celebrate his birthday. It was a Sixties theme, the decade of his birth apparently, (making me feel really old). It was imperative that everyone dressed in 60s fashion and it was hard to recognize the Embassy staff who had decided to dress as hippies. Janice and I did our best to look the part in mini dresses and boots.

Culture is plentiful and relatively cheap in Eastern Europe and I made the most of it, going to the ballet and opera regularly and, living next door to the Philharmonic, was a frequent visitor to classical music concerts. Once the Scottish percussionist Evelyn Glennie was performing at the

Philharmonic and Archie and Cynthia organized a small party of us to go along and to show support. After the concert we were invited to an elegant salon upstairs where the Embassy was hosting a reception for the famous percussionist. She was very charming and she and Archie found they had mutual friends in common in Aberdeen. It really is a small world.

Having always been interested in fashion and clothes since my days as a 'Mod' in the Sixties, I noticed that Lithuanian women were well dressed with a unique sense of style and I found some interesting shops - Armani, Escada and Max Mara, and many small boutiques. D'Alby, a boutique on my street, always had a cat asleep in the window. It sold French-designed clothes using Lithuanian fabrics and I came to know the young sales assistant well. She knew my size and advised on colours and styles, rejecting those she thought didn't suit me, and I enjoyed calling in on Saturdays. On Town Hall Square was the shop of Ramuna Piekutitai, a famous Lithuanian designer whose collection sells like hot cakes in America. She designs and makes unique one-off pieces in linen or silk, always quirky and individual, and I cherish the few items I bought from her. Elementas, a small boutique on a crooked street in Old Town, was another favourite, owned and run by an American/Lithuanian woman whom I often encountered at social functions. Born in Lithuania, she had left the country with her family before the Soviets moved in and only returned to Vilnius after independence. She sourced unusual clothing and home interiors. There are dozens of amber shops in Vilnius – it is mined on the Baltic coast - and I had several pieces by the time I left. They say if you wear it next to your skin it has healing and calming effects, and once I had a facial using amber crystal. My Lithuanian friends told me I would not survive the winter without a fur coat and Neringa (who had three) drove me to a huge Russian market on the edge of the city, where I bought one for less than two hundred pounds. I was unsure about the ethics of wearing fur, which the Lithuanians could not understand at all; the farming of mink in the countryside supports the local economy.

We drove to the market twice more, when friends from home came to visit - Pat and Barrie from Hartlepool and Collete and Barrie from Blackpool. Both men also bought heavy winter coats and tell me they still wear them. Collete even bought an evening dress, trying it on in a freezing cold changing cubicle!

No sooner had I bought my own mink coat than Jacqui King gave me one. It was vintage, longer and warmer than mine. When my friend Myrna came to visit in winter she wore one and I the other, as did Grace who also appreciated it, missing the warmth of Malta. They both agreed there is nothing to compare with the warmth you get from real fur.

Frank and Grace Farrugia came to visit just before Christmas 2004. They were very excited to find a city buried in snow. Frank went out to buy a Christmas tree and when I returned from work the apartment was decorated with fairy lights everywhere. During their visit I was holding a Christmas party to thank my colleagues at the Board. Jim and Julia Spinks and Oonagh were also in town so we were quite an international group. Frank and Grace were popular with everyone and Feliksas, the Chairman of NCRPB, was good fun. Well, he was once he had recovered from a shock on arrival. Frank, eager to meet new people, had rushed to be at the door to greet the Lithuanians. Feliksas headed up the delegation, as it appeared, very formal, handing me flowers and an elegant glass bowl, gifts from him and his staff who stood behind him. He looked askance at Frank, knowing him not to be my husband, having already met Alan. I began the introductions. Just at the point when I was saying 'I met Frank in Malta when we...' Frank chipped in, saying, 'Yes that was when we became lovers'. There was a stunned silence – until I introduced the lovely Grace, his wife. Most Eastern Europeans don't really understand our sense of humour; irony and satire don't work at all. Being Maltese, Frank is influenced by the English and does. Feliksas looked completely shocked. He then saw the joke and roared with laughter and relaxed after a few vodkas. The evening was a success - the Lithuanians like a party and know how to have a good time. At the end of the evening we all took turns in singing national songs - Jim, Julia and myself sang *Jerusalem*, Frank and Grace sang in Maltese and the Lithuanians sang the folk songs outlawed during communism. Oonagh danced an Irish jig. It was a fitting end to a memorable year.

CHAPTER ELEVEN

Standing at the Centre of Europe

LITHUANIA IS FULL of surprises. I am standing on a newly laid circle of stones, surrounded by flags from the countries of Europe. Nearby is a small hut where the solitary assistant carefully writes my name on a certificate, taking out an official stamp to complete the process. (it seems every document in this country must have an official stamp.) The certificate confirms that I have stood at the centre of Europe. Lithuania claims to be the geographic centre of Europe, according to the French National Geographic Institute.

In the company of six colleagues I have just completed a week's training in the regions of Lithuania and having read about this landmark we decided, as Europeans, it would be a fitting end to our tour. The tour of the regions had not been included in the original terms of reference and was only made possible because we had funds to prolong the project. Initially I signed up for eighteen months and expected to leave Lithuania in the autumn, but a three-month extension kept me in Vilnius until Christmas. The European Commission, having allocated a specific amount of money to fund the activities requested by the beneficiaries, expect at least 90% of the budget to be used and any remaining funds must be returned to Brussels. In Lithuania we realized we would have a substantial surplus and began to think of an extension (or prolongation to give its official description). The Director had not been in post when the original project was drawn up and welcomed this as an opportunity to have additional activities. I was happy to acquiesce, even though it would mean a lot of extra work and delaying the start of my next project. Brussels requires a detailed Addendum to be written, detailing the work to be done that must be in line with the original objectives, accompanied by a new budget. This was my first experience of the bureaucratic procedure and I vowed never to go through it again; instead to make sure the money is spent by the time the project ends. The three-month prolongation was worth the effort though, especially the training presentations and conferences in the regions to support the newly appointed regional directors.

The previous year Neringa and I had organized some round table meetings in the regions in order to meet businesses and NGOs, and found them to be an enthusiastic audience. With the benefit of extra time we could build on these contacts and do more. I designed a programme that would take us around Lithuania and the regional directors helped us to find suitable conference locations and hotels to accommodate the speakers. The team consisted of me and Neringa, Mike Kitson (a lecturer at London University and European expert in consumer education), Jim Spinks and Robin Croft, Product Safety experts, plus translator Greta and Dianius who did an excellent job driving us around Lithuania on roads clothed in snow and ice. At this time there were no large hotels in the provinces and in some towns I had to share a room with Neringa and Greta. Driving around Lithuania it was impossible to ignore a landscape scarred by vast derelict factories, all the windows smashed, little left of the roof and a broken railway line that now ended at the factory gate rather than transporting goods across the mighty USSR. The countryside possessed a ghostly air. These empty factories bear witness to the cost of independence and democracy – the Russians did not just pull out of running the country after 1989; they also withdrew from running industry and thousands of people were put out of work overnight. Factories that would have provided employment for an entire town were now replaced by 'Business Incubators' – small but well resourced units that encourage entrepreneurs to start up a new business. We were able to utilize their training rooms for our seminars. Another feature of the landscape, in common with other countries in Eastern Europe, are the towers of concrete block housing that encircle towns and cities, rising in the distance as you approach a regional city or town - built by Soviet planners to look the same and house the workers.

On our journey we visited some of the lesser-known cities and each had their own unique feature. In Kaunas we met representatives from the textile industry who manufacture clothing for British high street chains such as Jaeger and Next. They were amused when I showed them the 'Next' label in my jacket and speculated whether it had its source at their factory. The city has a reputation as being a centre of private initiative and home to numerous small and medium enterprises, helped by its convenient location and good transport links. The Via Baltica motorway, which links Helsinki with Central and Eastern Europe, passes through Kaunas. It also has a Museum of Devils with a large collection of pieces of art and crafts representing the devil.

Panevėžysis is halfway between Vilnius and Riga and a stop is made here when travelling by bus between the two capitals. It's an industrial city, not attractive but a good place to talk to entrepreneurs. This is where most of the linen is produced – and I had already bought plenty of this good quality fabric to be made into summer dresses by my dressmaker.

Klaipėda – known as Lithuania's gateway to the Baltic - gave us a welcome breath of sea air. Walking along a pier jutting out into the cold Baltic Sea, it sparked memories of home on the north coast of England. We were taken for lunch on an old sailing boat, now a restaurant moored on the quayside. Our hosts urged us to visit Nida on the Curonian Spit, accessed by a short boat ride across the lagoon. A UNESCO World Heritage Site, it is sixty-two miles long and no more than two and a half miles wide, connecting Lithuania with Russia at Kaliningrad. It has been described as looking like an outpost of the Sahara - home to the highest drifting sand dunes in Europe, which reach from thirty-five to sixty metres high. Sadly there was no time to visit on this occasion and I had to wait a few more years until as a tourist on a Baltic cruise I finally stepped on to its fine white sands beside the fishing village of Nida and saw sand forming huge walls that brush up against fragrant pine forests. Knowing you are in Lithuania – not far from the so-called centre of Europe – it is odd to see a sign saying 'Welcome to Russia'. It would not be a good idea, however, to step across the boundary. A short drive north of Klaipeda is the seaside resort of Palanga, once a favourite holiday destination of former Soviet leader Leonid Brezhnev, whose former villa is now a hotel. Unfortunately I visited out of season and the resort looked rather faded and in need of restoration.

We made a detour in order to visit the Hill of Crosses at Šiauliai, a truly awe-inspiring experience. This small hill is scattered with tens of thousands of crosses, placed there by ordinary men and women. It is thought that people began to put crosses here in the nineteenth century but the area gained special significance during the Soviet period after 1944. The authorities continually destroyed the crosses, burning those made of wood or throwing them into the river, yet people continued to leave crosses at night. The authorities continually flattened the hill with bulldozers, even considered flooding it, then tried to ban people from the site, and when this didn't work issued false announcements alleging there was an epidemic of rabies or Black Death. After the restoration of independence the Hill of Crosses received greater significance. All visitors to Lithuania should allow a day to visit the Hill of Crosses and reflect on the tenacity of people to fight for their beliefs.

Our road show included a presentation by one of the regional directors and our British team spoke about new European initiatives in consumer education, networking with stakeholders and product safety. We were enthusiastically welcomed everywhere. All the seminars were well attended and participation in debates so good it was difficult to end the discussion. Our hosts, representatives from the Board in each town, made sure we saw the local sights and after the training arranged visits to places of interest. In Rokiskes we visited a cheese factory, where we donned white overalls caps and boots to see how the cheese was made. After the tour we were ushered into their VIP room where a banquet of cheese, wine and fruit was laid out for us. It is excellent cheese and I always look for it whenever I am in the Baltic States. In another town we had a tour of a factory making oak furniture for export to the UK, at another a brewery.

After the tour all that remained was to write the final report and organize wrap-up events. We held the closing conference at the Radisson hotel and I invited Colin Roberts the British Ambassador to Lithuania to speak again. In his speech he reminded us that his first engagement in Lithuania had been at our opening event, praised the work of UK experts and thanked me for meeting British trade delegations that came to Vilnius and attending functions at the Embassy. In my closing speech I went through the main achievements of the project and acknowledged all those who had supported me. They knew that I had become attached to Lithuania and was sad to leave. To express my feelings about the city I had come to love, I decided to adapt a well-known anecdote and began, 'When Napoleon was in Vilnius he admired the Gothic church of St Anne so much he told people he wanted to put it into the palm of his hand and take it back to France'. Everyone was familiar with the story and nodded and smiled. I could feel all eyes on me, adding, 'I have come to love this city that has been my home for almost two years and will be sorry to leave; I would like to put *Vilnius* in the palm of my hand and take it back to England; it will always have a special place in my heart.' There were many damp eyes. Afterwards my friend Nijole said, 'Well, Carole, I see you are more ambitious than Napoleon. He only wanted a church – you want a whole city!'

Neringa, Greta and I had got along very well on the tour of the regions and just before leaving Lithuania we decided to have a farewell party at Pablo Latino, the most popular nightclub in Vilnius. Janice Ramsey and her assistant joined us and we all met at Janice's apartment for drinks. Greta gave me a present of a red necklace, and from Janice I received a small painting of Vilnius. Greta confessed she had another surprise waiting for me at the club. Not only had she booked a good table on the edge of the dance floor but also a private dance tutor. This slim young man taught us how to salsa and other Latin dances, first in a group and then by taking each of us up on the floor individually. Janice couldn't get into the swing of it at all and sat down, but I love dancing, especially salsa and took her turn for a second session with our private dancer. Never before have I been swirled around a dance floor by such an expert – a young and handsome one at that.

The conference marked the official end to the project but I also wanted an informal party with close colleagues and to mark the end of our twenty-one months' collaboration in style. La Provence is regarded as the premier restaurant in Vilnius and we booked a private room for selected invited guests. The restaurant lived up to its reputation and served excellent food. Feliksas made a speech and presented me with a silver and amber bangle and also gave a present to Oonagh, which she tearfully accepted. All the men stood up to give toasts and it appeared as if the glasses were going to be smashed against the wall in true Russian style. Feliksas and Jim made short speeches but I declined, having said enough at the closing event. Everyone was very emotional as they came to the realization that the project was coming to an end. I knew Lithuania would always have a special place in my heart and that I would miss these friends and colleagues, but it was time to move on.

I look back on the twenty-one months in Lithuania as a milestone in my life. I had accepted the work with scant knowledge of the workings of the European Union, Eastern Europe, or role of Resident Twinning

Adviser, and had worried whether I had the capability to deliver such a large project. Another challenge had been living on my own for the first time since I was twenty, away from family and friends. I had managed the work of thirty short-term experts, from a judge, university lecturers to Trading Standards Officers. In meeting these challenges I learned far more about consumer protection than I had over the past twenty years. I also learned a lot about myself and emerged from the experience a more confident, strong and knowledgeable woman.

It was almost time to step off the Baltic Road, for a while anyway.

CHAPTER TWELVE

Hot Baths in a Cold Forest

DRUSKININKAI: A SMALL TOWN 130 kilometres south of Vilnius, one of the oldest spas and recreation resorts in Eastern Europe. The curative effects of its mineral springs and salts were declared in the 18th century and the resort now has several sanatoriums and numerous hotels with spa facilities.

There remained one last place to visit before I left Lithuania. Over the past year and a half I had spent many weekends in this charming spa town near the Polish border, which had been very popular with Russians. There are many good spa hotels in the town but I always went to the same one, taking advantage of a special weekend offer of two nights with accommodation, food, Saturday evening entertainment and five treatments for under a hundred pounds. Apparently it is now more expensive and difficult to get accommodation due to its increasing popularity. My first visit was in deep snow and there were fantastic ice sculptures throughout the town. On arrival I booked my treatments and this determined the weekend programme, fitting in swimming and the gym round them. The town is famous for the healing powers of its water and mud from seven mineral springs. Presenting myself for a mineral bath I had no idea what to expect. With no privacy I was ordered to strip off and enter a large bath, whereupon a stout lady turned on the hose and tipped in strangely coloured mineral powder. The bath faced large glass windows that looked out into the forest. It was a charming view but right in front of the window was a public footpath and many people walked by! The minerals possess a unique odour and cause the water to appear brown but the result is soothing and cleansing. Other treatments included sitting in a salt room wrapped head to toe in a white robe and slippers; a paraffin wax footbath; inhaling vapours through a tube, and a massage. I also took the opportunity of having various beauty treatments, all reasonably priced. After a few more visits I was accustomed to the routine of mineral baths and massages and during the summer I took my sister Heather for a visit and we hired bikes and explored the country lanes and forests around the town. In the winter months it was bitterly cold and froze my eyelashes.

The journey from Vilnius to Druskininkai was far from relaxing however and I longed for the speed of my sports car back home. It was necessary to take a very old minibus and be bumped along for two hours. On the way back it was always packed full of people with baskets laden with fruit and vegetables they were taking to the market in Vilnius. They placed the baskets and bags in the centre aisle, making it impossible to walk down the bus without putting your feet in a basket of strawberries or pumpkins. Returning from the visit with Heather we found all seats were taken and we had to sit crouched on the floor next to the driver, constantly thrown from side to side. There were no seatbelts on any of the buses (or taxis for that matter) and the driver smoked and talked on his mobile phone for the entire journey. I once commented to Neringa that we had a law in Britain forbidding drivers to speak on their phones. 'Yes, we have that law also,' she replied sardonically.

One summer weekend Jim and Julia Spinks accompanied Alan and me to Druskininkai and we took the bus to Grutus Park, an unusual outdoor museum a few miles away. An enterprising millionaire, his fortune made from mushrooms, had created this sculpture park after independence was restored. Citizens had pulled down statues of Lenin, Stalin, soldiers and other members of the Communist Party - erected during the Soviet era in the parks and cities in Lithuania – and they have ended up at Grutas, which has become a major tourist attraction. The order in which the monuments are displayed in the forest is based on the fact that all of these people took part in the organization and implementation of terror. It's quite unnerving when confronted by them, especially since there are graphic descriptions of the horrific behaviour of each man – and the occasional woman. As there were more statues of Lenin than anyone else, he seems to be everywhere; his penetrating eyes follow you, which I found unnerving. The park also has a series of large wooden huts that contain substantial archives, artifacts and propaganda from the Soviet occupation, intended to provide a historical record of a terrible time for Lithuanians. Propaganda of every kind is on display – rugs, art, household objects and posters – all celebrating 'Mother Russia' and urging people to work hard in the fields. The message is reinforced by music piped from speakers on the watchtowers, guarded by waxwork figures of soldiers in uniform, pointing their guns down at visitors. In earlier times the towers were manned by real armed soldiers of course, ready to shoot comrades in the fields who didn't work hard enough. Two of the original cattle trucks that were used to transport people to Siberia are on display. It is impossible not to be moved by the numbers who were forced into a small area, with no light or sanitation.

The establishment of the park and museum is controversial and many Lithuanians object to making a theme park of tragedy, but it's important for new generations to understand the history of their country. The museum does a splendid job of explaining how the communists manipulated people and held faux elections. Having grown up in a democracy, I did feel chilled by the place, finding the atmosphere of terror and death disturbing, but it is also place of entertainment, not just a museum, having a small lake and a few children's attractions. Stopping for a coffee at one of the outdoor kiosks, we couldn't help but smile at a large group of Lithuanians who had invaded several picnic tables and benches. They brought out baskets of food and copious bottles of wine. It was a wedding party with the bride and groom, plus guests, all dressed in their finery. I tried to picture the scene when the wedding was being planned. 'Where would be a suitable place to hold our reception?' the groom might have asked his bride. 'I know, let's all go to Grutas Park, we can frolic among the Soviet artifacts of torture and occupation, sit at wooden tables with muddy soil underfoot with Lenin gazing down at us'. Did his bride reply, 'It sounds absolutely perfect darling'? I would have loved to have asked them why they chose this unusual venue, but have to say they were clearly having more fun than I have seen some bride and grooms have at expensive weddings back home.

Refreshed by the spa treatments at Druskininkai, I now felt ready to move on to the next challenge. It would take me south to the Balkans, to work in a country that only a few years previously was ravaged by civil war. Now a candidate country hoping to join the European Union, the Republic of Croatia was making great efforts to meet the exacting standards required by the EU to modernize its administrations and, most important, if it was ever to get the green light from Brussels, give up its war criminals. There was a long way to go but progress was being made. It was the turn of the Consumer Protection Unit in the Ministry of Economy in Croatia to receive assistance from Europe. It was time to pack my bags again, this time to live in a warmer climate.

CHAPTER THIRTEEN

Communicating in Croatia

LITHUANIA WAS TO HAVE been my one and only long-term project but a few months before I finished my work in Vilnius a company based in Vienna contacted me. Human Dynamics were tendering for a project in Croatia and wanted to include me as a key expert in communication and public awareness. I was surprised but said I would think about it and sent off my CV as requested. They then asked for written confirmation of everything I had included on the CV. It was quite a task to supply it, as I was in Lithuania and the evidence was located at home in Hartlepool. Fortunately I have a good filing system from my training as a secretary and was able to tell Alan where to find everything, which he then scanned or faxed to me. He had to go to the Civic Centre to ask my former manager to write a letter confirming how long I had worked for Cleveland and my tasks there, and eventually we got it all together. It taught me a lesson – to have everything in a portfolio in readiness for future offers of work. The scanned documents are now held electronically on my computer.

In 2005 Croatia was in the early stages of transition to a market economy. The EU White Paper of 1995, regarding the preparation for accession of Central and Eastern European countries stated, '*Consumer legislation has begun to be put into place but tends to remain a dead letter where consumers do not understand their rights and no mechanisms exist for exercising them.*' The country had signed a Stabilization and Association Agreement (SAA) with the European Union as a step towards membership and had started the process of harmonizing legislation and aligning consumer protection with the EU Acquis. The first consumer protection law had only been adopted by Parliament two years earlier and the Croatian Government had now begun to create institutions in order to strengthen the role of consumers. It would be exciting to be a part of this transition process, since our consumer laws and institutions in Britain can be traced back to the 19th century. The objectives of the proposed project included assisting administrative structures to ensure market surveillance and law enforcement, encouragement of active participation of consumers through information, education and development of NGOs.

Human Dynamics asked me to write some of the terms of reference from an original brief report, something I had not done before and am in no hurry to do again as it proved more difficult than I had anticipated, requiring me to spend a long weekend isolated in a cold apartment. It may have been early April but outside in Vilnius it was snowing heavily and bitterly cold. Inside the temperature seemed just as low because the State-controlled energy supplier had turned off the heating due to a warmer spell the previous week. With no heating, I stoked up the stove with logs, set up a makeshift table to take the laptop in front of it and tried to keep my fingers warm enough to type. It paid off and Human Dynamics won the project. They brought in other institutions such as the Hungarian Trade Inspectorate and Consumers International as junior partners in the consortium to supply short-term expertise. My job as 'Key Expert' would be to improve communications, build public awareness, train staff and organize seminars, round tables, workshops and conferences.

I flew to Zagreb for the kick-off meeting in July from Vilnius. As I had to change flights in Vienna I decided to stay over on the Saturday night, booking into a small hotel. This was the first time I had stayed anywhere as a tourist on my own and I still find it a lonely experience, preferring to have a travelling companion, but it was a good opportunity to explore Vienna. On Sunday I took a sightseeing tour by bus, visited the Lipizzaner stables, and ate chocolate torte in the park next to Mozart's golden statue before taking the train to the airport. I had arranged to meet Roman and Lukas from Human Dynamics at the departure gate to fly to Zagreb together. We met up with Malcolm Adams at the hotel, who was to be team leader, and Rok, our IT expert from Slovenia. The next day we had the kick-off meeting and met our future colleagues. It would only be a short visit as I was still working in Lithuania and for the next few months had to shuttle back and forth a few more times between Vilnius and Zagreb. On the next visit I met the team's legal expert, Yvonne Stein from Sweden, a first class lawyer who strengthened the team, having worked in Brussels at the European Commission for several years combining a career with bringing up a young family. We got on well from the start and have stayed in touch. After the project she went into politics and became the elected Mayor of her town.

I had to interrupt my work in Vilnius again to attend the opening conference of the project held in the theatre of the Ministry, formerly used for communist rallies. We had a big budget for this and were able to provide a three-course lunch for everyone. Our project assistant Tihana Stipeca arranged everything as I was held up in Vilnius. Each member of the project team gave a presentation about our key expert area and it's probably the largest venue I have spoken at. Ministry buildings in Eastern Europe tend to be built on a large scale - intended, I suppose, to remind citizens of the importance of the State and to ensure workers and visitors know their place. In the grandly titled Ministry of Economy Labour and Entrepreneurship (MELE) where we had our office there was a spacious entrance, theatre, several conference rooms and a canteen where we took our lunch.

In the centre of the building was a coffee bar, a large open space with leather sofas where we met other English-speaking people working in the Ministry. It didn't just serve coffee; you could have every possible alcoholic drink from eight in the morning until it closed before five. Every day there would be one or two men enjoying a glass or two of brandy or vodka at 8.30 a.m. but after work when we could have had some team socializing over a glass of wine the bar was closed. We used the coffee bar a lot, not being allowed to have a kettle in our office - dubbed the 'brown box' by Yvonne, as it was so drab and, well, brown. Another feature of the Ministry that I found amusing was a notice on the front door – a picture of a gun with a red 'not allowed' sign struck through it. Obviously people needed to be reminded not to bring their guns to the office. Smoking was allowed of course. There was no building, restaurant or anywhere that you could not smoke. Entering a bar or restaurant I would scan the place for smokers and keep well clear. It made no difference - as soon as the food arrived a smoker would inevitably sit as near to me as possible.

Part of my work was to organize public events and I sourced different historic venues in the old town, never using the Ministry again. We also put on training events throughout Croatia on market surveillance subjects, plus a train-the-trainers course, and I did some media training. After my work as an RTA in Lithuania it was good to return to training and deliver work within my consumer protection expertise. The Hungarian Trade Inspectorate and Consumers' International, as consortium members, assisted in the training and being part of an international team enhanced my personal knowledge and horizons. Short-term experts were booked into the Astoria Hotel where I was a long-term resident, having failed to find an apartment like Malcolm and Yvonne. The first expert to come out was Colin Brown from the Office of Fair Trading who chaired one of the public meetings. The project terms of reference asked for public debates, seminars, round tables and conferences but it was up to me to design a varied programme and find alternative ways of debating consumer issues. For the public debate I drew up four motions and invited representatives from business, non-governmental organizations and the Ministry to speak for and against each motion. I sought out the manager of the largest supermarket chain and he agreed to participate immediately. He told me it was the first time that anyone connected with consumer protection had spoken to him, yet he had sound views of what was required to improve the rights and responsibilities of consumers and businesses. The idea of a debate was an alien concept for the Croatians and they required a lot of persuading to speak against a motion. Colin was an excellent chairman, telling the audience from the start, 'I will be tough on time, and the causes of time.' It is unlikely that the audience understood his reference to Tony Blair, then British Prime Minister (speaking of crime, not time). He was right, though, to remind them they each had an allotted time and not to exceed it, otherwise they were likely to go on for hours. It went well, but those speaking against a motion were rather too timid and stepped back from controversial statements.

Next to step into the chair's role was visiting expert Julian Edwards, a former editor of *Which* consumer magazine and author of books on consumer matters. It was fascinating to have the opportunity to talk about issues in consumer protection with experts from outside Trading Standards, especially after work over dinner. At the time Julian was writing a consumer reference book and outlined to me his theory that there are three distinct strands of consumer protection in the UK. In the first group are academics, usually delivering a consumer degree at University level. The second group includes people like himself, either self employed or working with consumer NGOs or lobbying at EU or international level. The third group comprises those who work directly with the public, e.g. in Trading Standards. It is likely, he said, that people in these different groups never meet or share ideas. I was interested in this line of thinking and would have liked to hear more but Julian's visit was short. The next expert sent by Consumers' International was Robin Simpson who joined us as a trainer. He had also edited *Which* and knew Colin and Julian. Representing Consumers' International, he was an excellent trainer, well versed in European and international consumer rights and EU treaties and seems to spend most of his time travelling around the world.

The first round table was held in Rijeka in Istria. Accompanied by several of our colleagues from the Ministry, we drove through spectacular scenery and along good roads. The meeting went well and on the way back we took a different route through the mountains, stopping for lunch at a Croatian restaurant in the hills. We noticed how close it was to an island called Krk. At Easter and at a loose end in Zagreb over a public holiday weekend, Malcolm and I decided to hire a car and drive to Krk to do some walking. We stayed at Baska, a charming resort at the south of the island facing the beach and the island of Rab - on the Dalmatian coast there is always a view of an island it seems. On Easter Sunday we had a full day's walk to Vela Luka, elegantly situated in a bay though remote. It required us to walk, and climb, over white rocks described by locals as a 'lunar landscape'. It was an apt description and one I had come across before, though not in relation to this island in Croatia. George Orwell used the term 'lunar landscape' in his book *The Road to Wigan Pier* but was referring to the less picturesque slag heaps of Lancashire. That evening we had a meal in a restaurant right on the harbour where the fish was brought in fresh, washed down with Croatian wine. On Sunday morning we came across an artist's studio. The artist was displaying some of his work outside and I bought an oil of a local seascape, which he signed on the back for me. The paint was still slightly damp, as he had only completed the painting the previous day.

We went to Zadar, a seaside town on the Adriatic, for another round table. We tried to time these working visits close to a weekend and Yvonne and I would usually stay until Sunday at our own expense, even if Malcolm and Tihana returned to Zagreb after the meeting. Our venue in Zadar was the County Hall and on arrival we were taken to meet the Head of the County and his staff, who were pleased we had chosen their town to hold the round table. We had our coffee break on a terrace overlooking the sea and the presence of sweet organ music within the background was a welcome touch. I was told this was the sea organ and presumed there was someone down on the seafront actually playing it, but in fact it is entirely natural. Pipes have been built under the sea and promenade; the movement of the waves makes the 'organ' play. When it is choppy the sound gets louder. It's a bit like whale music, but better. We had lunch at another restored historic building, the Arsenal. Over lunch a Janis Joplin tribute band rehearsing for a concert that evening entertained us. The lead singer really did look and sound like Joplin and I congratulated her, whilst hoping she had a longer life. Yvonne and I helped the local economy by purchasing bracelets made from Murano glass from the craft shop.

After the training a young man called Zoran, who ran a local consumer association, begged us to visit his office and witness the splendid arrangements he had for advising consumers. I had taken on an additional task for the Ministry of assessing new Consumer Counselling Centres, NGOs that were now receiving funding from the government. Zoran whisked us off in his car to an Internet café, behind which, in a tiny room with few facilities, he dispensed advice to the consumers of Zadar. He was a serious but attentive young man, an excellent guide to the area and clearly proud of his town, rightly so as the Dalmatian coastline in this area is just wonderful. First though he insisted we meet his family. As we pulled up outside his home they were lined up at the gate waiting to greet us, as if we were royalty. Aunts, uncles, cousins apparently lived on the same road, occupying large houses with gardens. After introductions and shaking of hands, we were invited into a shed/workshop in the garden where his father and uncles carved objects large and small from wood. They told us no other woman had ever been allowed inside this shed, not even their wives! They insisted that we select a piece to take home. It was very embarrassing because it had taken them six months to produce some of the pieces. Imagine asking for one of those! We were modest in our choice. I chose a wooden fish with intricately carved scales that now hangs in my kitchen. That evening Zoran collected us from our hotel and drove us up the coast for more sightseeing. Our first stop was to see the smallest church in Croatia, called a Coronation Church because it was where former Kings paid homage after their crowning. The church is topped with a roof shaped like a crown. We continued to the small town of Nin where we bought Zoran dinner, then drove down the coast, stopping to see a fabulous sunset and pick bunches of wild thyme – the scent was amazing.

Once again the sun ensured its burning presence when we visited Split for a five-day visit, this time to train staff from the State Inspectorate. Tihana's uncle met us at the airport, a knowledgeable architect who also happened to be entertaining. After we arrived on Sunday afternoon he gave us a tour of Diocletian's palace in Split, then drove us to Trogir, a much prettier town with beautiful Roman architecture and a marina. During our walking tour we bumped into the President of Croatia who like us was being given a guided tour. We were looking forward to our hotel in Split, which was on the beach and boasted (on its website) a swimming pool, spa and other facilities. The reality was somewhat different, being built in the old communist style with none of the afore-mentioned facilities, unless you count a swimming pool with no water in it and a spa centre that was closed. I did have a naked man outside my room though! Returning to my room one afternoon I found him strolling up and down the corridor, without a stitch on. When he saw me he smiled, completely unabashed and sat down on the sofa outside my room. I went down to reception to ask if this was normal behaviour of their guests; the manager shrugged, unsurprised. Yvonne and I had already complained about our rooms and when we threatened to leave they gave us better ones with a balcony overlooking the sea. I think this was the first time I had walked along the beach to work. Returning after my training session, usually alone because Yvonne would have taken over, I would be greeted by a group of older people in their swimsuits, friends who were sunbathing, barbecuing food, laughing and obviously enjoying themselves. They invited me to join in but it was far too hot for my pale English skin. I envied them – a mature group of friends hanging out at the beach every day - not a bad way to spend your retirement. Why should it only be young people who have fun on the beach?

In Split we were fortunate to be allowed to hold our training course at the beautiful Villa Dalmatia. This was one of several grand houses owned or occupied by former dictator of Yugoslavia Marshall Tito. Although a communist state, citizens of Yugoslavia enjoyed a less severe form of communism than their neighbours in the Eastern Bloc and Tito was a popular leader. The union of Balkan countries comprising Yugoslavia disintegrated after he died of course and fought each other in a terrible war during the 1980s and early 90s. I saw plenty of evidence of this, though not in this beautiful place. The Villa is not opened to the public nor available to rent and is normally only used by government institutions. The day before our training there had been a conference attended by the Czech President and it was still decked out in fragrant flowers. We had met the manager, Ante Titic, who was also President of the local NGO, in Rijeka and he offered it to us as a venue. He gave Yvonne and me a tour of the house and we were shown the bedroom where Queen Elizabeth II had slept. They were very proud of this, and of a later visit by Prince Charles. The grounds, edging the sea, provided a cool and relaxing walk when not training and we had our breakout sessions on the terrace looking out to sea. Training venues don't get better than this I thought. Our Hungarian colleagues joined us halfway through the training. I had got to know them quite well when we trained together in Zagreb and admired them for undertaking the project for little profit or fees from their institution once they had paid their expenses. As a new Member State they did it for the experience. They never ate in restaurants, having little money, and instead had snacks in their hotel room. Only one member of their group spoke English so they brought their own interpreters, it having proved on a previous training course in Zagreb to be too complicated to interpret Hungarian into English and back into Croatian. In Split I found them wandering along the beach trying to find the Villa Dalmatia, which being private was not signposted. Malcolm and Tihana had returned to Zagreb and I opened up their product safety training and introduced them to the delegates. There seemed little point in staying because it was being delivered in Hungarian and translated into Croatian, so Yvonne and I went down to the marina and took a boat to a nearby island for the day.

When abroad it's always interesting to discover national artists or poets, not always known to the wider world. Usually by the time I finish work the museums are closed but during a break from training in Split we found time to visit the former home of Croatia's famous sculptor, Mestrevic, someone I confess I had not heard of. We visited the museum and both the house and gardens were full of his wonderful sculptures. One of the exhibits was his best-known sculpture - the Vestal Virgins. I bought a small copy of another of his famous pieces called the History of the Croats.

Jelena, a young woman we had met at the round table in Rijeka, attended the training and during the week I visited her Consumer Counselling centre in Split as part of my evaluation work on these centres now being funded by the Ministry. She was very committed to her work and I watched her going to great lengths to mediate with a utility company on a client's behalf. After the training she showed us round her town and we went out in the evenings to eat together. She spoke perfect English, having lived in Bristol for many years with her fiancé. Just before they were to be married he died tragically and she had to return to Croatia because she didn't have a visa. She kept in touch with his family and visits Bristol regularly but has never been able to get over his death or consider another relationship. We met again at other events and before I left she gave me a little ceramic plaque to remind me of the Dalmatian coast.

In September 2006 we went to Pula for five days to train NGOs, joined again by Robin Simpson. He proved to be an interesting companion, having spent many years in Europe and several continents furthering the cause of consumer rights. Our hotel was actually located at the seaside town of Medulin, next to the beach, and we took advantage of the swimming pool and the sea. One evening Vladimir and Bruno, consumer association representatives on our course, drove us into the town. We arrived at the Roman Amphitheatre (Forum) at dusk when it was due to close and I thought we were too late. However Bruno is a well-known local figure and we were waved in and had the place to ourselves just in time to see the sunset flooding through the arches. It is one of the best-preserved and intact Roman forums in Europe, seating three thousand people in Roman times, now used for opera and concerts rather than gladiator fights. After we wrapped up the training at the end of the week, Yvonne and I transferred to Scarletti hotel in the centre of Pula. On Bruno's advice we took a bus to Rovinj, an Italianate hilltop town in Istria that used to belong to Italy. It is a charming place, with streets that wind up round to a church at the top with spectacular views of the Adriatic all round. On Saturday we took a taxi to Fazana where the boat departs for Brijuni Island, said to have been Tito's favourite residence where he entertained world leaders, film stars and royalty. Along the pier are blown up photographs of famous politicians, princesses and film stars who had taken the trip from the same pier in the 1950s and 60s. Princess Margaret and Sophia Loren were regular visitors. The house contains a museum dedicated to Tito. I had not realized quite how revered he was, still is, by Croatians. The tour included a ride on a little train taking us to a small safari park. Tito stocked his private zoo by asking visitors and foreign leaders to donate animals as a gift and the offspring of those original donations can still be seen. Some of them however don't look too healthy and large animals such as the elephants and giraffe had insufficient space and I felt very sorry for them. There are Roman remains on the island and of course it has great views of the Adriatic. Back in Pula we were caught in a spectacular two and a half hour thunder and lightning storm whilst making our way into town, yet strangely there was an absence of rain. The next day was fresh and sunny again and we walked across to the other side of Pula to the beaches, where we swam for an hour in the Adriatic. We had only our swimsuits and no towel so used a local hotel toilet to change and wash ourselves down after the swim and the sun aided in drying us off.

   In complete contrast, on our next training we had no sea view or the dazzling bright blue sky typical of the Adriatic. Osijek is in the poorer north east of Croatia, close to the Serbian border. We held a round table at the Chamber of Commerce there. The town suffered badly during the Balkan war. During a break in our training, we took the local bus to nearby Vukovar. It was here that the worst of the bombing and fighting between Serbia and Croatia took place and most of the city was destroyed. The devastation was left as a deliberate reminder of Serbian aggression although there are now some renovations taking place. It's strange to see new buildings with smoked glass exteriors beside others left in a bombed out state. The population is almost evenly divided between Serb and Croat but they live separately with minimal contact. It was an interesting place to visit and we walked along the Danube, but you wouldn't want to stay too long, the dissonance of the past lingers in the air.

The time spent away from home on this project was enhanced by the many excursions, both in the course of work and at weekends with Yvonne, an excellent travelling companion. One weekend we decided to visit Venice. There are good train links from Zagreb to European cities but our Slovenian colleague Rok offered us a lift in his car to Ljubljana one Friday afternoon and from there we joined the train. Rok took us to his office to meet his colleagues and his young wife came to the railway station, giving us an apple cake she had baked for our journey. Yvonne and I laughed about this – two young people who were not yet thirty, waving off two middle-aged women as if we were embarking upon an epic journey, ensuring we had sustenance. One of the best ways to arrive in Venice is by train (the other being by boat across the lagoon). Stepping outside the station on to the Grand Canal, boarding a waterbus is a perfect introduction to this magical city. We disembarked at the Rialto Bridge; from here it was a short walk through the wonderful fish and vegetable market to our hotel. We did all the sights, wandered around the winding streets and canals and took the boat to Murano. It was Palm Sunday, the churches were full and everyone clutched real olive branches, so much better I thought than the plastic crosses given to worshippers at home. We returned, very tired, to Zagreb by train on Sunday evening.

The best excursion was a visit to Dubrovnik, or *Ragusa* to give it its Italian name until 1918. It fully deserves its place on the list of UNESCO World Heritage sites and I fell in love with this walled city as soon as I crossed the moat. Stradum, the main street, is made of polished marble from Roman times and motorized vehicles are not allowed inside the walls. The city suffered extensive damage and loss of life during the Balkan war. It was not liberated until 1992 and most of the damage has now been repaired. It's possible to pick out those buildings that have been restored due to their bright coloured roofs. An enduring memory is a magical balmy evening, walking along the old walls then dining outdoor at a fish restaurant, gazing out over the Adriatic.

The following summer Yvonne and I spent a weekend at the Plitvice Lakes – another World Heritage site. There are no cars in the protected area - electric buses take you to a starting point for a walk and you must stay on the paths. Halfway round we met a couple from South Africa. They were travelling around Europe and both being over sixty, joked that they were the oldest backpackers in the world. By coincidence they were staying in our hotel and joined us for dinner. They had lived in South Africa since the Sixties. Ken was a Yorkshire miner, his wife from Nottingham and they had set up their own company in Cape Town and become prosperous. They obviously had a good life there but told us some dreadful stories about the violence against white settlers and had to live in a gated community. Ken held up a scarred hand. 'I wound down the window of my car whilst stationary at traffic lights near my home,' he told us. 'A local man forced himself through the open window, intent on robbing me; As I tried to wind up the window to stop him, the man bit my hand so badly the bone was exposed and I ended up in hospital'. Yvonne and I were shocked but his wife said, 'He doesn't deserve any sympathy; it was his own fault for having the window open so he could smoke. He knows he is not allowed to smoke in the car.' She told us of other occasions when, returning home from shopping or visiting friends, she would be unable to open the automatic gates to their property because of local men hanging around. 'If I open the gates they will be in the compound and I would not be safe.' Ken and his wife obviously had a large house and good lifestyle but were lacking in fundamental freedoms. They were travelling around Europe on a rail pass and hadn't decided where to visit next, so we suggested they have a night in Zagreb and stay at the Best Western Astoria. Ken was carrying around large quantities of South African wine in his case and asked the waiter to open one for us at dinner in the hotel. They resumed their travels the next day, insisting we visit them in Cape Town.

On Saturdays in Zagreb I met Yvonne for coffee in Jelacica Square; we would wander around the open market and look at the shops, although they closed mid afternoon on Saturday, not to reopen until Monday morning. On Sundays we usually took the tram to the foot of Mount Slimje to walk up to the top. In winter we watched the skiing and snowboarding, sometimes using the cable car if the tracks were too icy to walk but in summer the forest was cooling. A tram in the other direction took us to a large lake on the outskirts of the city, used by national athletes for practice and there was often a sailing regatta or canoe race at weekends. Although I love walking and had my hiking boots with me in Zagreb, I most envied and wanted to join the large numbers of people rollerblading. Designated paths had been sectioned off around the lake so they could skate at speed without pedestrians getting in the way. I had watched them in Vingis Park in Vilnius, wanting then to participate in the sport, and now had an overwhelming urge to join them. I went as far as visiting a sports shop with a view to buying a pair of blades but in the end felt it was too risky. I had, after all, had a couple of falls off my bike in Vilnius and it's very difficult to cope with injuries when you are in a foreign country on your own and contracted to work each day. I persuaded myself it would not be a sensible decision, but have always regretted it nonetheless.

In Zagreb I discovered that going to the cinema was something one could easily do alone and there was a multiplex just a five-minute walk from the hotel. I saw practically every film released in 2006. Unlike Vilnius, the opera house in Zagreb is in the grand Austro-Hungarian style and in fact is a smaller version of the one in Vienna. I saw good productions there, particularly during the Mozart festival. I also watched England compete in an international football match for the first time. Malcolm, Yvonne and I bought tickets to watch England play Croatia at the Maksimir stadium in Zagreb. All the shops were decked out in the colours of both teams and there was a carnival like atmosphere in the city the week leading up to the match. England played very badly and lost, after putting two goals into the opposing net. Breakfast in the Astoria hotel the next morning was enlivened by a large group of England supporters analyzing the match.

Croatia proved to be a wonderful country in which to work and play. People are very friendly and English is widely spoken. It was a change to work in a constantly warm climate from April to October. Very different from the Baltic Road, along which I was soon to travel again. First, though, I had agreed to make a short trip to Turkey.

CHAPTER FOURTEEN

Better Regulation in Zagreb

FIVE YEARS AFTER LEAVING Croatia I was asked to be a short-term expert on a new twinning project, again based in Zagreb, this time on the development of Regulatory Impact Assessment (RIA). My work was to develop and implement a PR campaign for raising public awareness on Impact Assessment, working alongside British civil servants, experts in the area of Better Regulation, who were harmonizing Croatia's law in this area and training Ministry personnel. This time the project was based in the Prime Ministry in Zagreb. I was still in contact with people I had previously worked with and it would be interesting to see what progress had been made on the country's path towards joining the EU. David Baker, husband of Beth, was project leader.

In short, impact assessment is a process to help policy-makers think through and understand the consequences of possible Government regulatory intervention in the public and private sector. It is used to enable the evidence on positive and negative effects of such intervention to be considered before legislation is implemented, explaining why the Government is proposing to intervene, how new policies may impact on public services and the estimated costs and benefits. Unintended consequences can be identified at this stage and avoided. The aim is to introduce proposals that best achieve the Government's objectives whilst minimizing costs and burdens on business. In Britain this includes reducing burdens that affect business and the public sector, improve accountability and transparency.

My first visit in 2011 was during a cold spell and I found Zagreb very much as I had left it five years ago. Jelacica Square is still the focal point of the city; the gun that is fired every day at noon still makes me jump; Dolac market is as colourful and full of fresh fruit and vegetables as ever and everyone still meets under the clock in the square. Some of the small shops have closed for business but the shopping mall has doubled in size – it seems wherever you go it's the malls that increase in size, while the smaller shops find it hard to compete. One shop that is still in business is the hat shop in Flower Square. I called in wearing the hat they had made for me five years ago and came out with a new one!

The 'kick-off' meeting was held during my first visit and I was pleased to meet up again with Suzana Kolesar, who I had worked with on my first project in Croatia. Suzana is a lawyer working at the Chamber of Trade and Crafts, which represents ninety thousand small enterprises in Croatia and is regarded as one of the stakeholders in terms of RIA. We spent a long time chatting and agreed to meet again. A meeting was also arranged at the Ministry of Economy, Labour and Entrepreneurship where I had previously been based. I didn't actually see any of my old colleagues – most having moved on to different areas of work – but the Ministry remained the same. It's an odd feeling to return somewhere that you had assumed you would never see again and memories came flooding back.

This time I stayed at the Dubrovnik Hotel facing the square – an excellent base and short walk to the old part of town where our office was based. In the evenings I re-acquainted myself with Zagreb, walking around the city to look at the main sights. I found a new museum in the Upper Town called the Museum of Broken Relationships established by a Croatian couple after they split up. It grew from a travelling exhibition revolving around the concept of failed relationships and their ruins – 'a poignant trail of broken hearts, all on display', states the brochure. The idea behind it is that unlike self-help instructions for recovery from failed loves, the museum offers a chance to overcome an emotional collapse by donating to the museum artifacts symbolizing painful reminders of a failed relationship. People from all over the world have contributed items – wedding dresses, photographs and personal memorabilia such as a collar for a cat, letters and pictures – even an axe. Some of the exhibits are tragic, others humorous. One was a Bible; the broken relationship in this case was the Catholic Church, which the man had left. A married woman had donated letters secretly written to her lover. She was 62, he 34 when the affair began and she always called him number 34. It had been a deep and passionate love but she had destroyed all evidence so that her family would not discover the affair after she died. Another wrote, 'Can I donate myself to the museum with the name branded as "duped by the one she loved most"?' Each exhibit is displayed with a card explaining the significance of the item and many include a name and their town/country.

I was back in Zagreb in June 2011 and my visit coincided with that of Pope Benedict XVI. There was great excitement in the city and a huge stage and altar were set up in Jelacica Square. The entire population of Croatia seemed to have converged on Zagreb and the parks were full of young people singing and dancing. As the Pope left, Bon Jovi flew in for a concert and the hysteria continued. During his visit the Pope strongly backed Croatia's bid to join the European Union, stating it was 'logical, just and necessary'. A few days later, on 10 June, the European Commission announced the date that Croatia will join the EU – 1st July 2013. There will be a referendum but people I have spoken to seem enthusiastic about joining Europe.

CHAPTER FIFTEEN

A Turkish Escapade

BECAUSE MY OVERSEAS PROJECT work is funded by the European Union people always assume I directly work for them and cannot understand why some of the countries I visit are not, or ever likely to be, in the EU. In fact the Commission gives assistance to countries all over the world, not just to those aspiring to join the 'club'. Turkey, however, has had aspirations to join the EU for decades – they made an application when the Baltic States were still behind the Iron Curtain and Croatia was part of Yugoslavia. On an official visit to Ankara in 2010 British Prime Minister David Cameron referred to their long wait: 'We know what it's like to be shut out of the club', reminding them that Britain also had a long wait. Turkey applied for Associate membership of the European Union back in 1959, an Association Agreement was signed in 1963 with additional protocols a decade later and in 1984 it applied for full membership. In 2005 it was officially designated as a 'candidate country'. Those against Turkey joining the EU tend to cite two arguments: the size of the country – its population is over 72 million and its inclusion would greatly extend the EU – and religion. Officially Turkey is a secular state with no official religion, Islam being the largest, and most citizens register as Muslim. In fact this is not why membership has been blocked. Turkey, and any other candidate country, must guarantee that its laws are in harmony with those of the EU. This process can take years.

Whilst working in Vilnius in 2005 I took a diversion into Turkey. NI-CO were tendering for a twinning project based in Ankara and Beth Baker was lined up to be the Resident Twinning Adviser. She went out on a scoping visit and decided she disliked Ankara and could not see herself living there. She withdrew, leaving NI-CO without a proposed RTA. They persuaded me to replace her on the bid, even though I was not going to be available when the project was due to start. I made it clear that if, like Beth, I didn't like the city I would also decline the posting but agreed to attend the interview. At the time I had no other offers of work after the project in Lithuania was completed. I flew out one Saturday morning from Riga to Ankara via Istanbul, wishing I could spend some time in that city, which has long fascinated me, but I had to be in Ankara later that day to meet Malcolm Adams and Oonagh McAliskey.

On the flight from Istanbul to Ankara I was seated next to a middle-aged charming man who introduced himself as a doctor. He said he was in a party of ten doctors who were attending a conference in Ankara that weekend. He gave me some background information on his country and then questioned me about my onward travel arrangements from the airport. I told him that the Hilton hotel where I was staying was sending a taxi. I had insisted on this with Oonagh because I didn't want to have to buy any local currency for such a short visit. The doctor kept expressing concern about this throughout the flight but I assured him there would be a taxi driver waiting for me, holding up a card with my name. When we landed he took down my small case from the rack. 'I'm going to watch you very carefully when we leave the plane,' he told me. I was beginning to think he may be a problem, perhaps he wasn't a doctor at all, and I would somehow have to shake him off.

After clearing passport and customs I emerged to the waiting crowd scanning the boards in search of my name. Nothing. I waved to the doctor and his colleagues as they went ahead to get into their minibus, indicating I was fine. In fact, I was suddenly alone with no taxi in sight. Having received no assistance at the taxi desk, the doctor noticed I was still waiting and returned, insisting I go in his group's transport; they were staying near the Hilton and would drop me there. While I was thinking about it he grabbed my case and suddenly I'm on a minibus full of Turkish men. It was dark but fortunately my vision could just about make out the road signs. When we came to a 'T' junction that indicated Ankara to the left but we turned right I did start to worry, particularly as the road became potholed and we seemed to be in the middle of the countryside. After a few minutes the doctor said 'You may have noticed we have not taken to road to Ankara.' 'Yes, I had noticed,' I nervously replied. 'The direct road is very busy because President Putin arrives tomorrow to meet our President, so we take a detour.' Was this true, I wondered? Actually it was, the traffic came to a standstill the next day when the Russian president and his entourage moved across the city to high-level meetings. Eventually we arrived at my hotel and all the doctors led me out, kissing my hand, and were really very charming.

I checked into the Hilton expecting Malcolm to be there as his flight was due in before mine but he had not arrived. Eventually I went down to the bar, ordered a drink and positioned myself near the entrance to wait for him. I suddenly realized I was the only woman in a sea of men in suits and the subject of attention. Perhaps the drink was not such a good idea in this country. After about an hour Malcolm turned up. He had arrived at the airport later than expected and, noticing my flight was due within the next half an hour, decided to wait so that we could share a taxi. He rang the Hilton to cancel my taxi. After waiting a long time he checked with staff and they suggested that perhaps I was arriving at a different terminal – domestic, as I had come from Istanbul? Malcolm had not realized there were two terminals, having arrived at the international terminal from a connection in Munich. He was quite shocked when I told him my tale of being abducted by Turkish doctors in a minibus, but we have laughed about it since.

I made the most of my unexpected weekend away from Vilnius and swam in the hotel's beautiful pool and of course a Turkish Hamman. The next day we had a walk around the area but it wasn't very exciting. At the interview on Monday a representative from the British Embassy joined us to support the UK bid. The EU Delegation representative questioned me about my availability and I told them frankly I would not be available for several months. They awarded the project to our competitor, the German consumer protection authority. I didn't mind because, like Beth, I was not sure Ankara was for me, though brief glimpses of a city are never a good indication. I had enjoyed this experience and the opportunity to visit Turkey but was pleased that on this occasion we didn't win the project. The jury is still out as to whether Turkey will ever get the green light to join the EU. Many argue that Turkey is in Asia and not Europe.

CHAPTER SIXTEEN

Further Travels Along the Baltic Road

BETH BAKER, WHO HAD delivered a full twinning project in Latvia around the same time as I was doing the same in Lithuania, moved on to her second twinning based in Warsaw whilst I was working in Croatia in 2006. Her new project was based in the Office of Competition and Consumer Protection, the objective to improve alternative dispute resolution (ADR) -namely to find ways of resolving consumer disputes other than in a formal court of law - and invited me to train with Danish lawyers. Using a court to resolve consumer disputes is lengthy and costly and most countries have found a way to provide simple low-cost solutions. Over the next eighteen months I also trained in credit and debt as well as alternative dispute resolution and thoroughly enjoyed the experience of working on a well-run and interesting project.

My first visit was to Warsaw. Always efficient, Beth had arranged for a taxi at the airport to take me to the Marriott hotel. The next day I met the two Danish experts I would be training with – Tina, a lawyer at the Consumer Ombudsman office and Benedicte Federspiel from the Danish Consumer Association. We would each describe different European models of resolving consumer disputes and how the principles may be applied in Poland. The Danish model of consumer redress is interesting and Tina convinced me, and the delegates I'm sure, that theirs is an inexpensive and effective method of resolving disputes, backed up by a government agency. Benedicte is a board member of Consumers' International and consequently has a wealth of experience in consumer education and dispute resolution throughout Europe. It was a risk allowing three people, consisting of two different nationalities who didn't know each other, to train together. Nor is it easy to plan and design training courses that will have relevance to both ministry personnel and NGOs, some of whom work in large cities, others in small provincial towns, but in fact it all went well. Project assistant Karolina drew up a timetable of the cities where we would train taking charge of booking hotels, planes and trains, accommodation, training rooms and translators. Like Beth, Karolina's efficiency ensured that everything went to plan. She always travelled with us, providing consecutive translation during our training seminars, along with Tida, a professional interpreter.

We kicked off the training in 2006 in Warsaw to a receptive audience of State Inspectorate staff then moved on to Poznan, a provincial town. The hotel was quite basic, to put it mildly, and on the second day of training I was locked in my room for two hours. I had pulled the door handle to go downstairs after breakfast to begin training when the handle came off in my hand. I rang reception to report it but was an hour before the joiner arrived and another before I could leave. At the end of the day they still hadn't repaired it and I was moved to another room.

Beth caught up with us at Gdansk, where our training room at the Poseidon hotel boasted an aquarium right along one wall, which was strangely soothing. The hotel had access to a 10km beach walk and after the training we walked up to Sopot, a popular seaside resort that lays claim to having the longest pier in the Baltic region, providing good views. In 1939 Hitler spent a week here on holiday while his army marched on Warsaw. In happier times on a hot summer's afternoon in 2006 we paddled in the Baltic Sea, joining the thousands of Polish families on holiday, and sampled some of the cafes and restaurants. When we returned to deliver credit training in the winter months it was a very different place. We braved the bitterly cold winds, walking along the boardwalk to a fish restaurant right on the beach. On a bitterly cold night it was packed with locals. We took a tray, ordered and paid for our meal at the counter, the price depending on the weight of the fish, and received a numbered ticket. When your number was called you went to a hatch and the plate was handed through from the kitchen. After finishing the meal you returned the plate and cutlery to the hatch. Sitting at a window seat, the sea seemed to come right up to the building, but inside it was wonderfully warm and full of laughter. After the final training session Beth and I took a taxi into Gdansk -an elegant town with many smart cafes and restaurants. Entry to the Old Town is through a 16th century gate, there are neat cobbled streets and restored Burgher houses. My work meant that local sightseeing had to take place after museums and galleries were closed and I was disappointed not to be able to visit the *Roads to Freedom* exhibition. I like Lech Walesa's description of the monument to fallen shipyard workers as 'a harpoon driven through the body of a whale'. There is so much history in Gdansk, not just because of the shipyards and Solidarity, but it was where World War II began, on 1 September 1939 when the Germans launched their attack on Westerplatte. It's a smart town and with low cost flights from the UK, it's a good place for a weekend break.

After completing training with our Danish colleagues I left Warsaw, assuming my work in Poland to be done, but the following year Beth invited me to train on credit and over-indebtedness, to be delivered to State Inspectorate staff, Consumer Ombudsmen and consumer associations. The credit and debt training spanned a total of eight weeks to an audience of local Consumer Ombudsmen, representatives from the State Inspectorate and consumer associations. We ran three or four courses over a two-week period. After piloting the course in Warsaw we headed to twelve cities. In Poland the regions are called Voivodeships, administered by a Governor who represents central government at regional level and an elected assembly called Sejmik that elects an Executive. The second level of local government is the Poviat, similar to a County or District in Britain. Every Poviat has a Consumer Ombudsman office that protects consumer rights and arbitrates on consumer disputes. We trained in Bialystok, Olztyn, Wroclaw, Rzeszow, Gdansk, Poznan, Krakow, Katowice, Szczecin and Lublin, travelling by train or plane and mostly staying in Orbis hotels, a chain previously under central control that still had a communist feel.

Research shows that Poland has low use of credit, but the Office of Competition and Consumer Protection (an institution similar to our Office of Fair Trading) had the foresight to see they may follow the way of other European countries that are witnessing an increase in the use of credit and consequently the number of people becoming indebted. It was appropriate that English trainers would be delivering the training – we have the largest market for credit in Europe and the most personal debt. I was unsure whether participants would be able to relate to this training, particularly as a survey showed that less than half of consumers had a current account or bank/credit card, compared with 82% in the UK and 93% in Sweden. Polish consumers seem to prefer to pay for a significant purchase in cash but of course the possibility of getting into debt is no less likely.

I delivered the credit training, taking them through the new EU Directive that Poland would have to implement, as well as the British model. Our credit legislation was introduced in the 1970s and goes much further in terms of regulating credit and protecting consumers than other countries. My co-trainer, a specialist debt worker, did the over indebtedness part of the course but we were both present at all the training sessions and group work. None of the delegates confessed to having experienced debt problems but they had begun to receive requests for help from the public and wanted to know how we solve problems, as there are few routes for Polish consumers to complain when they have received poor treatment by banks. We took them through the debt management process: preparation of an income and expenditure budget statement, dealing with priority debts (taxes, unpaid fines) first before offering creditors a share of the available income after all household expenses have been paid. We designed a debt self-help pack for consumers as many of the State Inspectorate and Ombudsman staff lacked the resources to give individual help. One Consumer Ombudsman told me that if the training meant she would be able to help just one person, it would have been worthwhile.

My first co-trainer Debbie worked at the Money Advice training centre in Birmingham. I had attended a course there ten years ago and before we began the training I decided to go down to Birmingham for an update, joining one of Debbie's training courses. It was a good chance to meet each other but otherwise the trip yielded little except to confirm that the process of helping people with debt problems had not changed. After Warsaw we headed to Bialystok, a city tucked up in the north east of Poland only thirty miles from Belarus and also close to the border with Lithuania, not far from my favourite spa town of Druskininkai. This part of Lithuania, including the capital of Vilnius, was once ruled by Poland and delegates on the course knew it well. How I longed to visit that wonderful town again, but there was no time. When working it's rarely possible to see all a city has to offer and this was the case in Bialystok, which apparently boasts many fine art galleries, museums and architecture, but I saw no further than the training room. It narrowly missed out being shortlisted for European Capital of Culture in 2016. My own region had been similarly disappointed in 2008 when the Newcastle-Gateshead bid was beaten by Liverpool.

For the second course Maria, a bubbly CAB Manager experienced in training and debt management, joined us. Maria's parents were born and grew up in Poland but they managed to escape just before it came under communist rule and restrictions on travel were imposed. They lived for the rest of their life in the West Midlands where they raised their family. Maria had many relatives in Poland and consequently spoke the language fluently but she chose to deliver her training in English using an interpreter, like myself. She was able to pass on comments made by the group during coffee breaks, but there was nothing of a derogatory nature fortunately. I persuaded her to 'come clean' at the end of the two-day course and speak to them in their own language. The group was stunned at first, immediately followed by embarrassment when they realized Maria had understood all their comments made over coffee and lunch. We decided to do this for the rest of the training courses and the reaction of the group was always the same and they wanted to know more of Maria's history.

Maria and I started training at Wroclaw (formerly Breslau) southeast of Warsaw and fourth largest city in Poland. If you believe the description in the guidebook as being a mini Prague you may be disappointed, but as a provincial Polish town it's pleasant enough. We arrived on Sunday and enjoyed tea and cakes in the medieval market square (Rynek) complete with Gothic arch. Yet again, most of the square had been levelled during the war and later rebuilt. I can appreciate the rebuilt ancient squares, but once I know I am looking upon a replica and admiring restoration techniques rather than the work of original craftsmen, such as Durham or York cathedrals or our Saxon church at Hart Village, I am drained of inspiration. On the corner of a busy crossroads, we came upon *Anonymous Pedestrians*, a memorial of fourteen lifelike bronze statues, including a child, only their upper bodies visible as they descend into the ground. It commemorates people taken by the militia in the middle of the night in 1982. The sculpture likewise appeared in the middle of the night on the anniversary of the introduction of martial law. It was located between our hotel and the town and became a landmark for us. By this time I had stayed in so many towns and cities in Poland it was getting hard to distinguish one from another, so identifying landmarks back to the hotel were essential, plus carrying the hotel details just in case we lost our way!

We reluctantly said goodbye to Maria after the two-week training course. She was a good trainer and had been an excellent companion whilst travelling around Poland. We would have used her for the rest of the training but she had a holiday booked with her family. Her replacement was my old friend Jacqui King and we met up at Stansted for a direct budget flight to Rzeszow. Not having seen each other for a while, we had a lot to catch up on and started chatting as soon as we boarded the flight. We were oblivious to the fact that the cabin crew had already begun their safety presentation – I usually try to look interested, safety being of the highest priority of course. But as I was taking flights every two weeks I could probably step in and do it myself word for word; whatever they say, every airline has the same message. Deep in discussion with Jacqui, the girl stopped her presentation and reprimanded us. 'Stop talking and pay attention,' she said, as if we were children. We got our own back later by ignoring her when she tried to sell us overpriced food and scratch cards.

Rzeszow is a quiet small town near the border with Slovakia and with not much to do we decided one evening to see the film *Notes on a Scandal*. Finding the old fashioned cinema somewhat deserted, we assumed it to be closed until an old lady came out to sell us tickets. She then accompanied us into the large auditorium, switched on the lights and showed us to our seats. She returned with a tray of ice cream before and during the film and at the end turned out the lights. We assumed she was also in charge of the screening. It would have been a private and exclusive viewing apart from one other person. Quite what the Polish people thought of the British educational system portrayed in this film, I can't say. Our final training was in Szczecin and Lublin, towns on opposite sides of this large country, requiring another long train journey. Fortunately Jacqui is a great raconteur and entertained us en route. Szczecin is in the north-west corner, almost in Germany and here we were driven around the area by our translator Andrej's friend and taken to a typical Polish restaurant. Lublin, near the Ukraine, was our next venue and bears a striking similarity to Vilnius old town and brought back fond memories as I walked along the cobbled streets and alleyways. They appear charming now but hide a dark history. During occupation in World War II the intention was to turn Lublin into a German city. It was also the German headquarters for *Operation Reinhardt* (the execution of all Jews in Poland).

The war and the fate of the Jewish population cannot be avoided in Poland; everywhere you go you are confronted with memories of the Holocaust. Poznan, our next destination, was no different. It appears to be a quiet market town where very little happens but in common with other cities it suffered terribly during the war. It was annexed and incorporated into the Third Reich in 1939 and many civilians were killed. In 1943 Himmler delivered a speech here declaring Nazi intentions to exterminate Jewish life, and little survives of Poznan's Jewish heritage. Although most of the city was destroyed during the war, there is a reconstructed and picturesque Old Town Square in Baroque and Renaissance styles, with museums and restaurants. I was interested in the City Scales building behind the Town Hall. It once housed the hardware for weighing merchandise on its way to the market and I would have liked to find out more about this – my Trading Standards background coming out – but it was closed. In this

17. Beirut 2007: Train-the-trainers group – with local Market Surveillance Inspectors and Roy Simpson

18. A meze in Beirut with Market Surveillance Inspectors

19. Sitting on Lenin's foot – Grutas Park, Lithuania

20. Pula 2005: Enjoying a drink with Yvonne Stein and James Joyce

21. Poland 2006: Paddling in the Baltic Sea with Beth, Karolina and Benedicte

22. Riga opera house in the pink

23. Vela Luka – a lunar landscape

24. Beautiful Rovinj

25. 2008: Training staff in Customer Care skills with Michele Shambrook from the Office of Fair Trading

26. Nick Riordan checking out the yachts during an on-site visit at a Riga boatyard

27. Showing off my 'Soviet' cast

28. With Alan and Lelde at the office Christmas Party

29. Robin Croft in a wintry Riga

30. Bridge over the Daugava, Riga

31. One of many bridges in Riga that are covered in locks

32. Lovers' locks. I hope they don't lose the key

square on a balmy summer's evening in 2006 I sat with Danish colleagues at a restaurant watching yet another World Cup final on a large screen in the square. After a tense penalty shoot-out Italy defeated France. On my next visit the winter sales were in full swing and our two interpreters took it in turns to check out the local shops. When the training finished we had less than an hour to pack up and get to the railway station for our train to the next city. Tida returned from the shops with exciting news of amazing bargains at a boutique's closing down sale. I joined her and Karolina in a mad dash to the Stary Browar shopping mall, housed in an old brewery, where we picked up some bargains before running to the station, catching the train by the skin of our teeth. I always enjoyed their company and we spent many hours chatting about fashion on our long train journeys.

I enjoyed the training in many regional cities of Poland and saw a lot of this interesting country. I can attest that Polish people are very hardworking, well educated and skilled – as we have seen from those now working in Britain.

CHAPTER SEVENTEEN

Warsaw and Krakow - A Tale of Two Cities

VISITING WARSAW IMMEDIATELY AFTER the war, US General Dwight Eisenhower remarked, 'I have seen many towns destroyed, but nowhere have I been faced with such destruction.' Eight-five percent of Warsaw was in ruins and twenty percent of the population lost their lives in the war. At the time of my first visit in 2006 the city was undergoing a modernization programme and the Royal Castle and Monte Cassino monument had been restored. The Old Town, completely destroyed by the Nazis, was rebuilt by using rubble and materials from demolished historic buildings in regional cities.

One of the pleasures of working overseas is the opportunity to sample a city I would otherwise not have visited. There are always surprises to be found when you stay for a longer period and get to know local people through a working environment, rather than as a tourist. Warsaw is a good example of this. It is not a pretty city and first impressions failed to arouse my interest, but it has a powerful history. Modern skyscrapers dominate the landscape, along with the usual grey concrete apartment blocks. There are luxury hotels and shopping malls, trendy bars and gourmet restaurants among traditional small shops and artisan workshops. I always stayed at the

Marriott Hotel, opposite the Palace of Culture, a colossus of a building that dominates the city skyline. The so-called Palace, an example of socialist architecture, was commissioned by Stalin as a 'gift' from the Soviet people and was intended to serve as the Communist party headquarters. Similar, though smaller, buildings in the same design can be seen in other Eastern European cities, for example Riga, and are equally disliked by their citizens, seen as a reminder of communism. The people of Warsaw, in common with other cities hosting one of Stalin's 'gifts' considered demolition after gaining independence, but the cost was prohibitive, and they remain.

During several visits I became familiar with Warsaw and unearthed something of its history. Visiting the Warsaw Museum of Uprising I learned about the extent of the suffering of Polish people and the bitterness felt toward Britain at the end of the war. The Uprising began in 1944 when the Poles rose against the occupying German forces. They assumed the west would come to their aid but this didn't happen and the Nazi army crushed the rebellion. On Hitler's orders, the entire city was to be destroyed. Buildings in order of cultural importance were numbered and systematically blown up. Soviet tanks, parked on the other side of the river Wisla, watched the destruction and by the time they chose to enter Warsaw most of the city was in ruin.

A visit to the former Gestapo headquarters is disturbing, as you would expect. It was one of the few buildings to survive, its original purpose being a centre for religious beliefs, but during Nazi occupation became a brutal interrogation centre. Cells have been left as they were, bullet marks scar the walls and manacles, bullwhips and other instruments of torture can be seen. Another poignant memorial is 'The Little Insurgent', commemorating the children who were killed during the Uprising, often used as messengers. After this, a walk around the landscaped gardens of Lazienki Park and the Chopin monument is a good idea.

Krakow escaped the wholesale destruction of Warsaw and has many original buildings of interest, not least Wawel Castle and Cathedral. The medieval market square is one of the largest in Europe. The huge Cloth Hall in the centre of the square was effectively the first shopping mall and today it is crammed with shops and stalls selling amber, lace and wood items. Maria wanted to buy Burstyn (amber) and there was plenty of choice. Our training went well but the timing of our visit was not so good. It was the school holidays and the hotel was full of French and Italian teenagers on an educational tour. We were kept awake all night as they ran amok down the corridors, banging on our doors. We complained all night to the hotel staff but they were not prepared to do anything and the teachers couldn't be found.

Maria and I stayed on in Krakow an extra day in order to take a tour out to Auschwitz (or Oswiecim, to give it the Polish name Maria always used). Members of Maria's family had died during the Nazi occupation of Poland and this visit was difficult for her. She told me that whenever her father had taken the family back to Poland to visit relatives he always opened the window of the train when entering his country and shouted abuse. He was addressing the occupying forces of Germany and Russia. Sadly he had not lived to witness Poland's independence in 1989.

Nothing really prepares you for the horror of Auschwitz. A video played on the bus taking us there set the scene and was very graphic. You enter through the infamous gates with its dishonest sign *Arbeit Macht Frei* (Work sets you free), a notice tells you that the camp orchestra played music when prisoners went to and from work - apparently it kept them in step and helped guards to count them. Prisoners were escorted out every morning to work in the fields, returning in the evening. The long low blocks of buildings in matching red brick don't immediately look menacing, being separated by green grass and tall trees, but the double fences of electrified and barbed wire leave you in no doubt of their purpose.

Inside the blocks are long glass walls containing mountains of human hair. Another has piles of suitcases that prisoners had been told to pack, their names written on the front and sometimes a date of birth, containing their treasured possessions. There is a small mountain of children's shoes. Other displays contained spectacles, shoes, toothbrushes and prayer shawls. It's almost too much to bear. Explanations are given about the lethal Zyklon B gas used to kill large numbers of people at a time; we were shown the shower blocks, gas ovens, torture cells, the building where Dr Mengele carried out his evil experiments and the execution yard. As if this is not shocking enough, a bus then takes you three kilometres to Birkenau, containing three hundred barracks. Entering through an arch onto a railway track, overlooked by the SS watchtower, it looks oddly familiar. This is the scene used in countless films, where prisoners alighted from a train at the end of the track to face a selection process. Murder was committed here on an industrial scale. Over half were sent straight to the gas chambers, the rest used as slave labour until they dropped. They say a lake near the crematoria is still a cloudy colour, from human ash. I found Auschwitz II-Birkenau even more distressing than the main camp. No one spoke on the return bus trip to Krakow.

I have met people who won't go to Auschwitz or other camps, and respect that, but we need to be reminded of man's capacity for wickedness and never be allowed to forget what happened. I recalled a famous remark, *'All it takes for evil to survive is that good men do nothing.'*

At the airport on my return from this trip I had just cleared security and was putting myself back together after removing coat, boots, belt etc. when I heard a man shouting my name. As Karol is a Polish name I didn't take any notice at first but turned to see Feliksas Petrauskas from Vilnius running toward me. He literally swept me off my feet with hugs and kisses saying, 'Vilnius is waiting for you, when will you return?' Dalia, who had worked with me in the office in Vilnius, was with him and it was just lovely to see them again. They had been attending a meeting in Krakow and were on their way back to Vilnius, proving that it really is a small world.

My final visit to Warsaw was in 2007, to write public awareness materials for the Consumer Protection Authority. The project was nearing an end and some spare money had been found to design and print a range of brochures on credit and debt avoidance. By this time I had warmed to Warsaw and enjoyed my free time at the Marriott, using the swimming pool and having spa treatments after work. I worked on the brochures with Jim Spinks and two Danish lawyers - teamwork that produced good results. Beth later sent me copies of the printed brochures – in Polish of course. The range of work and the opportunity to learn about the history and culture of this country had proved an interesting and enjoyable experience.

CHAPTER EIGHTEEN

A Middle Eastern Sojourn

BEIRUT: CAPITAL OF LEBANON is dubbed the 'Pearl of the Middle East' and situated on a peninsula extending westward into the Mediterranean Sea, flanked by mountains.

Sandwiched between work in Poland and visits to Riga in preparation for a long-term project in Latvia, I agreed to spend a few weeks delivering a train-the-trainers course in Lebanon. I had never contemplated working this far from home and was mindful of the fact that a posting in Beirut brought its own fears and complications, not least because initially my family was not keen on the idea. I had been working for NI-CO for some years as an overseas expert when they won their first project in Lebanon. The question everyone asks is why the European Union gives funding to an unstable country in the Middle East, and surely Lebanon had more serious problems than consumer protection anyway. The answer of course is trade. The EU is Lebanon's largest trading partner. Further ties are through the EU's European Neighbourhood policy.

Oonagh McAliskey called to tell me about this project, having been on a scoping visit to Beirut, inviting me to be a short-term expert. She enthused about the French inspired architecture, exciting nightlife and sunset strolls along the Corniche. The Lebanese had shown her the best of their city, which in 2006 had been rebuilt and settled down after decades of war. I was not entirely convinced, only being able to associate Beirut with hostage taking, having followed the kidnapping of British and Americans during the 1980s, later reading the memoirs of Terry Waite, John McCarthy and Brian Keenan. However, never one to turn down prospective work outright, and tempted by Oonagh's exotic portrait of Beirut, I said I might consider her proposal. In the end I had to refuse, as I was already committed to work in Poland on the proposed dates. I had a lucky escape because in July 2006, when I should have been there, Israel launched a ferocious attack on Lebanon. The airport runways were bombed and there was a long delay before people could be evacuated. I was very concerned for my friends Robin Croft and Mike Hanson who were working in Beirut at the time. They had no choice but to remain in their hotel whilst bombs and gunfire rained all around them, until they were able to persuade a taxi driver to take them to the Syrian border and after a long walk eventually made it to the airport where they managed to get a flight home.

The following year Robin persuaded me Lebanon was now completely safe and I should consider participating in the project. 'It's safer than going to Egypt at the moment,' he insisted, knowing I had recently been there on holiday. Another incentive was that I would be working with Roy Simpson, a training expert from Northern Ireland, who had been proposed as a short-term expert to work on my next project in Latvia. I had not met him and this would be a good opportunity to do so. In July and September of 2007 I went to Beirut, with the support of my husband, though not necessarily my daughters – that was because I didn't actually tell them I was off to the Middle East. They assumed I was working in Poland. We are not a family who keep secrets from each other but if I had told them where I was going they would have been worried. Alison had expressed relief when I had narrowly avoided being caught up in the Israeli bombings the previous year, saying, 'Well, Dad never wanted you to go anyway.' Not true actually, but it was an odd statement from an avowed feminist who may listen to her husband's advice but will ultimately make her own decision about a proposed action, which is exactly as it should be. After I returned from the first mission I did tell them where I had been and that I would be going back to complete the work providing the country remained peaceful. This time I was amused by Carolyn's comment: 'As long as Dad is happy about you going.' I'm quite sure she doesn't always seek her husband's permission for proposed actions and would agree that marriage should not be based on one partner telling the other what they can or cannot do. However, I was very pleased to have their support. Alan's response was that if I were to be kidnapped he was not paying the ransom. He was joking – at least I hope he was!

I agreed to meet Roy at Heathrow. Not having seen a photograph of him I took a chance when standing in a queue at the check-in desk I spotted a man holding what looked to be a NI-CO ticket and introduced myself. He was an excellent travelling companion and the long flight simply flew by. Having lived in Belfast all of his life, Roy was the best companion I could have had in Beirut because he never underestimated the danger of violence, which is always present there, and he could recognize gunfire from miles away. Prior to our first visit a politician had been assassinated in a restaurant and whilst we were there fighting broke out in the north of the country and there was trouble in the refugee camps, but fortunately we encountered nothing dangerous. We emerged from Beirut airport into a hot and sultry late evening and hailed a taxi. I thought that taxi drivers could not get any worse than those I had experienced in Poland, but the Lebanese were crazy, driving at high speeds, constantly changing lanes, and the cacophony of car horns was deafening.

Working with Roy was the most relaxed and easy work I have ever done overseas. We were there to deliver a training-of-trainers course for senior staff of the consumer department and he went about the preparation and delivery of this in a relaxed and unrushed manner. I realized that this was a course he had delivered many times and could probably have done without notes, but at the same time his delivery was so fresh no one would have known this. I was in the company of a master and a gentleman. After work he was good company, a raconteur with fascinating tales to tell from his early career as a priest in Northern Ireland, his work shadowed by the 'Troubles', and of the house he and his wife are now building in France. After leaving the church he worked for Shell as a management executive before embarking on a career overseas. His humour and obvious charm with people almost made me forget I was in a dangerous country and that those at home were probably quite worried about my welfare and safety. Robin Croft and Mike Hanson were also working there during my first visit and we all went out to eat in the evenings. They knew the city well and recommended places to visit at the weekend.

Lebanon is a complex but fascinating country and I was fortunate to visit many of its historic sites. With no public transport system we had to hire a private taxi to get around. The hotel organized this and Roy politely bartered over the price. We found a driver whose skills were good, an improvement on the usual taxis that we picked up outside the hotel, and used him for other weekend excursions. The first was to Byblos, a charming fishing port believed to be the oldest continued civilization in the world. It is famous for its archaeological site and its spectacular setting on the Mediterranean. We walked among the ruins, the only tourists, and saw evidence of various digs over the last century, taking lunch at a quayside restaurant. We were the only visitors at the old souk, as the stalls were doing no business - the Israeli bombardment of the previous summer having all but killed off the tourist trade. At every stall we were offered coffee and the entire family would be brought out to meet the special visitors from England. At another small shop we bought fossils and objects crafted from cedar wood; again the owner insisted on making coffee. When we passed his shop a couple of hours later he darted out with two chilled bottles of water, pressing them into our hands but refused to take any money, further evidence of warm hospitable people. After this we visited the Jetta Caves, fantastic grottoes with a subterranean lake and vast caverns sculpted by water. You take a ride up the mountain, by cable car or small train, reaching the upper gallery to view the stalagmites and stalactites. A small boat takes you into the lower grotto.

A long and tiring journey took us through the Bekaa Valley, to what is referred to as Lebanon's greatest treasure - Baalbek, formerly Heliopolis. This archeological site beside the Syrian border is truly stunning. A day is not sufficient to take in the history and archeology of Baalbek, which contains the best-preserved and largest Roman temples built. I particularly liked the Temple of Jupiter, with its six magnificent Corinthian columns, and the *'Stone of the Pregnant Woman'* – said to be the largest hewn stone in the world weighing in at one thousand tons. Driving there we knew we were in Hezbollah country when the roads were covered with yellow and green flags atop large pictures of their leaders, and before we could enter Baalbek we were required to walk through one of their camps, a small cave set into the ancient wall. Money had to change hands before we were permitted to pass through and Roy approached them and made a purchase. This is unofficial, I don't think they own the site but it would have been foolhardy to ignore them. On the way back we stopped off to visit the Kasara vineyard, makers of fine white and red wines. It was very well organized and we were taken on a tour of the cellars followed by wine tasting – and buying. Lebanese red and white wines are very good. Our taxi driver would occasionally stop point and announce 'Palestinian refugee camp'; another stop was to point out a huge bridge scanning a valley - the problem was the middle part of the bridge was missing. 'Israel did that, summer of 2006, you will want to take photo,' he ordered. I got out of the car and took a photo just to make him happy. Roy had fallen asleep as soon as the car went into motion and I had to keep up the conversation with the driver, a polite young man who told me of his impending marriage, passing photo after photo of his fiancée to me in the back of the car. On the way back he took a detour to show me the house where they would begin their married life.

In Beirut we stayed in the Gefinore Hotel, located near the sea and very smart, part of an Arab chain. The English manager took care of us exceptionally well and Roy charmed and chatted with the staff, gently asking questions about their work and family. It was the first hotel I have stayed in with an infinity swimming pool on the roof; the water from the pool seemed to fall right into the blue sea. On the tables were dishes of fresh gardenias – their smell divine – and we often took dinner by the pool. Moving around the city was interesting, armed soldiers on every corner and my bag searched every morning on the way to the office. Reminded of the fact that Beirut was once called the Paris of the east, I saw some examples of this, but the bombings of the previous year had destroyed many buildings. The streets in the government area were scattered with razor wire and the Hezbollah camp outside Parliament was difficult to ignore. I became accustomed to seeing bombed out buildings and bullet holes everywhere, often next door to a new skyscraper with glass fronts, yet it is also the only city where I have seen traffic lights being dusted down with a feather mop! The people were wonderfully friendly – hard to reconcile with their reputation and turbulent past, not to mention kidnapping foreigners. An oasis in this troubled city was the American University of Beirut, where Brian Keenan was employed as a lecturer before being taken as a hostage. The University gardens, close to the sea, are peaceful, with views of the Mediterranean and containing many exotic species of plants. There was a Banyan tree with a plaque dedicated to a man who had died young. It simply said, '*He lived life abundantly*', which I think is a fitting epitaph for anyone.

    At the train-the-trainers course, held at the Chamber of Commerce, we were impressed by the commitment shown by market surveillance staff. Teamwork was not a problem, remarkable when you consider the huge political and religious diversity in this country. Everyone participated and applied their new knowledge when asked to design and deliver a short presentation on an area of their work. Two women even attempted role-play – not easy to pull off but it worked. Another duo gave a presentation aimed at training new inspectors and brought in lots of bottles of wine and spirits, describing how to identify if they were counterfeit. It seems in Lebanon they do, after all, have similar consumer problems to those in Britain. Their colleagues decided that samples must be tasted to distinguish authentic from counterfeit.

    After one of the training sessions Roy and I were whisked off to enjoy some Lebanese hospitality. The RTA was leaving, the Inspectors had organized a lunch in his honour and we were invited. We were driven up the coast and taken to a restaurant by the beach, where we joined a group of about thirty people already there. The meze was amazing with dish after dish dancing out of the kitchen. There was much excitement when one plate of meat was brought out and it was soon devoured. I'm glad I didn't partake – it was raw liver. The lunch lasted nearly four hours, followed by complimentary fresh fruit and liqueurs, which is the custom in Lebanese restaurants. When we finally departed no bill was offered, nor payment requested as far as I know. Someone joked that the restaurant was unlikely to be inspected for a long time. Had we participated in something that would be regarded as fraudulent in Britain? In local government we had to declare even a box of chocolates given to us by a grateful consumer.

Working in the Middle East is not for everyone and I never did grow accustomed to the UN tanks on the streets and armed soldiers everywhere, but I'm very glad I made the decision to go. The experience has changed my view of this region and of Lebanese people and that of course is the true value of travel. When I think of Beirut now I no longer think of hostage taking but of the man dusting the traffic lights with a feather mop! In spite of their history, improving consumer protection is seen as an important feature of modernization and reconstruction. At the same time I was relieved to land back in England safe and sound. I bought a book for Hannah's international bookshelf –I hope she keeps it and remembers the trouble her grandmother took to buy it. A Lebanese colleague wrote her name in Arabic and also gave me a small wooden cedar tree. It had been a brief, but fascinating, glimpse into a completely different culture.

CHAPTER NINETEEN

Four Excursions to Riga and a Day in Belfast

I FIRST HEARD about the possibility of another twinning project in Latvia during the summer of 2005. I was working in Vilnius; Beth Baker had recently finished her project in Latvia and put my name forward to speak at a product safety conference. There was no speaker's fee but as long as my travel costs were reimbursed I was happy to accept. The conference was held at the Reval hotel – fast forward three years and I would be a frequent visitor to their Skybar - but not on this occasion. I arrived the evening before the conference just as everyone was sitting down to dinner. My late flight meant that I had missed the pre-dinner cocktail party but Linda Rinkule, the organizer, had kept some champagne and immediately pressed a glass in my hand. Over dinner I met the other speakers, who had travelled from various parts of the EU, and learnt that I was also expected to run a workshop for business representatives, which was rather unnerving.

The next day I gave a presentation that focused on how businesses and consumer associations can assist in ensuring only safe products are placed on the market. Noel Toledo from Malta was also a speaker, a well-known and respected expert on product safety, who later brought me up to date with the changes taking place in his country following accession to the European Union. After completion of the presentations we joined our respective workshops. I was directed to a conference room and introduced myself to the translators sitting in two booths ready to give simultaneous translation. In a workshop situation they don't have the opportunity of reading the material beforehand to clarify unusual terms of phrases, so it helps if they can talk informally to the speaker and assess the range and speed of their vocabulary. After some initial trepidation – there were more businesses present than I had expected - I relaxed and enjoyed my role of facilitating discussion and chairing the workshop. Over lunch I was seated next to Baiba Vitolina, the new Director of the Consumer Rights Protection Centre, the main beneficiary institution. She outlined to me an application for second a Twinning Project that was currently being drafted for submission to Brussels. The principal objective would be to train staff in technical areas of market surveillance, as many were new to this work. Not for a moment did I think this would be of interest to me.

After the conference wound up we were taken over to the Ridzene hotel on the other side of the Esplanade, the park that separates the Old Town from the rest of the city, for a cocktail party and dinner. Our hosts were gracious and made us feel very welcome and appreciated. It was a hot sultry evening and Anna, a Danish woman representing a business federation and familiar with Riga, suggested we walk over to the Old Town. I was struck how different it was from Vilnius, yet the cities share a similar culture and history. Riga has medieval defences, influences of Gothic, Baroque churches and Art Nouveau architecture - all amid the legacy of the recent Soviet era. We lingered at Pilsetas Kanal that flows through the centre of town to watch people negotiating their rowing boats around the fountains, their shrieks of laughter carrying through the air when they got too close and were sprayed. Street musicians performed on the bridge and the grassy banks of Bastejkalns. It seemed a much livelier city than its Lithuanian neighbour, particularly as there were several stag parties in town. Every bar, café or restaurant had an outdoor terrace and it was a perfect summer evening. Before leaving for the airport the next day I had time to explore the Old Town's cobbled streets, visit the stunning Russian Cathedral with its golden domes and cross the tracks to shop in Stockmanns, the Nordic departmental store. When visiting a new place I seem to have an eye for the best shops even without a guidebook; I must have a built-in homing instinct to shop. I made the most of my visit because after this midsummer stopover I was not expecting to return to

Riga. It was back to work in Vilnius and another sub-zero winter to look forward to.

The following year, Brussels gave approval for Baiba's Twinning Project to go ahead and it went out to tender in the member states. I was surprised when NI-CO asked me to be proposed Resident Twinning Adviser but my work in Croatia was coming to an end and I accepted. I began researching the numerous EU Directives included in the Fiche, mostly on areas of consumer protection that were unfamiliar to me, but it was just as well because we received short notice that our attendance was required at an interview in Riga in October 2006. I had to make two connections from Zagreb to Riga, thinking, 'Why are my travel arrangements never straightforward?' I always seem to be in the wrong place, somewhere other than home, when called upon to make these trips.

Jim Spinks, proposed as Project Leader, plus Graeme McCammon representing NI-CO, joined me in Riga. We had prepared a presentation and sent it in advance for translation. I smiled when it came up on the screen – this time my name was shown as Caroli. My father called me this when I complained that someone had dropped the 'e' from my name. I can't say we put up a very good presentation at the interview. The specifics as to how we would plan the work and achieve the results was not in sufficient detail, probably because the three of us had not had the opportunity to meet beforehand. It seemed to me unlikely that the United Kingdom would win it, having already delivered a big twinning project a few years earlier. Beneficiaries often prefer to choose a different country the second time round so they receive a different perspective on how to deliver consumer protection. The twinning project that followed ours in Croatia, for which NI-CO also made a bid, had been awarded to Germany, disappointing many of the short-term experts who were looking forward to trips to Croatia. I had a few reservations about leading this project. Reading the terms of reference my immediate reaction was that they needed a Market Surveillance expert as RTA. This was because most of the work entailed a working knowledge in unfamiliar subjects like gas appliances, recreational craft, and pressure vessels. However Jim and Graham disagreed and I appreciated their support and confidence in me.

This visit was to be no repeat of my summer sojourn the previous year. We arrived into an early winter chill and torrential rain; in fact it rained for the entire two days and in the old town that means your feet get soaked because the drains can't cope. I had come from Zagreb where we were enjoying a sublime warm and sunny autumn, and shivered. We had been booked into a so-called boutique hotel but never could the reality have been at such divergence from the description. It was cold and inhospitable. The Ministry of Finance in Smilsu Street, where the interview took place, was grim in the old Soviet style, guarded by unsmiling people who appeared unfriendly and almost hostile. Immediately entering the building a stern unsmiling guard demanded our passports, scrutinizing them before exchanging it for a badge. Even Baiba Vitolina, the Director of the Consumer Rights Protection Centre where I would be based and whom I had met the previous summer, seemed more subdued than at our first meeting and seemed to have lost some of her earlier enthusiasm. The damp atmosphere outside seemed to have affected those round the conference table. Did I really want to work here? And the litmus test – could I see myself living in this city for a year? It wasn't grabbing me, as Vilnius had done on those first visits. I was relieved to return to the warmth of a Croatian autumn to complete my work there, determined to put Latvia out of my mind, telling everyone that I thought it unlikely that we would be awarded the contract. However, we were not to be let off so easily. A week later the Latvians told us they would be interviewing the German team, the only other bidder for the project, the following week and would like us to prepare a more comprehensive case of how we would deliver the objectives of the project so they could have a proper comparison. We resubmitted our proposal and a month later received a decision from the European Commission that we had won the contract.

I completed the work in Croatia at the end of 2006 and after two days at home took a flight to Riga to meet the Latvian team I would be working with and begin to write the Twinning Contract. We tried a different hotel, a former convent and historic building, but still not to my liking, and again it rained constantly. The bedrooms are located in courtyards and some distance from the main building so I was soaked just getting to breakfast. Joanne Lenzi from NI-CO accompanied me this time but was unwell on arrival. I had to ask the hotel to bring a doctor and she spent the next two days in bed. I felt so sorry for Joanne; she had taken two flights from Belfast, arranged childcare for her young son, only to be ill and didn't leave the hotel bedroom until she returned to the airport. I went to the meeting at the Ministry of Finance on my own and did my best to answer the questions regarding finance and project management, normally taken by NI-CO. After the meeting I took Baiba out for lunch and she expanded on the structure of her department and what she wanted to achieve. She told me that she and her colleagues had always preferred the

UK tender and that was why they had given us another chance to improve our presentation. I'm sure this was due in large part to Beth Baker having delivered a good project for them previously - astutely we had named Beth as a short-term expert on the bid. Baiba made no mention of potential delays; in fact she indicated a preference for starting immediately as she had appointed new staff and they urgently required training. As we parted we looked forward to working together in a few months' time.

We then began the laborious task of writing the Twinning Contract. It took longer than necessary due to poor communication on the Latvian side, which was never really explained. The European Commission expects a twinning project to be started within six months from the award of the tender, but in this case fifteen months were to pass from winning the project to starting. The European Commission is the principal funder of projects in candidate or new member states but the beneficiary country also has to guarantee to provide substantial funding from its own government. My guess is that this was not in place and the delay in agreeing the Contract may have been deliberate. To maintain the momentum on our side I invited Jim and his wife Julia to visit our apartment in the Lake District so that we could work on the Contract detail together. Electronic communication is a wonderful thing but sometimes you need face-to-face discussion. Inspired, I am sure, by the fells and beautiful scenery we were able to complete the Project work plan by the end of this visit and all that remained was to agree a start date with the Latvians.

By the summer of 2007, convinced the Twinning Contract was almost ready for signature and would start in the autumn, Jim and I flew out to Riga to meet Baiba and her colleagues. Linda Rinkule, now Baiba's deputy and my former host at the product safety conference two years previously, met us at the hotel, and I was delighted to hear that she would be my counterpart in the project. We took a taxi to their new offices on the outskirts of the city where we received a warm welcome by Baiba and her senior staff. Jim had the advantage of having been Project Leader on Beth's project and was therefore well acquainted with the structure of consumer protection in Latvia and was familiar with many of the staff. Our meeting was friendly and constructive and we were all confident the project would start in the autumn, allowing me to complete my short-term work in Poland and Lebanon.

This time we stayed at a new hotel, the Albert, and liked it so much we negotiated with the manager to get special rates for our visiting experts. It was close to Valdemara Street that had a tram and trolleybus link direct to the office. The weather was hot and sunny and I warmed to Riga. Jim knew the city quite well and was an excellent guide to parts I had not visited before. He always knows the best teashops, places to eat and what's on at the opera or ballet. He pointed out the huge central market; a giant bazaar contained within five huge aircraft airport hangers, and on the other side of town the Art Nouveau architecture, the best examples being in and around Alberta Street. The florid decorations on the buildings are amazing and it surprised me that so little is known of Riga's treasures, as opposed to Prague where everyone seems to visit. Noticing that one of the most spectacular buildings housed the Danish Embassy, Jim rang the doorbell, as he knew Beth Baker's previous assistant now worked there. Zinta answered the door to us and was intrigued to find Jim, someone she had not encountered for a few years. She welcomed us in and introduced us to the Ambassador. I was impressed that he was hunched over a computer in the main office writing his own emails. It's not generally the image you have of an Ambassador, assuming they have an army of administrative staff, though in fact Zinta told us they were a small team and His Excellency took care of his own administrative duties.

After lunch sitting in the sun on Dome Square, Jim and I visited the Tourist Information Centre nearby and noticed there was to be a concert that evening. Not in the city, but at the seaside town of Jurmala (which means 'seaside' in Latvian). I was disappointed, assuming there was no time to visit the coast, but Jim said 'It's only a twenty minute train ride from Riga, let's go.' It was to be the first of many visits to Majori, the principal town at Jurmala, which boasts a 33 km sweep of golden sands on the Baltic Sea. The Dzintari Concert Hall is set in a beautiful garden by the beach, and we were treated to wonderful classical music played in a marvellous environment. The concert hall has an open-air stage with a roof that protects performers and audiences from bad weather, and wooden cladding said to ensure perfect acoustics. The sides are open and the warm evening air, scented from the fragrant gardens, wafts across the audience. As ever in Eastern Europe the audience was all-embracing, from babies in prams to concertgoers in their best frocks and suits.

This short visit had been productive and enjoyable, due in large part to Jim's excellent planning and knowledge of Riga, and I felt more positive about working and living in Latvia. The next morning I said goodbye to Jim; my plane was due to leave earlier than his and he would spend the rest of the day in Riga. At the departure gate, getting ready to board, we were told there was a technical fault and after hanging around the airport for several hours KLM announced there were no more flights to the UK and I would have to stay in Riga for an another night and return to the airport for a 6 a.m. flight the next day. I was sent back into the city to the Radisson hotel and an early flight the next morning; Jim's flight of course had left on time and he was already back home in Croydon.

In the autumn of 2007, I had completed my short-term work in Poland and Lebanon, yet there was still no sign of starting Latvia. There was a worrying silence in the Consumer Protection department and it began to look as if the project would never get off the ground. It was now a year since we had been awarded the contract. Perhaps they had changed their mind and didn't need help with consumer protection in Riga after all? Suddenly, just after I had booked a short pre-Christmas break to New York, they wrote asking if I could start in early December. I packed a case so as to be ready to leave for Riga at short notice. I thought if we could start the project in the first week of December I could get the first month's activities out of the way: find an apartment, set up the office, appoint a project assistant, then return home for Christmas and bring out the first short-term experts in January. It seemed a reasonable plan. I flew to Belfast for a meeting with Jim and Graeme at NI-CO to sign my contract. Although none of us wanted another delay we realized that to start at the end of December would present difficulties and that it would now be preferable to wait until January, if the beneficiaries agreed. They did, and with a resigned sigh at yet another delay I made my way back to Belfast airport, only to find the flight had been delayed by several hours. Oonagh came to the rescue, taking me to her house in Belfast and for a meal at her local, very Irish, pub. I had to accept that the project would now not start until after the New Year, and put the suitcases away.

CHAPTER TWENTY

Sveiki! Latvia

LATVIA: A SMALL COUNTRY with a quiet verdant countryside, golden beaches on the Baltic Sea and a hint of a mountain in Sigulda, where skiing is possible. Commerce and business is centred in Riga, the capital city, which has a charming Old Town with cobblestones and boasts impressive art-nouveau architecture.

Starting work in a new city in the middle of winter, particularly in the Baltic, is not ideal but once the European Commission has signed off a project the RTA is expected to begin work immediately. Alan flew out to Riga with me in January 2008, arriving in sub zero temperatures and deep snow. On the first day I took a taxi to the office of my beneficiaries at the Consumer Rights Protection Centre. I felt nervous, not by meeting them again but about the type of office accommodation I would be provided. In previous projects I have been forced into cramped unsatisfactory accommodation, and it's not a good start. So I took a taxi on that first day and held my breath. Baiba Vitolina and her team welcomed me, we had coffee, she took me on a tour of the building to introduce me to every staff member (though it's impossible to remember everyone's name and rank on these occasions) and then escorted me to my new office a few minutes' walk away. I was amazed and delighted when I saw it. It was on the fourth floor of a newly built modern office block, winner of architectural awards, very spacious with a separate office for me. It was light and airy, with glass windows floor to ceiling, wall to wall – a huge bonus in the dark days of winter. They had engraved my name on the board downstairs and outside the office door and fitted it out generously for six people with all the equipment and stationery I would need for a year. Baiba even gave me two mobile phones, for the project assistant and me. I could not have expected more, yet they insisted I must say if there was anything missing. There was even an excellent canteen downstairs serving good food all day. It was a superb working environment and worth having to catch the trolleybus to work each morning, even though I often missed the stop when it was dark and the windows had steamed up. More than once I found myself in a strange part of town, having to return to the centre and start again. In the spring most of the short-term experts decided to walk back to the Albert Hotel rather than take the trolley-bus and I joined them, though my walk was longer to the Old Town – an hour door to door. For over a year I enjoyed every day in the office and was sad to leave.

This project was unique in that over the next year I appointed four project assistants. The young woman I initially selected was ideal and had recently completed a twinning project, but she never actually started because she was offered a job in the Ministry of Agriculture, providing more permanent employment. We continued to meet for coffee and she gave me advice about administrative procedures in Latvia. The runner up was Laura, but she couldn't start for a month so I appointed Lelde in a temporary position. Laura had previous project experience and settled in straightaway. She was a serious young woman, an academic. After work she rushed off to the University every night, where she was studying for her second Masters degree in Literature, so rarely came out with us after work. Nor could she seem to give much local information, suggest where to go at weekends or what number bus to take, and I had to find everything out for myself – often the best way. I had no complaints with her work and she was an efficient and supportive assistant. She had already signed up to go to Norway for a further course of study when the project was due to end and for the final month I had to look for a replacement, someone with experience, as there was no time to train anyone. Laura sent out some emails to other project assistants and found Mara Rozenberga who had recently completed work on a Greek twinning project. A bright friendly girl in her twenties, she was extremely helpful in organizing social events as well as activities concerned with the project, and was well liked by the beneficiaries and experts. She is confident in a quiet way, comes from an academic and close family, the youngest of four daughters who all sing with choirs. I would like to have met her family and heard her perform in the choir but there was no time during the last month of the project. She aided me in organizing a closing conference and dinner at the Frog restaurant and when I left gave me a satirical book *Latvia Too,* and in the inscription wrote 'To the best and last RTA in Latvia' – a reference to the fact that Latvia no longer qualified for EU assistance. Mara's favourite band, Antony and the Johnsons (whom none of us had heard of) were playing the Sage in Gateshead in June 2009 and she was determined to see them. We invited her to stay with us for a few days and I went to the concert with her. She also experienced English village life by coming along to our bingo and fish and chip supper at the village hall!

Soon after I arrived in Riga the Ministry of Finance organized a seminar in order to instruct those of us running EU projects on the correct administrative and invoicing requirements. Many issues were clarified at this meeting but the Ministry of Finance and Central Financing Contract Agency were not easy to deal with and the procedures were unnecessarily bureaucratic. The meeting was helpful in another respect however as it brought together all the Resident Twinning Advisers and their project assistants and we bonded over a meal after the seminar. Two of them left soon after, when their projects completed, but Keith Mellor, from the UK National Audit Office in London, stayed in Riga until the end of 2008 and we met up occasionally. It's always good to be able to discuss your project with someone who is experiencing the same problems. I was later able to transfer some of this experience to a new RTA, David Sterret, an ex Special Branch policeman from Northern Ireland, now working with NI-CO and about to start a project in the Police Authority.

The first short-term expert to come out from England was my good friend Robin Croft and he returned most months until the end. Robin had worked on two previous projects in Latvia and possessed more knowledge about their consumer regime than I did. As ever, he was an excellent colleague and companion and produced first-class work. One of his first tasks was to design and deliver in-depth training to staff of the Consumer Protection Directorate. He suggested to me that the training would be more interesting and beneficial to staff if it were conducted by two trainers rather than him alone and proposed Mike Hanson as co-trainer. I had met Mike in Lebanon who, like Robin, is a retired Chief Trading Standards Officer, also now working for NI-CO as a consultant. I had no doubt that Mike would be a valuable member of the team. Experts such as himself and Robin formed the backbone of the project, supplementing Trading Standards Officers who worked for local authorities in Britain who were only able to commit to one or two weeks at a time, but initially I wanted to avoid the bureaucratic procedure necessary when introducing a new short-term expert. There are letters to be written, a financial statement prepared, the reasons as to why a change in the Twinning Contract is necessary and the agreement of the Ministry of Finance and the beneficiaries are necessary. An expert's CV, however good, will be placed under scrutiny. However these '*Side Letters*', as they are called, cannot be avoided, as modifications to the Contract are inevitable. People move jobs, their employer may not release them for work overseas, the nature of their expertise may have changed or the beneficiaries will suddenly ask for a departure in the work plan. So long as it does not affect the overall purpose of the project changes will be ratified but gaining agreement can take time and the expert cannot be contracted or his or her flight booked until the Side Letter is approved and contains the appropriate stamps. They are very keen on their stamps in Eastern Europe.

Every week I had one or more short-term experts in the office, designing or delivering training on various aspects of market surveillance: pressure vessels; construction products; gas appliances; child articles; recreational crafts etc. The Twinning Contract simply stated that staff should receive training on these subjects; it was silent as to how this was to be done, the duration or nature of the training. It had to be challenging and interactive, providing more than a just a lecture from a British expert. Most of all I wanted the participants to go away from the training feeling they had learned a valuable lesson and now had the skills to be an effective market surveillance officer. This was likely to be the last EU-funded project the Consumer Protection Directorate would receive, so the training also had to be sustainable. I set about designing a two-day training course. On the first day of training the visiting expert would deliver presentations on relevant European Directives and enforcement methods, with some group work. On the second morning we arranged for the participants to visit the premises of a local supplier linked to the subject of the training and to carry out a market surveillance inspection under the guidance of the expert. After all, how can you learn how to check compliance against EU Directives of, say, a yacht or pressure vessel from the training room? After an on-site visit they returned to the training room after lunch and spent the afternoon discussing the findings of their visit. The training culminated in a quiz to be completed by all participants in order to receive their training certificates. Most of the training courses were held at the same hotel, near to the bus and railway station, not the best part of town but a convenient and familiar environment for staff. It was important that all the technical training followed the same template as it gave consistency and everyone knew what to expect – and what was expected of him or her. The only change was that the trainer would be different. Mike Hanson delivered a lot of this training, as well as the introductory course with Robin.

Over the next few months we followed the same pattern. I would walk across town to the venue to arrive by 8.30 a.m. Laura would already be there to ensure the technology was in working condition, the refreshments were adequate and distribute the training packs. I would open the training, introduce the trainer and the interpreters, remaining until I was sure they had everything they required before returning to the office. On the second day of training Laura accompanied the group to the on-site inspection, later helping the trainer mark the test papers during the afternoon tea break. Delegates took the test seriously, treating it as an examination and wanted to get good results. I arrived at the afternoon coffee break to hear the trainer announce the results of the test. I closed the training, thanked the trainer and interpreters and presented the certificates. They always appeared enthusiastic and appreciative of the training and when I presented their certificates would give me a standing ovation. I felt I was conferring a degree on proud graduates! I noticed that whereas on the first day of training the participants seemed unsure and reserved with the trainer, when I returned on the second day they were all on good terms and the atmosphere was light-hearted.

The first of these two-day training courses was on the Recreational Craft Directive and Nick Riordan from Hampshire Trading Standards was more than qualified to train in this complicated subject. He was a member of the relevant EU group in Brussels, a sailor himself and a trained small crafts instructor. Participants were amused by his first PowerPoint slide - a picture of the *Titanic* - Nick was demonstrating his family connections to the shipbuilders. Nick also brought with him the detailed checklists used throughout the European Union to ensure a boat was in accordance with requirements. We organized a visit to a boatyard on the second morning of training, Nick reminding female staff to leave their high heels at home that day – otherwise they would not be allowed near a boat. On the day of the visit there was a yacht at the yard valued at over a million Euro and the entrepreneur was quite nervous about our group going anywhere near it. The group used the checklist successfully on this first training, so in future training I always asked the trainer to prepare a checklist, as well as a test, in addition to their PowerPoint presentation.

Arranging visits to business premises could have been problematic but Laura worked with staff in the Consumer Protection Directorate to identify and persuade entrepreneurs to allow a group of people from the enforcing authority to wander around their warehouses and identify goods that may not be in compliance with the law. It helped that from the beginning of the project we had encouraged business representatives to participate, putting on a breakfast seminar at the Albert hotel to explain product safety law and the consequences if they were found to be negligent. Robin and I also visited a couple of importers, who were grateful for Robin's expertise and advice on recently purchased goods that may have safety issues.

When the contract was drawn up Jim had persuaded the UK Health & Safety Executive to participate in the training on a range of technical areas such as gas suppliers. One of their officers, Steve Shaw, was named as trainer and had been included in the twinning contract. After the project started we were disappointed to learn that work pressures at home meant he would be unable to fulfil this commitment. However I persuaded him at least to come out for a few days and made the most of his time by arranging four lectures over two days. It was worth it because his training was very specific and gave Baiba's staff another dimension in respect of the technical subjects listed in the project contract.

It's always good to bring out people you have worked with before and now regard as friends. I include Helena Twist in this category – she had worked with me in Lithuania - and was included into the project to train Judges. Helena used to run a large legal firm and now trains European lawyers and consumer associations in Brussels. As well as being a first class lawyer she is great fun and excellent company. We are the same age but she has led a very different life to my own. The daughter of a diplomat, educated privately at boarding school, she lived in India at the time of independence, where her parents entertained royalty and politicians. She has travelled widely and is often invited, through her position as Chair of the National Consumer Federation, to chair conferences in Africa. She lives in the Barbican in London with her partner Joe from Liverpool and they are a wonderfully bohemian couple. Helena came to train Judges of the Civil and Administrative courts and we went along to the Judges' Training Centre in Riga to ask how many Judges would wish to attend and the type of training they required. We were told *all* the Judges and they offered to send out a questionnaire as to the subjects they would like included. It would prove difficult to accommodate such a large number in two sessions so we decided to do four. In return the training centre offered to provide a venue for two of them. It was not fair to expect Helena to train on her own and for the first sessions Richard Ferry from Gateshead Trading Standards and a lay Magistrate trained alongside her. For the next sessions we brought out a clever young lawyer from the Office of

Fair Trading - Barrister Jason Freeman. His professional expertise from both a governmental department and the British High Court was well received. He was also popular with the young lawyers in the Consumer Protection Directorate and generously gave them extra training sessions and answered all their questions.

Beth Baker and Roy Simpson came out a few times to deliver an excellent train-the-trainers course for senior staff. Baiba was meeting the cost of training venues and generously suggested we hold the course outside Riga so the staff would have no external distractions. A hotel in Sigulda was booked for two weeks to deliver two four-day courses. It was May, the weather and the surrounding countryside painted a fine image, though I was only there for the final afternoon sessions. It was a joy to work with Beth and Roy again. Beth also came out a few more times to write a qualification framework for CRPC staff, something they had never previously had and hopefully this is now in place. One weekend Beth and I took an overnight ferry from Riga – just along the river from where I lived – to Stockholm and Yvonne, my colleague in Croatia, joined us on the Sunday.

I also had to find new short-term experts to fill gaps. Gordon Robb and David Mackenzie, Trading Standards Officers from Scotland, were new to overseas work but adapted well, did everything I asked of them and were popular with CRPC staff. They worked for Inverness Trading Standards, who were happy to allow them leave of absence to work in Latvia. Gordon brought along a plaque, complete with the Highlands' crest and suitably inscribed to mark the liaison between the two market surveillance authorities. I organized an informal presentation at the Consumer Protection Directorate with senior colleagues to celebrate the occasion and in addition to the plaque, which Baiba displayed in her 'trophy' cabinet, Gordon also gave her a bottle of malt whisky. David Mackenzie was equally generous and brought all the delegates on his training course a miniature bottle of whisky. He also gave Laura and me a book each written by a Scottish author (mine was *The Prime of Miss Jean Brodie*) as well as plenty of shortbread. David is expert in E-commerce and the Distance Selling Regulations and gave an excellent training presentation to over twenty staff. This is a complicated area, encompassing buying on the Internet, cross border sales and mail order, potentially changing not only the way we buy things but how market surveillance is carried out. It was obvious that the CRPC staff needed more than one day's training to absorb the rules and regulations so we decided to set them a piece of research, to be undertaken over the next month, returning for individual sessions with David in the project office on his next visit. I put some topics in a hat and asked each delegate to draw one out and use that as the basis for their work. We were not sure if they would all complete the 'homework' but in fact everyone did. When David returned I had to allocate timed interviews over three days and he continued to give more assistance on subsequent visits. On his first visit David had shown me some photographs of the Highlands on his computer, which were stunning, and I suggested he run a slide show of them during the coffee breaks. Latvia has no mountains to speak of – apart from a small one where they ski in winter, but nothing like Scotland. People were stunned when they saw the magnificence of the Highland scenery in summer and winter.

    I encouraged more experts to give Latvians a flavour of their local area in Britain. Wherever I go in Eastern Europe, when people tell me they have been to England it is always to London, rarely do they venture further north. Robin, being from Liverpool, always had an opening PowerPoint slide that included the Beatles and other famous people and landmarks. Not to be outdone, when his friend Mike Hanson came to visit he illustrated his introduction with scenes of Yorkshire. I talk about the Lake District (my second home) endlessly and always give colleagues coasters made of Cumbrian slate with a view of the fells etched on it. Over the years I have bought lots of these coasters and like to imagine them in the offices of various countries across Europe.

    Robin and Mike were good company and I often joined them later at the Frog restaurant or in Old Town for dinner, as I did with most of the short-term experts. Some joined me at the opera or a concert after work. The diverse talents and experience of the experts always made for entertaining evenings. Jim Spinks, often joined by his wife Julia, enjoyed visiting Riga and they were often in town, and were very kind to me.

    We had a month's extension of the project, made possible by judicious budgeting. It was a bureaucratic procedure and overlooking my previous decision never to do this again, Jim and I wrote an Addendum to seek approval from the European Commission for a prolongation. It was up to the beneficiaries to decide what activities they wanted to include and they asked for UK expertise on financial and regulatory matters. Latvia's economy had grown by fifty percent between 2004 and 2007 but the global financial crisis was hitting the country hard in 2008-9 and the government was pushing through unpopular austerity measures, including cuts in the salaries of civil servants, in order to rescue the state from bankruptcy.

Most of my colleagues at the Ministry of Economy were affected, whose jobs were at risk as their salaries plummeted, but to their credit they still gave full participation to the project. The anger of people toward the government erupted one night resulting in street riots that scarred the Old Town with shattered windows and damaged buildings. I was caught in the middle of it and had to ask a line of armed police to break their cordon and allow me to walk across Dome Square back to my apartment. The social turmoil, triggered by the financial crisis, led to the fall of the government just before I left Latvia and unemployment soared to twenty percent.

Two representatives from the UK Financial Ombudsman Service came out for a short visit and held meetings with Ministers and the banking industry, answering their many questions. David Thomas continued to correspond with Latvian banks and businesses after his return to London and his help was appreciated. Better regulation for businesses was also becoming important and Graham Russell from the UK Local Better Regulation Office led a round table and met key civil servants and Ministers.

Despite social turmoil and economic gloom of that time, it seems Latvians have not lost their sense of humour. Last year the country was still in recession but the female population brought a smile and lifted the national spirit by staging a Blonde Parade. Participants, all blonde of course, took to the streets in Riga dressed in pink and wearing high heels. There were parties and concerts and it was so successful the 'Latvian Association of Blondes' announced they hope to stage a two-day festival this year.

At the closing conference I presented the results of the project. With the help of an excellent project leader, short-term experts and staff from the Consumer Rights Protection Centre we had worked together to build capability and provide a strong foundation to sustain the business economy and protect consumers. We had organized thirty-five training seminars conferences and workshops, leaving CRPC with a highly trained workforce, capable of enforcing consumer protection legislation to EU standard. Our experts had written guidelines for entrepreneurs to allow them quick access to product safety regulations, so that products are legally compliant. The new accident notification scheme in hospitals will enable the authorities to take quick action to remove unsafe products from the market. This is a cost-effective way of identifying unsafe products without the need for more costly inspection and testing procedures. This information had been loaded onto a USB key and all market surveillance staff received one. Checklists to help market surveillance officers in their job were produced in 'Filofax'-type folders.

At the closing conference I wanted to leave a symbolic message of my time in Riga. When you have lived and worked in another country for over a year it is always sad to say goodbye, but you leave with many good memories, of people and places, and they remain with you. There are many people to thank and it's important I think to let them know how much you have enjoyed living in their country. I decided to build my speech around a unique attraction in Riga. There are several bridges that span the canal weaving its way through the centre of Old Town. The railings of these bridges are densely covered in padlocks, left there by newly married couples as a symbol of their love. It is common, especially at weekends, to see wedding parties having their photographs taken whilst placing their locks on a favourite bridge. For other couples it is a private gesture. I told my audience that every day when I walked over Bastejkalns Bridge I stop for a moment to look at the view of the canal, to read the names and declarations of love etched on these locks. At the end of a happy year I too would have liked to declare my affinity to this lovely place, but knew it was not appropriate, it being a marriage tradition. I went on to reflect on the similarities between marriage and twinning - both have two partners, in this case the republic of Latvia and the UK. At the outset the parties discuss their terms of reference, what they hope to achieve in their future relationship. We had done this in a series of meetings before commencement. A contract is drawn up and signed by both parties. In marriage and twinning it is important to ask what the other party wants, not just tell them what you think they should have, and to listen. I said that I hoped the Latvians agreed that our project team had followed this principle – asking them what kind of training and expertise they wanted us to provide. At key points in a marriage we reflect on the outcomes and achievements, and this was such an occasion. My final side was a beautiful photograph of the sun setting on the river Daugava, the view from my apartment. 'As the sun sets on the Daugava,' I said, 'So it does on our project.'

CHAPTER TWENTY-ONE

Living in Old Riga

FINDING AN APARTMENT IN Riga was not as easy as it had been in Vilnius. I began the search immediately and had almost despaired of finding anything suitable when an agent took me to an old building near Dome Square, the centre of old Riga, dominated by the cathedral. It didn't look very promising from the outside, with a yard in poor repair and no secure entrance. The yard was full of potholes, the entrance door was smashed and walking up a dark dingy spiral staircase I told the agent I couldn't live in such a place as this. Many of the concrete steps had worn away (when my granddaughter visited I warned her about these 'naughty steps' which could suddenly cause you to fall). There was an unpleasant odour upon the staircase and it was in desperate need of redecoration. To be polite to the agent, who never tired of showing me apartments, only to have them rejected, I continued the viewing, convinced I would not like it. I changed my mind once I entered the sitting room and bedroom. There was a clear uninterrupted view of the river Daugava immediately in front of me; my eyes were constantly drawn to it. The apartment was simply decorated and furnished in a modern style. The landlord was English, living in Bristol with a Latvian wife he had met whilst working in Riga.

This made negotiation on the rent and facilities much easier and I was able to persuade him to include utilities in with the rent in exchange for me buying new linen and crockery that I would leave on departure. He was a good landlord, always responding immediately to any problem by sending his mother-in-law and her boyfriend round to put things right. Neither of them spoke English and I failed to master much Latvian, so it was interesting to say the least when they called round. Lots of sign language!

I was very happy living in this cosy apartment greeted by the river in the heart of Old Town. It was not the most luxurious or well-equipped accommodation I have had and the lack of security was a worry, nevertheless I loved living there. I felt I belonged, that it was my home. In the summer I watched the riverboat cruises sail past my window and there was once an aerobatic display of low flying aircraft, similar to the Red Arrows. Church bells serenaded me on Sunday mornings and although I had been warned that Old Town could be noisy at weekends, the apartment was in a quiet spot behind Dome Square. In the winter I watched the snow fall and freeze the river and when the bridge was illuminated I never closed the blinds. The fact that the front door into the building was not secure did lead to a problem just before I left. I unlocked my door on to the landing early one morning to find a tramp – an extremely smelly tramp - sitting outside, hugging a radiator for warmth. It was minus fifteen outside and snowing and he had obviously come in from the cold. Finding no heat in the hall he had come up the stairs and was now leaning against my door. I went back inside, not sure what to do, but had to go to work so held my breath and went out again. He shuffled to one side to allow me to pass. After work Robin gallantly walked me back to the apartment but the tramp had left.

Old Riga has ancient alleyways and narrow cobbled streets that twist and turn. Unusually the Castle is not on a hill, but by the riverside (not far from my apartment) and is the official residence of the President of Latvia. Also nearby is the oddly named House of Blackheads, a beautiful building with a Dutch Renaissance façade.

I didn't buy a bike this time but during the hot summer months I would take the short train journey to Jurmala to walk along the beach most weekends, calling at the Baltic Beach hotel for lunch. There was a wonderful family atmosphere on the long sandy beach with all kinds of sports taking place. It reminded me of childhood bank holidays at Skegness, when my family and relatives went en masse to pitch our windbreaks on the beach and play rounders or cricket. In June Latvia celebrate *Jani* (St John's day) – a sort of pagan summer solstice. It is an important celebration, a public holiday, and most people go to parties in the countryside, light bonfires, wear flower garlands and stay up to watch the sun rise. At a meeting at the Ministry the day before midsummer a banquet of food and drink was spread out on the conference table in honour of *Jani* and I was offered a special apple cake and a spice drink. Baiba explained the evening rituals, with a perfectly straight face: 'we light fires in the forest, eat and drink before going off into the woods to have sex. I met my husband on *Jani's* day'. My concession to the celebration was to bring home the wreath of oak leaves they place on their heads and some apple cake. We were having a small party of friends in our garden to celebrate Alan's retirement and the wreath was passed around every head – that and the apple cake was our offering to *Jani*.

As in other Eastern European cities, culture was cheap and plentiful and living in Old Town I never had far to walk to it. The week I arrived the Kings Singers, a British choral group, was performing at the National Opera House and this was the first of many subsequent visits. During the season I attended most of the ballet and opera productions, alone or accompanied by my experts. Music is important in the Latvian culture: there were weekly organ concerts at Dome Cathedral, classical music in various venues and summer festivals. During the summer months there were concerts to attend at Jurmala - one that stands out for me was a 'Music of the Movies' concert conducted by English conductor Carl Davies. Another was an Elvis tribute – backed up with an orchestra - and they even had pink Chevrolets lined up outside the concert hall.

Eating out was inexpensive in 2008, with many good restaurants in Riga. Ask any Latvian to name the best one and they will answer 'Vincents'. The chef has cooked for Presidents (including George Bush) Rock Stars (Elton John) and Royalty (Prince Charles) and having enjoyed a birthday meal there I can attest to its deserved reputation. I regularly bought the best croissants and pain au chocolat outside of France at a boulangerie in Riga – made fresh throughout the day by the French owner. My favourite restaurant though was Carpe Diem. As well as serving up good food, jazz is played by a live band most evenings. It's easy to find by looking for the 'Cats House'. There are two black felines perched on the points of the towers of this building. The legend is that the owner was excluded from the Guild opposite so he ordered the cats to be turned around tails high as an insult to his enemies. However, the short-term experts were loyal to the 'Flying Frog' restaurant near the Albert Hotel. If ever I wanted to find them in the evening I knew were they would be.

During the summer Alan came out to visit and we took the coach to Vilnius for a weekend. Going by road allows you to see more of the two countries and I was tired of flying anyway. Others may argue that the Latvian and Lithuanian countryside is the same, but I could tell the difference as soon as we crossed the border. The coach made a brief stop in Panevėžys, a welcome break on a four-hour journey. In Vilnius Neringa was waiting to greet us at our hotel and we took her out to dinner. The next morning she returned with her car to drive us out into the countryside. She pointed out the renovations in Vilnius since my last visit, partly due to the city having been European Capital of Culture in 2009. Despite the economic recession, the main square had been restored; new fountains had sprung up around the city; paved pedestrian areas and more shops and hotels were being built. The following January Neringa came to visit me in Riga for a few days. We went to the ballet and on Sunday morning to a service at the English church on the riverside near my apartment. British traders built the church in the mid 19th century, importing English soil from the UK. I had been once before, on Remembrance Sunday, and found it to be very moving, partly because of an inspirational speech given by the priest. Classical musicians played at the service, something I have never known during Sunday morning services at home. I regretted not having attended more often.

Again I was forced to experience the local health services. Early in the project I had a medical problem and the British Embassy gave me the name of a private doctor. From her I was referred to a surgeon at the hospital, accompanied by Lelde, who found it to be a rather bleak place, but the doctor was fine and for future visits I went to her private clinic in the evenings rather than return to the hospital. Some months later one of my fillings fell out and I visited a dentist who replaced it. Having had a morbid fear of dentists from childhood, I was quite nervous, especially as her equipment seemed archaic, but she did an adequate job and at a fraction of the cost at home. The most inconvenient health problem was a fracture I suffered just before Christmas. I had just said goodbye to Alison and her friend who had been staying for the weekend and went off to join Mike and Robin for a meal. They kindly offered to walk me home through the park and I managed to slip on a tiny area of ice. Feeling embarrassed at falling, I insisted it was OK (why do I always do this?) but realized overnight I had probably broken my wrist. My assistant was not in the office the following day so I said nothing to the others about it, pulling my sleeve down to hide the bruise and typing with my left hand. Two days after the accident I finally went to hospital and the X-ray showed a break in my right hand and small finger —a classic 'boxer's break' they said. They put on a heavy plaster cast up to the elbow, a typical Soviet cast Laura said. It was difficult to get dressed as I lived alone and I had to learn to type with my left hand.

Thanks to cheap flights from Stansted, I had many visitors in Riga. Ann Kaye was not working on this project but wanted to visit the city. The weather was good and we decided to take the train to Jurmala. Unfortunately Ann fell whilst stepping off the train, damaging her leg. It was with supreme effort and considerable pain on her part that we managed to get her back to my apartment and up the winding staircase. She spotted a long-handled broom and used this to get around. Her partner back home contacted the airline (one not known for its customer service) to ensure help was available at Riga and Stansted airports and she still tells the story of two burly Latvian men carrying her on to the plane, where they gave her a row of three seats to stretch out. Sadly she missed out on visiting the museums – one of the best is the Occupation museum showing the brutal occupation by Nazi and Soviet occupying forces.

There were also many visits from family and friends who found plenty to do whilst I was at work. The Christmas markets in Dome Square and New Year's Eve celebrations at Freedom Square, where as a family we saw in 2009, are particularly memorable. Before flying home for the Christmas holidays I decided to hold a party. My colleagues in the Ministry had been told they would not be allowed celebrations because of the economic crisis and they were disappointed. Eastern Europeans love to party so I decided to have one in the project office to thank everyone for their help over the year. At the time I had four experts in the office – Robin Croft, Mike Hanson and two young women from Consumer Direct in London, plus Alan, who made sure everyone's glasses were topped up. We tucked into a mix of Latvian and English food, with mince pies and the Christmas cake I had made three months earlier; Mike and Robin were in charge of the music. It was a great party and most of us finished up at the Frog for dinner before heading home for Christmas. After the Christmas and New Year celebrations it was back to work to prepare for the final weeks of the project. Soon I would be heading south again, to the land of the vampires.

CHAPTER TWENTY-TWO

The Travails of Travel

I LOVE TO TRAVEL and, stretching out my arms, welcoming the morning sun in a new place, but the actual act of getting there is not something to be relished any more. I used to enjoy flying. There was the anticipation of a holiday booked some months previously and the excitement of exploring a new country. You could virtually drive right to the door of the airport, stroll through check-in, passport control and security. How times have changed. Now you must make sure your handbag can be slipped into your carry-on case, since the rules insist on only one piece of hand luggage. You must *never* make a joke to the check-in staff when they ask if you are carrying dangerous weapons or if anyone may have interfered with your luggage, and you are not allowed to complain about having to remove coats, scarves, shoes, belts but meekly accede to their demands. Liquids more than 100 ml, (though few of us actually know what this is in relation to our cosmetics) must be bagged - if you haven't had the foresight to place them in a clear bag you will be charged a pound to buy one. Invariably I'm called aside to be frisked and feel quite exhausted by the time I get on board. Then there is the worry whether your luggage will arrive, not to mention subjecting yourself to a taxi driver who thinks he is competing on the Monte Carlo rally. You can't even rely on your boarding card being correct. I used only to glance at the seat number but recently at Bucharest airport, checking in with my colleague Malcolm Adams, we asked for seats together. Whilst waiting at the gate he happened to look at his boarding card and saw that it was in my name, not his, and also had the same seat number. Malcolm had to retrace his steps back to the check-in desk to have a new boarding card issued, this time in his own name and a seat to himself.

  I have had more than my share of lost luggage and delays, to the point that if my case doesn't come on the carousel straight away I'm looking around to locate the desk where I will have to report it. In Poland

and Riga it was an inconvenient but relatively simple process of filling in forms and assuming the case would be delivered to my hotel the following day, but different rules applied in Lebanon. Usually delayed luggage is delivered to your hotel by taxi but three days later it had not arrived and I was still wearing the clothes I had travelled in. When the airport confirmed they had located my case and that Zahi, our project assistant, could collect it with my written authorization he drove off, only to return without the case. They had changed their mind and wanted to see me. Off we went back to the airport – a white knuckle ride as he drove at high speed, one hand on the wheel and the other holding his mobile phone to his ear while he talked to his friends, changing lanes and swerving as if we were on a slalom down a ski run. I was regarded suspiciously by airport staff, asked to sign lots of forms written in Arabic though I had no idea what I was putting my signature to and followed the guard through a tunnel to a holding pen where eventually I was reunited with my case. Normally passport and travel documents suffice as identification but for some reason they also wanted to know my parents' date of birth and death and their wedding anniversary, which was written by hand into a large register. It was impossible for them to check this information, but there was no point in arguing.

Flight delays have blighted my travels over the past few years, usually when routing through a connecting airport. Whilst working in Latvia I regularly left Teesside airport on the 6 a.m. flight for Amsterdam to arrive in Riga in time for lunch, but the flight was frequently late, missing the connection at Schipol. Once I left home at 4.30 a.m. but didn't arrive in Riga until 4 p.m. the following day due to snowstorms and delayed flights. I reckoned I could have travelled to Australia in the time it took from Teesside to Riga. Another time, accompanied by my friend Myrna, a delay meant we missed our connection in Amsterdam, were re-routed via Copenhagen to connect to a Latvian flight due to arrive early evening. It was Sunday, so we thought no problem, we will still arrive in time for dinner. No such luck – this flight was also delayed and another several hours were spent sitting in Copenhagen airport. Three airports and three flights later, we finally arrived in Riga in the early hours of the following morning. However, unlike someone I know, I have never fallen asleep at the departure gate and woken up to find the flight had left hours ago.

During my travels in Poland I had the unusual problem of a runaway case. A party of us was returning from training in the regions and on arrival at Warsaw railway station Benedicte insisted on going ahead to stand on the platform to receive our cases, which Karolina handed down from the train. We had several cases between us and had to take care because Polish trains stand high off the track with a severe drop to the platform. I heard shouting followed by laughter and made my way through the train in order to inspect what was happening. The case had been thrown down and with four wheels it continued to travel along the platform before spinning round and tripping over on to the rails. It was now lying on the track in front of the driver's cab, some two feet below the platform. The advertising for this new type of case featured the whirling dervishes and mine seemed to be acting like one! Benedicte was on the point of hitching up her skirt to go on to the track and retrieve it, but I stopped her because the train was due to depart. Suddenly out of nowhere came running a tall young man, mobile phone to his ear, who without hesitation jumped down on to the track, picked my case up and just as quickly departed, still talking into his phone. What a hero!

On another occasion, again at Warsaw railway station, I realized I had been robbed. Getting on the train at Poznan a crush had formed behind me - nothing unusual in this, people push to get on the train first, even before departing passengers have alighted. I was carrying a briefcase, small case and a shoulder bag strapped across my shoulder. I felt this bag move and brought it round to the front but thought nothing more of it and didn't open it on the train. On arrival at Warsaw I walked across to the Marriott hotel to check in, just for one night as I was leaving the next day. Only then did I notice that my purse was missing and so was my credit card. I then realized that someone had deliberately caused the crush in order to go into my bag. Fortunately I had some reserve cash in my case, just enough for one night's accommodation and Beth provided me with a meal that evening. The following morning I went to the local police station to report the theft, but they expressed a lack of interest, claiming there was no interpreter available to take a statement. The journey home was difficult, not having any Polish or English money. I had a four-hour wait at Heathrow with no money even to buy a cup of coffee or newspaper.

The most recent problem whilst travelling between Britain and Latvia was losing or having my passport stolen (I never did work out which). I remember having it on arrival at Riga airport but a week later couldn't find it. Eventually I had to go to the British Embassy and apply for an emergency passport. It was helped that I had a photocopy of the passport. I didn't intend making an insurance claim but they still required me to get a police report. The temporary passport was sufficient to get me in and out of European countries but we had a holiday booked to Russia where it would not be accepted, so I had to go through the same process again back home. It has taught me to guard my passport carefully, if only because the process to renew it is full of complications. I still worry that the old one is out there somewhere and I could be the victim of identity fraud.

Another passport problem was entirely of my own making. Arriving at my local airport for an early flight to London and then Beirut, I realized I didn't have my passport. I rang Alan, who searched the house for it and broke all speed limits to get back to the airport before the flight left. I was allowed to go through security but not board the plane until he arrived and they held it up for me. Alan now demands to see the passport before I leave the house.

CHAPTER TWENTY-THREE

A Balkan Assignment

BORDERED BY MOLDOVA, Ukraine, Bulgaria, Serbia and Hungary, Romania has many treasures - the Black Sea, Danube Delta, Carpathian Mountains, interesting cities and a gentle countryside. The capital city Bucharest is cosmopolitan and reasonably modern, whilst the regions remain predominantly rural.

After completing the work in Latvia at the beginning of 2009 I felt exhausted. The final two months of the project had been demanding, packed with extra training conferences and report writing. I had now been working overseas continually for several years and it was beginning to take its toll. Perhaps the time had come to throw in the towel and retire or at least take a rest, I asked myself. However, when you are self-employed there is always the thought that work refused may be the last to be offered. I still gained a lot of satisfaction from my job and enjoyed working with a diverse group of people of different nationalities. Although I had thought that Latvia would be my last big project I was open to short-term work.

I had been aware of a proposed consumer project in Romania some time before I was asked to participate in it as Robin Croft who was working with me in Riga had already accepted the key expert role as trainer and was looking forward to returning to a country where he had already completed three projects. With some surprise I received an unexpected phone call from Lukas Hoffman, formerly of Human Dynamics and now working for ATC, another Austrian company. He invited me to be key expert in Component 3 – Communications and Public Awareness, reprising the role I had performed in our last collaboration in Croatia. Initially I turned down the offer because this new project would start before my work in Latvia finished. I forgot about it until Lukas rang saying 'The tender has to be resubmitted and will now not start until your work in Latvia is completed, so you can join us'. Tempted by a new project in an unknown city I agreed and ATC won the tender. Robin didn't work on the project in the end, which was disappointing, but at least my old friend Malcolm Adams was project leader.

'Technical Assistance' projects, such as the one in Romania, start quickly once the tender is awarded, unlike Twinning Projects that can linger on for more than a year, as I know from my own experience of doing two of them. Although it was now only two weeks before Christmas, a 'kick-off' meeting was suddenly arranged and my presence required at the State Authority for Consumer Protection in Bucharest. As I had my right arm in plaster at this time I asked Lukas if I could be excused. 'No, you have to be at the meeting,' he said. 'The beneficiaries expect the entire team to be present and you would need to produce a doctor's certificate saying you could not travel.' Over the past year I had been required to have hospital treatment and I was not about to submit to the Latvian medical system again. Any letter would be in Latvian anyway, unable to be read by the Romanians. I agreed to go, as long as I was met at the airport. 'No problem,' said Lukas, adding, 'one of the consortium members will meet you and the beneficiaries will think highly of you for making the journey with a broken arm.' I was not seeking sympathy; I just couldn't work out how I was going to manage the journey with one arm in plaster. It was also bad timing because Alan was in Riga for a visit and instead of flying back home together for Christmas as planned, we would be going in opposite directions. We went as far as Riga airport together where I flew to Munich to connect with a flight to Bucharest. The journey was worse than I had anticipated, both to Bucharest and back to England, involving a total of four flights and lots of walking between terminals, carrying a case with only one good arm. On the return journey to Heathrow I landed at Terminal 5 confident that here at last I would find a trolley and give my arm a rest, only to be told there are none. At this newly opened 'state-of-the-art' terminal it seems that such passenger aids are a thing of the past. I have never been so pleased to touch down at Teesside airport.

Arriving in Bucharest I was met on arrival by an excited Adina Sasu, a slim energetic young woman with long dark hair who was a junior partner in the consortium. On the drive into Bucharest she chatted away constantly, telling me how she had set up her own company and worked with ATC to secure the tender for the contract. Malcolm Adams and Raymond O'Rourke were waiting for me at the hotel, ready to walk into the city for a meal. Reluctantly I had to decline as I was tired and needed to rest my arm. I had also seen the poor state of the pavements outside the hotel and didn't want to risk another fracture. It was mid December and the city was lit up for Christmas; it looked enticing but it would have to wait until tomorrow. We all met up again the next morning at breakfast, my appetite suppressed by a dining room engulfed in smoke. I was in another country that could not envisage giving up their cigarettes and smoked everywhere. I met the rest of the team: Lukas, Malcolm Adams (full-time Team Leader), Raymond O'Rourke (Irish Training Expert), Sylvia Zahia (Romanian Legal Expert) and our office manager Madalina Musetescu, a gentle foil to Adina but just as opinionated and strong willed. We took the subway to the offices of our beneficiaries, the National Authority for Consumer Protection (known as ANPC) where the Director Mr Mihail Meiu greeted us and introduced his staff. That night the project team got to know each better over a meal and drinks at Caru' cu Bere, a 19th century beer hall and restaurant in the old quarter. It's an interesting old building, popular with tourists, with murals on the ceiling and walls and lots of small rooms and balconies for eating and drinking that seem to go on forever. Every evening a small troupe of dancers perform and then pull diners out of the audience to whirl them around. My feet tapping to the playful rhythm of the music, I envied those chosen, but with a broken arm knew I would not be one of them.

This was a flying visit and there was no time to explore the city but Adina did drive me past the main sights, which were floodlit: pointing out the infamous Palace of Parliament built by Ceaușescu, Revolution Square where the former dictator had his final moments in power, the splendid Athenaeum concert hall, Royal Palaces and the surprising Arch of Triumph – all very impressive. At one point Adina enthusiastically told me that we were driving along the most fashionable and famous street, the Calea Victoriei and pointed out various designer shops. I glimpsed fine buildings alongside the usual communist-style bloc housing, and a large city with wide boulevards.

Adina and Madalina found and equipped an office in the city centre and the project team began work after the Christmas holiday. I didn't join them until March 2009 because I was still in Riga, but kept in touch by email, eventually arriving in Bucharest in time to celebrate St Patrick's Day. All the fountains in the city, and some of the buildings, were lit green, which delighted Raymond O'Rourke, a lawyer and food safety expert from Dublin. He invited us to celebrate at the Dubliner pub on the wettest evening I ever experienced in Bucharest. I felt I was back in Riga! The bar was packed and we were joined by the Irish Ambassador who had real shamrock in his lapel, something I had not seen before and flown in that day from Ireland - in the diplomatic bag presumably. At our previous meeting in December Raymond had told me something of Bucharest's history, having worked here before, and promised on my next visit to take me to the historic Athenée Palace Hilton Hotel for a drink. This he did and the English Bar became a favourite venue for a pre dinner drink, especially during the summer months when they opened up the garden bar.

Adina had booked me into the Minerva hotel but I set out to find an apartment because I would be here for nine months. ATC were paying my accommodation costs but agreed to allow a change in the contract so that I could rent. Malcolm recommended an agent he had used and I found an apartment on the Calea Victoriei, small but comfortable. It had a balcony at the front, though it was too noisy to remain out there for long. The Prime Minister lived in the same block so there was plenty of security around, which I found reassuring. I had an excellent landlord in Alexander who had fitted it out with new furniture from Ikea and provided everything I needed, including a cleaner who came in once a week. The day before I was due to move in I decided to take some of my belongings to the apartment after work, then return to the hotel and move everything else the following day. I had told the hotel manager of my intention to leave that morning. I packed a suitcase, exited the hotel and was walking down the street toward my new apartment when I became aware of a man running toward me shouting and waving his arms to attract my attention. I ignored him at first but he caught me up and barred my way. It was a bit worrying but I couldn't get away from him, it was dark and there was no one around. He was edging closer and closer towards me. Once he had caught his breath he accused me of leaving the hotel without settling my bill. 'Do I look like someone who would leave without paying the bill?' I asked. He looked a bit shamed but pointed to my case, 'But you left with luggage'. I explained that I was only taking some clothes to my new apartment and would be back at the hotel in half an hour and if they cared to look in my room they would find the rest of my belongings. He was very apologetic and offered me a better room if I would stay. 'Nothing would induce me to stay now,' I told him. When I mentioned this episode at work the next day, still bristling with indignation, I expected sympathy. Raymond laughed and said something on the lines of 'What did you expect, running out of a hotel with luggage and not having paid the bill?' I was then teased about it for the rest of the year and painted as a pay-dodger.

At the first project steering committee I was taken aback when the Director announced that he regarded my component as the most important one on the project. It wasn't of course but few state institutions can afford to pay for television and radio advertisements, publish a range of publicity material, let alone run a national campaign, and he needed EU funding for these activities. Also, he told me that his Inspectors in Bucharest and the regions couldn't cope with the number of consumer complaints and the campaign must not just make consumers aware of their rights but that they should be given the skills and confidence to try to resolve their own complaints before contacting ANPC.

My first job would be to organize a press conference to celebrate Consumer Rights Day (yet again!). I passed the EU Information Office every day on my way to work and noticed they sometimes had meetings there, so we hired it to hold our conference. Adina had contracted a young man called Marius to assist me with media activities and analysis. He would ensure the television radio and print media attended press conferences and produce an analysis of their coverage. He was a pleasant young man and we got along well, but he never really delivered the results as promised and this became evident at the first event, when too few journalists attended and he made excuses for their absence and lack of interest. Eventually another company took over this role.

The terms of reference allocated funding for two consumer surveys to be carried out at the beginning and end of the project. The cost of this was beyond the budget of ANPC and Mr Meiu told me it would be the first time such a survey had been conducted in Romania. Whilst still in Latvia I had been in regular contact with Malcolm, designing the questions and agreeing the sample and age spectrums for approval by ANPC, so that the first survey could be carried out soon after I arrived. Once in

Bucharest two representatives from Gallup, who had been awarded the contract, came to see me and we agreed the detail. The aim of the survey was to assess the level of knowledge among consumers across Romania as to their rights when buying goods and services, plus an understanding of where to get help and advice. The sample was 4,000 people over eighteen across social, geographical and age spectrums. Eight key questions were asked. Gallup produced a detailed analysis; the results revealing that there was a low level of awareness and half of the respondents stated they did nothing when they bought faulty goods. The results gave us a picture of consumer awareness and statistics we were able to use in our press releases.

The largest and most expensive part of my component was the design of a creative concept, campaign logo and slogan and production of TV and radio slots. Adina and I wrote the terms of reference and the contract went out to tender. We employed Silviu Balanica a local tendering expert to prepare the paperwork, chair the evaluation of tenders and handle the appeal procedure if the companies not selected lodged an appeal. The EU set down strict criteria for this process and even after awarding a contract the unsuccessful companies can appeal and cause lengthy delays. The EU is often criticized for uncontrolled spending but in my experience it keeps a very tight rein on money. Projects funded by the EU are regularly audited, required to show transparency and every Euro must be accounted for.

The project team assembled on the day tenders had to be submitted, between 10 a.m. and noon, and we all sat around nervously, wondering if anyone was going to arrive. Our office was on the third floor, the doorbell at street level. When the first company rang the bell it was quite exciting. Tenders could not be opened of course, they were sealed bids and Silviu logged everything, completing the paperwork and obtaining the necessary signatures. The doorbell continued to ring and the boxes piled up until noon, when Silviu announced the deadline for submission of tenders had expired. No sooner had the words left his mouth than the doorbell rang again. It was another submission and we had to decide whether to accept it. The company argued that they had initially rung the bell just before noon but we had not pressed for them to enter. There had been problems with the bell and we agreed to allow them to submit their tender. We went for lunch and reconvened in the afternoon to open the bids. The companies who had submitted tenders were invited to be present and Silviu chaired the meeting. The evaluation process was time consuming and bureaucratic, with spreadsheets having to be completed for each tender, but Silviu was efficient, noting the price of each tender, the number of boxes and files and dealing with arguments that flared up between companies.

In the terms of reference I had asked companies to use four topics to explain a consumer's rights: buying goods and services, financial services, unfair practices and unfair terms and distance selling. We received three valid proposals. One featured an alarm clock and called on consumers to 'Wake Up'. I liked the image but the company had not followed through with interesting TV and radio spots. Another featured a 'consumer champion' called Justin who rough-handled consumers in supermarkets and banks to make them think of their rights. His character confronted female shoppers but I disliked this, finding his character aggressive and unsympathetic. I used to feel the same about Esther Ranzten in her consumer programme *That's Life* many years ago. The BBC's *Watchdog* programme sometimes falls into the same trap, though I admit they expose unfair trading practices and 'name and shame' rogue traders. The third proposal from a company called Libra was better and when my Romanian colleagues saw it they fell about laughing and thought it a brilliant concept. It was somewhat lost on me but basically it featured the use of a large stick to claim your consumer rights (not physically I hasten to add but metaphorically). The stick is called a *'Teapă'* and originates from the legend of Vlad the Impaler who utilized sticks for a different reason altogether. Romanian colleagues explained to me how you use the *Teapă* against someone who has treated you badly and it's in their common language. Libra, the company who thought up this idea, thought it could win an award, as it was an original concept, *Teapă* never having been used in a campaign before. One of the storyboards for the proposed TV spot showed a peasant pulling a horse and cart containing milk churns. He opened for business in the market square, put up a sign for 'Honey milk' and had a queue of consumers. He soon sold out of milk and saddled up the horse to go home, promising to return with more milk the next day. He left telling his horse to 'walk on, Honey'. Would he have had so many consumers if they knew they were buying milk from a horse rather than a cow? It illustrated unfair commercial practices, but unfortunately our beneficiaries rejected it. The image of peasants pulling horse carts, although a common sight in the Romanian countryside, is not one they wished to project.

We evaluated the proposals fairly against the criteria and chose the Libra proposal, as they had understood and interpreted the terms of reference. We expected the beneficiaries to agree the *Teapa* concept was the one to use in our TV spots. Although they had been invited to participate in the opening of the tenders, ANPC had declined and rightly left the project team to make the decision and agreed to meet the successful company the following day. We took Libra along to a meeting at ANPC to outline their ideas, but unfortunately the beneficiaries did not like *Teapa* at all. By this time there had been a political change and members of the Cabinet were present at our meetings as well as the civil servants, and this slowed up decision-making. Being politicians they opposed anything creative, preferring it to be bland and inoffensive to everyone, and asked Libra to redesign the concept. After many meetings and some weeks' delay I finally had a slogan – *'Know Your Rights, Take Action'* - and a logo. This was a bag with coloured images of cartoon people jumping out – taking action. It's eye-catching and worked well.

There followed many more meetings at ANPC where we poured over books of actors, clothing and possible locations in order to chose the cast, location and even background music for the TV commercials. The process lacked any excitement but in the end the TV spots worked well, using an alter ego who emerged from a timid consumer's mortal body to explain their rights and urge them to take action, after which he/she became a strong consumer. I was invited to the filming of the first TV spot, shot in a real electrical store with a young actress playing a consumer returning a faulty iron, the seller refusing to do anything about it. It was interesting to see the storyline come to life; the director kept asking for reassurance that I was happy with the performance but after a while it became tedious watching take after take and I left them to it for the other three. Adina had the idea of producing a thirty-second commercial on the TV advertising monitors that flooded the country – in shops, restaurants, subway stations – and found an Internet company to produce the visuals. It cost quite a lot of money but our budget was generous and once they were ready you couldn't go anywhere in Bucharest without seeing our advertising campaign.

Libra's remit was also to design and illustrate the four pocket guides on consumer issues. I had written the text for these and again Libra proved they understood the messages I wanted to get across, coming up with good illustrations. On the front page was a trap; one had a gift-wrapped parcel inside it (distance selling), another credit cards and money (financial services). The most striking and colourful brochure, warning of unfair commercial practices, used the image of target boards. We commissioned exhibition stands and roll-ups were also produced with these images and transported around the country for our public events. At the end of the project the exhibition stands, brochures, posters and promotional material were handed over to ANPC and they will be able to use the *'Know Your Rights, Take Action'* campaign for some years.

  Libra handed over the management to Dana Maria Manu and we worked together over the next few months to design and deliver the campaign. Dana Maria is a larger-than-life character with strong opinions, is outspoken, charming and flirtatious with men. She has her own unique sense of style and we got along very well, sharing shopping trips together. Another good contact was Elena, a young journalist who worked for *Gandul*, a national daily newspaper. I met Elena at the first press conference I had organized for Consumer Rights Day. A tall, slim and attractive young woman, she had a huge smile and infectious personality and lit up the office every time she came to visit. She had a particular interest in consumer issues and wrote a weekly consumer page for her newspaper, frequently interviewing Mr Meiu. Her other passion was cars and she spent most of the week test driving sports cars and writing about them for her paper. What a great job, I thought. One of my tasks was to publish a newspaper supplement on consumer issues, something I had not done before but we had a budget for it, and we made a contract with Gandul. Elena and I collaborated to produce a four-page colour supplement to be included in the newspaper. I wrote the text on subjects agreed with Mr Meiu or suggested by Elena with her local knowledge of the type of problems experienced by Romanian consumers; she found relevant photographs to accompany the text and the result was far better than I had expected. The editing and setting up process was lengthy, after translation we had to wait for the beneficiaries to agree everything but it was all worth it. On the day it was published, as an insert into the Friday edition of *Gandul*, I was at a newspaper stand at dawn to purchase my own copy, even though Elena had promised to bring several copies into the office. It was very exciting opening up the paper to find my supplement in glorious colour, even though I couldn't read it. It was so successful we decided to publish a second edition before the end of the project, so I had to think up new articles to write. I still had the same thrill when it was published.

  As well as having responsibility for the national consumer campaign, my contract also specified the training of forty-five PR managers. It turned out there was the same number of ANPC regional offices and one person from each office was to receive training in media techniques. I suggested to Malcolm that we run two courses and invite Ann Kaye, our colleague from CSN, to lead the training. It was only for a week but it was good to have Ann's excellent company, not to mention her expertise, again. Malcolm and I also participated in the two-day training – it was an opportunity for me to tell them about the recent consumer survey and upcoming campaign. They were really excited about the campaign, never previously having had much in the way of brochures, posters and exhibition material and we received many invitations to visit their towns. Fortunately Ann suffered no falls this time.

CHAPTER TWENTY-FOUR

Bucharest - a Spoilt City?

I HAVE BORROWED THE title for this chapter from Olivia Manning's book (part of her *Balkan Trilogy*). In the early twentieth century Bucharest had enjoyed the sobriquet 'Little Paris' and was by all accounts a fine city. Photographs from that era show fashionably dressed people strolling up the Calea Victoriei or riding in their carriages. Even then it had an edgy reputation, described by one New York journalist as being 'delightfully depraved'. By the time Manning arrived in 1939 – stylishly on the Orient Express, proving the city was blessed with efficient transport links back then – Bucharest still had a King and royal family, though it had already begun to lose some of its former glamour. She described Bucharest as being on the margins: 'a strange half-oriental capital... primitive, bug-ridden and brutal'. Her time in Bucharest coincided with the outbreak of war in Europe and the rise of fascism, although Romania was ostensibly neutral.

Olivia Manning, a respected British author, based her novel in Bucharest at the start of World War Two. Later a film adaptation by the name of *Fortunes of War* was made. I only became aware of her work after I went to Romania and bought the book from the Antony Frost English Bookshop in Bucharest, a building that still bears the bullet holes from riots in 1989 that deposed Ceaușescu. The book was based upon her own experiences, living on the Calea Victoriei (like myself decades later) with her husband who worked for the British Council. It is peopled with colourful characters, Romanians and British Legation staff. My favourite is the wonderfully eccentric Prince Yakimov, who turns up again when they flee to Greece. Manning describes Bucharest as a hotbed of 'decadence, debauchery and espionage' with much of the action taking place at the English Bar at the Athénée Palace hotel, then said to be a place of intrigue, where British, Russian and Germans reputedly spied on each other and journalists wired their copy from the hotel bar to their newspapers. From the window of her apartment, she describes watching the abdication of King Carol II, forced to flee the country by the new dictator Antonescu when German troops entered Romania in October 1940, and the rise of the Iron Guard. When the German army reached Bucharest she describes witnessing the flag of the Third Reich being raised on the front of the historic Athenée Palace, a building I passed at least twice a day, never failing to look up and imagine how awful it must have been to see this terrible emblem of a brutal regime disfiguring a beautiful historic building. Even on a hot day in summer, when I crossed the square and thought of it hanging from the roof, it gave me a chill.

The city is very different today to the one described by Olivia Manning or as reflected in sepia print photographs displayed in local bars and restaurants. Sadly it seems that few of the buildings erected in the post-war years have enhanced the city. The most famous (or infamous) building is the 'Palace of the People', the second-largest administrative building in the world after the Pentagon, built on the order of Ceaușescu to house all the organs of state and accommodation for party officials. Returning from a visit to North Korea inspired, it is said, by that country's architecture the Dictator ordered the demolition of quarter of the Bucharest's historic quarter in order to build a vast civic centre. The project remained unfinished at the time of his downfall but past the point of no return. Today, renamed 'Palace of Parliament', it is host to the Parliament, Senate and the Museum of Contemporary Art and is hired out for parties and weddings, though it is so vast most of the building is unused. Before entering the Palace for a forty-five minute guided tour, I was a bit disconcerted when told to surrender my passport to guards, though it was returned at the end of the tour. Huge notices (everything is on a large scale) warn that leaving a tour, which is the only way to view the Palace, is regarded a violation of law and sanctions will be applied. The final part of the notice states: 'It is mandatory to keep clean'. Visitors are shown only a fraction of the thousand rooms spread over 14 floors that contain vast glittering chandeliers, silk wall hangings, hand woven carpets and marble staircases. I stood on the balcony where Ceaușescu had intended to address his nation, looking down his 'Boulevard to the Victory of Socialism' (now Boulevard Unirii), that he insisted be slightly wider and longer than the Champs-Elysees. A visit here is essential for visitors to Bucharest but I found the atmosphere disturbing and with a sense of revulsion, having read that twenty thousand builders and four thousand architects had worked round the clock to the whims of a dictator in terrible conditions with no concern for their safety.

Another notorious building associated with Ceaușescu's regime, and one I passed every day on my way to work, is the former office of the Communist Party Headquarters. Ceaușescu gave his final address to his people from this balcony in December 1989, expecting adulation. But the crowd turned on him. He and his wife had to be airlifted by helicopter from the roof, only to be captured outside of the city later. They were summarily tried and executed on Christmas Day. Many Romanians were shot during the protests and bullet holes are still visible in nearby buildings. The area has been renamed Piața Revolution (Revolution Square) and a monument is dedicated to those who died. The protests didn't end with Ceaușescu's execution however. Six months later students staged a protest at University Square against President Iliescu, who responded by bringing in miners to brutally put down the revolt. In a three-day riot up to a hundred people were killed and seven hundred injured. It's hard to believe this now, in a democratic Romania.

On the other side of the square is the elegant Royal Palace, built in the neoclassical style and now a museum of art. My favourite building in this area is the Athenaeum (home to the Romanian Philharmonic Orchestra) that resembles an ancient temple. Under its sublime Baroque cupola I listened to wonderful classical music. Built in 1888, it is free of communist overtures, having been financed with money donated by the general public. Citizens must have been more prosperous then. The gardens in front of the Athenaeum contain benches and are planted with flowers, so it's a good place to relax during a summer evening.

There are plenty of examples of ugly communist inspired buildings but many elegant private villas have survived from the 19th century, designed by French architects in the Neoclassical and Secessionist art nouveau style. The house that is now home to the George Enescu Museum on the Calea Victoriei is a good example of this period – I particularly admired the beaten silver canopy over the front door that I think resembles a lace doily. There are also many grand and historic buildings: the National Bank of Romania, the National Savings Bank with neoclassical facades and Corinthian columns, the National Art Museum housed within the Royal Palace, the Military Club and the Coltea Hospital, built in 1704. Unlike the New York journalist I didn't see any obvious depravity but I always think of Bucharest as slightly Bohemian, a little ragged around the edges, with an obvious energy and just that bit different from other European cities. It is not a popular tourist destination, in the way of other European capitals, but there are hidden gems to be discovered once you know where to look.

After the 1989 revolution there was a resurgence of religion and there are beautiful churches in Bucharest practically on every corner. It is the tradition of people to cross themselves when in sight of a church and therefore it's not unusual to see someone imitating the sign of the cross constantly as they walk along. It's hard to name a favourite, but one that provides cool shelter on a hot summer's day is Str. Stavropoulos in Lipscani, built in 1724. We usually lunched in this area and would then take a walk – inevitably ending up in the courtyard of this church. On Saturday and Sunday there would be weddings at the churches on the Calea Victoriei and I always stopped to watch when they came out. One Sunday I was invited to witness the wedding ceremony of my colleague Silviu and his lovely wife at a Romanian Orthodox church in the centre of Bucharest and was struck by both the informality and ritual of the service. There were few seats and everyone stood in groups around the bridal party, the bride and groom's small child asleep in a pushchair, being fussed over by everyone. Two priests officiated and I was fascinated by the blessing and exchange of the crowns, after which they all danced around in a circle. After the ceremony, on the steps of the church the men let off huge firecrackers.

I can't say I was impressed with Bucharest's historic centre, especially having seen so many beautiful 'Old Towns' in Eastern Europe. Lipscani is in dire need of renovation. Many of the buildings are crumbling; it is necessary to dodge large holes in the streets and pavements, which become treacherous when it rains. Raymond had first visited some years previously and said no progress had been made to restore the area, but suddenly during the summer of 2009 the city council sprang into action and as I left it was possible to see improvements. There is a wide range of cuisine in the city. I liked a chain called 'The French Bakery', where you could have breakfast, lunch or dinner though we usually ate lunch at the City Grill or a sandwich in the garden of the National Theatre. In the evening I often dined at the Bistro Atheneu, reminiscent of an English pub serving wonderful goulash, the Hungarian Kitchen or Trattoria Calcio, a football themed bistro where you are served by young waiters in football shirts. Malcolm was good at finding places to eat and there seemed to be new café or restaurant open every month.

Music did not disappoint. I went to many classical concerts at the

Athenaeum but during the summer there were concerts in the open air. Walking across the car park opposite the Hilton hotel on my way to work, vans would be unloading equipment and by the time I crossed again at the end of the working day the space had been transformed into a concert venue, with a stage, seating and covered areas. One weekend in June it was transformed into a fragrant garden and beach area complete with sand and deck chairs. There was what the British call a beer tent but most sales tended to be non-alcoholic. The concerts started in the afternoon and ended at 11 p.m. On the final evening the orchestra finished with 'Nessun Dorma' from *Turandot*. I spent almost the whole weekend listening to music; it was wonderful. The stage and tents went up again for two weeks in September during the Georges Enescu festival (Romania's famous composer) but with no beach this time. Crossing the square on my way home from work it was relaxing to sit awhile, listen to classical music and forget about work.

There was also music in Cismigiu and Heratstrau Parks. From May to October promenade concerts are held at weekends from 11.00 a.m. to 1.00 p.m. In common with other cities in Eastern Europe, where people tend to live mainly in apartments, Bucharest has many neighbourhood parks and open spaces. Cismigiu Park was a short walk from my apartment and I went there most evenings after work, just to walk or sit in the sunshine and read. The lake was popular in the summer, enjoyed by young and older people hiring a rowing boat and there was often a craft fair at weekends. In winter the lake was transformed into an ice skating rink and wooden chalets sprouted up in the park, selling winter delicacies. On Sundays I walked or took the metro to the larger Heratsau Park that boasts 187 hectares and a huge lake, aiming to arrive at midday to enjoy the concert at the bandstand. Sometimes classical music was being played, but I also heard modern music and once a Glenn Miller swing band. Elsewhere in the park families roller-bladed together, rode bikes, sailed their little boats on the lake, or held picnics. I found a Hard Rock café in the park, perfect for Sunday lunch. On the shores of the lake is the Village Museum with sixty original houses, farmsteads and churches from all of Romania's regions. The pretty houses and gardens are indicative of the former lives of peasants, but the reality in the Romanian countryside is far from idyllic and not all houses have running water. My final visit to Heratsau Park was on 11 November. It was a bright and sunny Remembrance Day, the trees covered in flame-coloured leaves - in contrast to Britain, which as far back as I can remember was always cold grey and miserable. As usual the park was crowded with families enjoying the autumn sunshine.

Bucharest is renowned as a safe city and I never felt afraid walking back to my apartment alone at night from an evening out. The men found it more difficult because they were continually accosted by 'ladies of the night', who openly walked the main streets stopping any man in sight. Even Malcolm, an elegant man and in his sixties, would be offered their services every few yards. You had to maintain a watchful eye on your belongings when using public transport or sitting outside cafes, but otherwise I did not experience any problem. Getting around Bucharest, on the other hand, can be a challenge. There are few directional signs and no published bus routes. The metro is cheap and clean and works well if you want to move around the centre quickly, although it was not designed with tourists in mind but rather to transport workers to jobs. Metro maps are not always accurate, showing stations that don't exist. I found the only way was to work out my own route and memorize how each station looked, but often got lost or found myself on the wrong line.

Living in Bucharest does require a strong sense of personal responsibility for one's welfare and safety in other ways. Dana Maria told me she wanted to move out because it is too dangerous a place to live. I assumed she was referring to crime but in fact her concern is that the city is subject to earthquakes. Driving around the city she pointed out to me the buildings that would be vulnerable when the anticipated earthquake came, indicated by a red plaque that tells you it is not secure against them; heaven knows why anyone would want to buy or rent such a building. It's also a mystery why the Romanians are so keen to build glass fronted high-rise blocks in Bucharest. Another hazard are vehicles that are allowed to park on the pavements and zebra crossings, forcing pedestrians into the road where you then have to dodge speeding cars, but you get used to it after a while.

Dogs area problem. When Ceaușescu built his grandiose Palace and ordered the destruction of several suburbs, those displaced simply left their dogs to fend for themselves on the streets. It's not unusual to see them trotting around in groups, crossing the road with a purpose en-masse, as if they have heard of a good party. Many have legs missing, presumably not having crossed the road quickly enough to avoid speeding cars. They appear quite docile but there are shocking stories of people being bitten. The civic authorities occasionally address the problem by removing a truckload of dogs and releasing them in another town, which seems cruel for the dogs and hardly fair to the community on the receiving end of the problem. As a dog lover I found it very upsetting to see so many dogs living on the streets, although people do feed them. When Britain introduced a law to fine owners who allowed their dogs to foul public places it met with initial resistance by less responsible dog owners but we now take it for granted that our pavements and parks will be clean. In Bucharest you have to constantly watch where you step, not just because of the street dogs but pets walked by their owners on leads. I was amused by one particular dog on my street though – when he wants to cross the road he always waits at the pedestrian crossing for the lights to change (they make a sound) before trotting across. I became quite fond of Bucharest but I never got used to the constant barking of street dogs in the evening.

CHAPTER TWENTY-FIVE

The European Debate

ROMANIA IS ONE OF the latest countries to join the EU (the other being Bulgaria) and a good place to consider the change from a command to a market economy. Among the people I met there seemed to be no nostalgia for a return to communist rule, on the contrary people seemed very comfortable being part of a modern, democratic society and member of the EU. Taxi drivers everywhere are willing to share their opinions on what is happening in their society. I met many and although they complained about their own politicians and government, I didn't hear any adverse comments about the EU, as you do in Britain. Malcolm found an enterprising man who owned a small fleet of well-maintained Mercedes cars whose drivers dressed smartly and spoke fluent English. They were happy to talk about the changes in their country and one of their taxi drivers, a woman, told me she was proud to be part of this new culture and optimistic about the future. This is a snapshot of public opinion of course – I met only a fraction of Romanians in Bucharest and other cities and was unable to read their newspapers or understand what was being said in television debates.

In Britain there is an ongoing debate as to the merits and demerits of the European Union and particularly Britain's place in it. I now regard myself reasonably well informed about European matters and while I am no apologist for the EU, nor am I convinced of the argument that the United Kingdom should leave it. One of its main achievements is the unity and peace that has been achieved, especially considering events that took place in the first half of the last century. At the same time we can acknowledge our differences - in traditions, national histories, culture and temperament. Britain joined the European Economic Community (as it was then called) in 1973 when the Treaty of Rome was signed. Ted Heath, then Prime Minister, had led the campaign to take us into Europe but in 1974 the Labour Party pledged in a manifesto to allow people to decide if we stayed in. A referendum was held in 1975 - uniquely both Labour Prime Minister Harold Wilson and Conservative leader Margaret Thatcher supported a 'Yes' vote. We all received a brochure outlining the pros and cons of membership and a lot of the debate centred on the fact that the EEC (as it was then called) had ensured peace in Europe. I was one of the 67% of voters who supported the United Kingdom's continued membership and despite its faults would probably do so again in any future referendum unless presented with a better option. I feel both British and European.

The UK, however, remains a nation of 'euro-sceptics' and many have lost confidence in EU membership. There is still debate as to whether we should withdraw, which would, of course, require an Act of Parliament and is unlikely to happen until the government of the day holds a referendum on membership. I'm not convinced that ordinary citizens think too much about the EU, except to lay blame at its door for things they dislike. Most of us are more concerned with the economy, health and education issues but the press likes to whip up anti-European fervour. Some time ago I wrote an article entitled *The good, bad and ridiculous* for the Institute of Consumer Affairs, trying to separate fact from fiction and myth. One example was a newspaper headline *'Brussels slaps a noise order on Scotland'*, announcing that bagpipe players would have to be quiet under health and safety laws. In fact, the proposal was simply aimed at protecting musicians from excessive noise by encouraging the use of special earplugs and sound absorbing material. It seems only negative headlines attract the reader's attention. Good news, such as the EU crackdown on lack of transparency when budget airlines use misleading advertising to sell 'cheap' flights that end up costing more or the successful campaign to bring down the cost of making mobile phone calls from abroad, the introduction of pet passports and compensation when flights are delayed just don't have the same impact.

Further EU enlargement is a thorny subject and opinion is divided as to whether it is a good or bad thing. From its inception in 1957, when six countries formed the European Coal and Steel Community, it now spreads from the west of Ireland to the Black Sea, taking in twenty-seven countries. The expansion into Eastern Europe on 1 May 2004 was the largest to date and welcomed by the West. I used to wonder why Lithuania readily agreed to change one master, the Soviet Union, for another in Brussels, especially as they had so recently gained independence. The answer of course is that being part of the Soviet Union was compulsory –

a referendum was necessary to take them into Europe. It can't be denied that among some older citizens there is nostalgia for the communist past, but I doubt that the communist system of central planning and lack of free movement of citizens and other freedoms is something they would want to return to. Romania and Bulgaria joined in 2007 and five candidate countries are currently working towards membership: Croatia, Macedonia, Iceland, Montenegro and Turkey. In addition, Serbia and Albania have submitted applications and other potential candidates (though they have not applied to join) include Bosnia and Herzegovina and Kosovo. The population (in January 2010) was estimated to be just over five hundred million – many would argue this is large enough and I am veering toward this point of view.

The arguments against enlargement include mass immigration; workers from poor countries taking jobs from richer ones; the subsidies needed for poorer states; lack of achieving integration and the difficulty in so many members being able to reach agreement on policy issues. Supporters say it reunites a continent divided by the Cold War and brings stability and prosperity. They point to the advantages of the single market and that Europe has more weight on the world stage. Despite Britain's reputation for being euro-sceptic, UK governments have been at the forefront of the enlargement process, citing that the single market has removed barriers to trade, offer greater opportunities to British business and benefits to consumers.

A European country that has voted *not* to join the EU is Norway. Along with Switzerland, Lichtenstein and Iceland they are members of the European Economic Area (EEA) and the European Free Trade Association (EFTA), whose members are able to participate in the European single market without joining the EU. The Association is based on the same four freedoms: free movement of goods, persons, services and capital. It promotes free trade and economic integration, has a worldwide network and could provide Britain with an alternative to the EU. I have visited Norway and found that their consumer protection regime has many similarities with Britain and Europe.

What does it actually mean to be European? To help me answer this question I have asked colleagues and friends in the new member states what it means to them. Their answers include: open borders; harmonization of laws and enforcement; freedom; democracy; justice; spirit of enterprise; no artificial barriers; exchange of goods; a passport. A middle-aged Romanian woman I know who runs her own real estate business told me she was not allowed a passport until the collapse of communism and could not travel abroad. She now regularly commutes between Paris and Bucharest. Discussing what life was like under communism, my interpreter Ovidiu, answered my question by removing my spectacles. 'I have decided I want these spectacles and will just take them from you - what do you think about that?' I replied, 'I can't see a thing.' 'That's communism for you' he said. Andrzej, one of my Polish interpreters thought about his answer for a while before saying, 'For me, being a citizen of Europe means I can move to another country without needing to emigrate and I now feel part of a larger family'. He also reminded me that it was not until the French revolution that checkpoints were in fact introduced – before that there were customs points but Europe was without frontiers. It's not such a new idea after all and of course it was Churchill who said 'We must build a kind of United States of Europe'.

For myself, having worked in consumer protection since the 1980s, it has meant better rights for consumers. The EU made a commitment to put consumers at the heart of its policies and has introduced new laws for the protection of European consumers. Membership gives us stronger influence in shaping global action and by removing barriers to trade brings access to fair and competitive markets. That's not to say the EU is a perfect organization. There will always be criticism and debate about its effectiveness and bureaucracy, but during working trips overseas I find it refreshing to see so much optimism, energy and enthusiasm coming from New Europe, where for many citizens looking west has been an inspirational model.

In the summer of 2011, some seven years after Lithuania joined the European Union, I asked Neringa Ulbaite, who now holds the position of Head of Food Products and Recreational Services Division at the State Consumer Rights Protection Authority, for her opinion of the changes that have taken place in her country since Lithuania gained independence in 1990 and the effects of membership of the European Union. She responded as follows:

> Since the restoration of the independence of Lithuania in 1990 our country has been facing a lot of challenges both in the political system and economic development. Lithuania's accession to the EU and NATO in spring 2004 marked the two most important events in Lithuania's history since 1990. Lithuania now enjoys the benefits of free movement of individuals, which creates a lot of possibilities for people to travel, find jobs overseas, participate

in youth exchange programs, etc. However opening of the borders also result in intensive migration increasing since 2004, and unemployment rate remains relatively high in Lithuania due to the closure of many industry sectors. Further structural reforms are needed in areas such as health care, social security and education. The progress of regulatory and administrative reform, the effective use of EU funds and further economic integration within the single market should be the priorities of the State in order to create new jobs and to prevent further migration of young people.

We are proud that in August 2011 Lithuania will host the 37th European basketball Championship 2011, and hope that it will provide a good possibility to promote Lithuania in Europe and present it as a destination offering sightseeing, tourist attractions and cultural heritage.

I believe we all need to make changes in our mentality and to develop more positive and optimistic approach in order to take the opportunities offered by developing society and internal market.

CHAPTER TWENTY-SIX

In the Footsteps of Dracula

THE FIRST OPPORTUNITY to venture out of Bucharest was a private weekend visit to the Saxon city of Brasov when Alan came to visit. In Transylvania the early autumn weather was perfect. The train from the capital took us through stunning scenery and as it was a fairly slow train, it was possible to see something of life in the rural hamlets we passed through. In the countryside farmers and their families were bringing in the harvest, using hand held scythes to cut hay, which they loaded on to a horse-drawn cart, with no mechanical machinery at all. Many of the small farms and houses still draw their water from a well and keep a couple of pigs and a cow for their personal requirements. It's common to see a cow being led from the field and down the main street to the family farm. We waved to elderly ladies dressed in headscarves and colourful aprons selling cheese or honey by the roadside and station platforms. This may be New Europe but the scenes looked vaguely familiar from my childhood. Arriving in Brasov we stumbled upon a music festival taking place in the town square and joined families with young children who were dancing to the music, finding this charming town in the Carpathian Mountains very different to Bucharest. Many Romanians had told me of their desire to live here instead of Bucharest and I can see why. The mountain that looks down upon the town can be reached by cable car or on foot and at the summit large letters spell out the city name visible for miles - inspired, one assumes, by Hollywood. We walked up to it, peering down at Brasov through the letters.

Transylvania of course is forever associated with the fiction and fantasy of Count Dracula and from Brasov we took a short bus ride to Bran, a charming town famous for its castle, the former home of Romanian royalty and certainly worth a visit. The castle has become associated with Bram Stoker's Gothic novel *Dracula* and indeed it does have the necessary pointy turrets and narrow winding corridors one would expect of a vampire's lair. It's a complete myth of course because Dracula is a figure of fiction – a bloodthirsty vampire who preyed upon the innocent and beautiful - and there is no historical record that Vlad the Impaler (who did exist and did terrible things) lived here. In any case, he was a prince of Wallachia, a region to the south, whereas Bran is in Transylvania. This fact does not interfere with Dracula tourism but it's a pity you have to walk through the market selling souvenirs associated with the Dracula legend to get to the castle, though I did buy some hand painted ceramics. I declare an interest in the legend of Dracula because Whitby in North Yorkshire (not far from where I live) inspired Stoker to write the novel in 1897. You will understand why if you have visited St Hilda's Abbey or St Mary's churchyard on the East Cliff. The town provided the setting for three chapters and, like Bran, capitalizes on the legend, describing itself as 'The true home of Dracula', offering the full 'Dracula experience'. Innocent and beautiful young women beware!

Other visits that took me out of Bucharest were work related and required hours of travelling, mainly by road, to reach our venues. The terms of the project required us to deliver a high impact national campaign. I interpreted this to be not just in Bucharest but also the regions, to inform and educate consumers of their rights so that they have the confidence to take action to resolve complaints. We had hoped to start this in the summer months but the mighty machine of Romanian bureaucracy derailed us. Politicians now worked alongside the consumer protection authority and this meant that every brochure I wrote, every public awareness event and all the promotional material for the campaign had to be scrutinized and deliberated over by members of the cabinet – in addition to the civil servants. Creativity often had to give way to fit into the political agenda. TV and radio commercials remained in the 'can' for months before broadcasting could go ahead and my programme of public awareness events was put on hold whilst they checked every detail of proposed tenders. The project had to end in December – there could be no prolongation - and at times it looked like my 'national' campaign would never get further than Bucharest. Summer gave way to autumn, then suddenly the political climate changed again and we had the green light to go ahead.

We went to ten towns and cities, disseminated huge amounts of publicity and promotional material direct to consumers. A contract with Carrefour hypermarkets allowed us to set up exhibition stands in ten of their hypermarkets around the country, another to purchase a stand at three major exhibitions. Dana Maria accompanied me to every promotional event as my Romanian PR expert and organized transport, the exhibition stands and promotional material we took everywhere. She also briefed the media in advance and prepared press packs to give them. A young team of promoters, students recruited by Dana Maria and trained by me, accompanied us. Romanians like to keep things in the family and consequently it was Adina's brother Bogdan who drove us around the country, accompanied by his girlfriend, Andreea Popa, who acted as a promoter. We all wore specially designed T-shirts and caps decorated with our campaign logo. The young promoters in our team always wanted to ask me about life in Britain and the type of awareness campaigns I had done. I told them of the first promotional campaign I had been involved with as a teenager in the Sixties. At that time I was working for a secretarial agency in Newcastle-upon-Tyne who were branching into PR and promotions. They won a contract from the Egg Marketing Board to promote eggs. I was recruited as one of a team of 'Egg Chicks', dressed as chickens and sent round the country during national Egg Week to knock on doors at breakfast time. If the householder answered a simple question correctly they 'won' five Premium Bonds. I was sent to Sheffield, accompanied by another 'chick' and an older woman, a sort of mother hen who drove the car and generally looked after us. She was lucky; she did not have to dress up. Our costumes took ages to get into. First a yellow furry leotard with plumped out breast, plus yellow tights, head cap and webbed feet. It was not easy to walk and we appeared to waddle, no doubt the designer's intention. The campaign slogan was 'Go to work on an egg'. This gave way to many jokes directed at us by the men of Yorkshire, such as laying an egg and what they would like to do with one.

Our promotional tours in Romanian towns were just as manic but at least our outfits raised no comment. None that I could comprehend anyway, as few people spoke English. Those that did were always amazed to find an English woman offering them advice about their consumer rights. 'What on earth are you doing in Romania?' they would wonder and I would call one of the promoters over to explain the object of the promotion, whereupon they would invariably tell me about a problem they had. Campaigns rarely venture into the regions and having an English woman there was even more unusual. At every event we were practically mobbed by consumers, mainly for the linen shopping bags, key holders with a detachable coin for the supermarket trolley, pens, bookmarks and fridge magnets we were giving away, plus the four Pocket Guides I had written about their consumer rights. We positioned our exhibition stand at the checkout exits, allowing us to target most of the consumers in the mall. They were attracted by the free gifts, but also asked for advice about their consumer problems and were genuinely interested in the information contained in the brochures. In small towns we caught the interest of television, radio and print journalists and the supermarket managers brought us coffee and cakes as sustenance. Dana Maria distributed her press packs and spoke to journalists at length about the campaign and what we were hoping to achieve and I would be interviewed, through an interpreter if necessary. She also gave legal advice, which rather worried me but as it was in Romanian it was impossible to know if it was correct. The beneficiaries at the Ministry in Bucharest have offices in most of the regional cities in Romania and their representatives came along to help and take advantage of giving interviews to the media about local issues in consumer protection. More than one of the regional directors rolled their sleeves up and helped to stuff the bags with leaflets. I doubt any of my previous bosses back home would have done the same.

We launched the campaign in the largest mall in Bucharest but thereafter we had to travel long distances, always by car as the budget did not allow for trains or planes and anyway it would have been difficult to transport all the equipment. The night before an event we would agree what time we would need to leave the office, allowing for the fact the cars had to be loaded up with the equipment. I followed these times punctually but was always the first to arrive and open up the office and it was not unusual to wait an hour before anyone else turned up and it could be another hour before we set off. At first I found this annoying, but later tried to follow their relaxed attitude to travel. When the team had assembled and I had my hat and coat on ready to leave, Dana Maria insisted we all sit down at a table to drink coffee together – a Russian tradition she said. On the way to our destination several stops would be made, so they could smoke but also to buy sweets and coffee. When we came out of the shop we would be surrounded by packs of stray dogs. They appeared to be tame but I was not keen to pet them. Dana Maria would buy packets of biscuits to feed them. On long journeys we needed to use the toilet facilities at petrol stations and usually found them to be clean but on one occasion I was horrified to find a stinking open toilet with a hole in the ground. Even Dana Maria was shocked - it was, she said, a 'Turkish toilet'.

 The drive back to Bucharest was the worst part of these campaign events, especially as we were all drained of energy by late afternoon. Once, driving through the Carpathian Mountains in torrential rain, we hit thunder and lightning storms and I feared we might go over a cliff. The roads twisted around the mountain for miles and miles and it was quite frightening sitting in the back of the car, worrying that we might not make it back safely to Bucharest. Suddenly Bogdan screeched to a stop. We were at an 11th century monastery and must all go inside to pay our respects and light candles. The monks who live and pray here wandered around, imposing figures in their long brown robes, oblivious to the pouring rain. The chapel was set among lovely gardens and contained stunning frescoes of saints. It enveloped me with its warmth, even on a cold wet evening. Many religious buildings are cold and forbidding, especially when you are not of their faith, but this was not the case here. My young colleagues and Dana Maria made their devotions and lit candles in the small chapel (on the right for the living but unwell, the left for those departed). I placed a donation in the box but they insisted I make a purchase in the tiny shop, where I bought a wooden bracelet for Hannah. We had a long journey ahead but none of us were in a hurry to leave this sacred place; the atmosphere calmed and embraced us. It was, I agreed, a very special and holy place and I wished we could have come earlier in the day, and in better weather, so that we could have spent more time to look around and meditate. But alas, I was not a tourist, free to wander about and explore the country.

 One of my favourite places on the tour was the city of Sibiu, a charming old town that had received an injection of funding when designated European Capital of Culture. It was money well spent - the

33. Jurmala 2008: Alison, Hannah and Carolyn with a turtle on the Beach

34. Alison and Hannah Borthwick and a grumpy statue in Riga

35. Latvians celebrating Jani Day on 23/24 June – the summer solstice

36. The family: Mark, Carolyn, David, Alison, Alan and Hannah asleep

37. Bucharest 2009: On my way to work across Revolution Square – where Ceauscescu met his downfall in 1989

38. The Atheneum – my favourite building in Bucharest

39. The car park in Bucharest, temporarily transformed into a fragrant garden for the music festival

40. Monument of Revolution commemorating those who died in the Romanian Revolution in December 1989. Locals have described it as an olive skewered on a toothpick!

41. Palace of Parliament, Bucharest – Ceausescu's folly

42. The former Bucharest secret police building, now occupied by the Architects' Union.
A modern structure on top of an old one.

43. Silviu and his new wife - a Romanian Orthodox wedding in Bucharest

44. With Mike Hanson and Malcolm Adams on the office balcony in Bucharest

45. The project team in Bucharest: Dana Maria, CB, Madelina, Adina, Malcolm Adams

46. 1970: CB on the beach in Mamaia, where this journey began

47. 2011: Hannah, aged 7, at Lake Windermere

48. 'I must go down to the sea again' - *back home in Hartlepool*

buildings have been restored to their former glory and there was a beautiful central square decorated with fountains, lots of art and pretty churches, cobbled streets and houses with odd slanted windows that appear to wink at you. We were staying overnight so there was time to appreciate the city. There appeared to be no litter or graffiti, very different from Bucharest, and put the capital city to shame.

After some hair-raising drives and long hours of travel to reach some of the towns in the north it was with some relief that when we went to the southern region of Romania –to Ploesti and Pitesti, both relatively short drives from Bucharest. These towns are more industrialized but the Carrefour hypermarkets were identical to those elsewhere. In Ploesti I learned about *Operation Tidal Wave* – a bombing raid by the American Air Force intended to destroy nine oil refineries, so cutting off Hitler's supply of fuel. The operation took place on what is now called Black Sunday because fifty-three aircraft and over six hundred airmen were lost. Pitesti is part of the Wallachia region; another industrialized city and manufacturing base of the car manufacturer, Dacia. Despite being defined by industry, Pitesti is also a wine making area, producing Stefanesti, and famous for its tulips. It also has the largest mall in Romania, providing plenty of space for our promotion.

We did a second and final promotion in Bucharest. I had hoped this would be the Carrefour in the centre where I shopped and could walk to, but in fact we drove to the outer suburbs of Colentina. This is a poor area and before we had even erected the stands we had big queues forming as soon as they realized we had free material to give away. There was some pushing and shoving, but once we spoke to people and asked them to form an orderly line, they were very polite. It was the right decision to take the promotion to a less prosperous area, where consumers needed the advice and appreciated the bags, key rings etc. The staff at this Carrefour were the most generous, bringing us plates of cakes and flasks of coffee to keep us going.

In addition to the Carrefour hypermarket events, we also took the campaign to three large exhibitions. Two are big annual events held at Romexpro, an international fair complex on the outskirts of Bucharest. We bought space at an agricultural and travel and tourism exhibition and distributed huge amounts of brochures and promotional material. Both gave me an interesting insight to two important areas of revenue for Romania. At Indagra, an agricultural and animal husbandry trade show, I spoke to farmers and those working in the rural community as well as taking time out to look at the cattle, hens, etc. The travel exhibition was a swish affair with hundreds of interesting stalls and entertainment from folk dancers over the two days and food tasting from countries around Europe. By this time we had our TV slots recorded on tape and were able to play the three scenarios of the informed consumer taking action on a monitor. It drew a lot of interest, particularly the 'alter ego', but we agreed that the *Teapa* would have made a better commercial.

Education fairs are popular in Romania, attended by teachers and students in large numbers. It's a showcase for companies to demonstrate new teaching aids for schools. For this event, with young people in mind, we purchased a large quantity of rucksacks printed with the campaign logo. Over the three days of the exhibition we were overwhelmed, not just for the free material but with questions about consumer rights – by teachers as well as students. If we were not to run out of material on the first day we needed a system to ration the rucksacks at least. I didn't want to hand out brochures or bags without trying to teach these young people something about their rights as consumers and went back to the office to design and print a consumer quiz. When I returned I had to fight my way through to our stand, such was the popularity of our message – or rather what we had to give away. I brought order, giving the teacher in charge of a group of students a quiz sheet and asked them to return to the stand after twenty minutes with the answers. When they did I told them about their consumer rights and handed out the rucksacks. It worked well and for the next three days I did more consumer education with young people than I have done in the last few years. The students were extremely polite, and asked lots of relevant questions, the teachers begged me to go to their school and give lessons in consumer rights. A group of 18 year olds were interested in training as market surveillance inspectors and asked for career advice. They all spoke fluent English so I took them off for coffee to talk about their future. They eschewed the rucksack though – it didn't have the right logo. Not cool enough.

I could not have done this alone of course. I was fortunate to have the help of Ovidiu, a young man who helped in the office with translation, acting as interpreter when required. He was a friend of Adina and Madalina, they had been to school together, and I assume he must have been paid for his help – I hope so anyway. After interpreting for me for the first two groups he said, 'Look I know all the questions and answers now so rather than interpret for you, why don't I just do it all in Romanian'. It worked extremely well; Ovidiu is an intelligent and good-looking man with a lovely warm personality and the students looked up at him adoringly as he checked their answers and handed out the rucksacks. I stood by to answer any supplementary questions about consumer advice but I wasn't really needed. With Ovidiu in charge our stand was crowded every day – in fact some of the other exhibitors came along to see what we were doing that made us so popular with teachers and students. Several teachers gave me the address of their school, urging me to visit them to teach consumer education. I wish this educational exhibition had taken place earlier in the year, as I would have liked nothing more than to accept their invitations, but the project was nearing an end and I was committed to the tasks outlined in the terms of reference. I did, however, make a recommendation in my final report that ANPC develop upon the enthusiasm shown by teachers and young people to know their rights, but of course they may lack the resources to do it.

At the end of the project we commissioned another survey from Gallup to assess the effectiveness of the consumer campaign. They conducted the survey in eight of the ten cities where we had delivered the campaign and concluded it had been a 'real success'. Almost half the respondents had heard about the campaign; television was the best medium for making consumers aware of their rights as 84% of those who were aware of the campaign had heard about it through that medium. We had distributed over 500,000 Pocket Guides, 10,000 bookmarks and the same number of linen shopping bags and keyholders, plus large quantities of rucksacks, pens and fridge magnets. It was estimated that we caught the attention at our exhibition stand of 1,000 people at each event.

We had now almost completed our consumer road show but there was one last place I had to visit before leaving Romania. It would be a sort of pilgrimage, to a resort I had come to as a young woman, barely out of my teens. I wondered if the mimosa would smell as sweet in the sand dunes, hoped that the prying eyes of the secret police were long gone and that the hotel bathrooms now had plugs. There would be no football World Cup to watch this time. It was time to return to the Black Sea coast.

CHAPTER TWENTY-SEVEN

Full Circle

THE LAST PUBLIC AWARENESS event was in the Black Sea resort of Constanţa, close to the neighbouring resort of Mamaia. It felt very strange to return to a place I last visited in 1970. Like Romania, I have also changed a lot in those intervening decades, though I like to think the young woman of that time is lurking within. It was apt that Alan was with me on this return trip to the Black Sea. We arrived on Sunday afternoon and checked in to the Simba hotel near the beach. It was modern but the breakfast was in true communist tradition, consisting only of a few small tomatoes, cold boiled egg, curled up cheese slices and very weak coffee. Bogdan and his girlfriend had driven us from Bucharest, Dana Maria, Adina and Madalina came separately. We were celebrating our wedding anniversary and they left us alone - insisting I must have time alone with my husband. 'Light some candles and have romantic moments,' Dana Maria insisted. It was a warm Sunday afternoon and we had a long walk along the beach. At dusk we found a decent restaurant overlooking the sea, reflecting on the four decades that had passed since our first visit to Romania.

Although some progress has been made to improve the infrastructure along the Black Sea coast, the resorts of Constanţa and Mamaia will need a huge injection of capital if they are to compete for tourists with other countries. Dana Maria told me she had been to Bulgaria for a seaside holiday and found the hotels and service there to be far superior compared to Romanian resorts. Cruise ships regularly dock at this ancient metropolis, offloading tourists who only have one day to spend in this corner of Romania. It saddens me that they may not get a good impression of the country.

I have already mentioned Ovidiu, who helped with interpretation, but I had not come across this name before. It was only after visiting Constanţa on the Black Sea that I realized he was named after the poet Ovid, who was banished by Rome to Tomis (as Constanța it was then called) and died there. I saw his statue on Piața Ovidiu, but despite its golden beach the city does not live up to its poetical connections, and is somewhat run down. It is in need of one of the poet's transformations. Ovid may have written about love, seduction and mythological transformations, but in Constanța the abiding influences are of the communist regime not romantic poetry. His namesake, my interpreter Ovidiu, was waiting for an internship and at a loose end so he helped out from time to time on the project. With degrees in law and economics he once explained venture capital and hedge funds to me over lunch, though I can't say I was any the wiser. He is full of all sorts of interesting information, particularly about life under the communist regime of Ceaușescu. He also had a fund of amusing anecdotes and the one I always remember was of an experiment he had seen on National Geographic TV. Three spiders were given a different substance in order to witness how it would affect their ability to weave a web. One was given an ecstasy tablet and went madly round and round, producing no obvious web; the second was given a coffee tablet and wove his web in straight high lines; but the one given chocolate quickly made a perfect web and then mated. It justifies my belief in a daily intake of chocolate, something I seek out in every country I visit. One must have some comfort whilst away from home.

The young Romanian people I came to know— Ovidiu, Adina, Dana Maria, Madalina and others who worked on the project – seem optimistic about the future and the new prospects opened up by membership of the EU. Dana Maria and Adina have set up their own companies to tender for European projects and entrepreneurs are opening new businesses. Madalina is now in Brussels, working for the European Commission. The infrastructure of the country clearly is in a poor condition; there is concern about housing and jobs – two things that were guaranteed under communist rule – and politics are in disarray. As I prepared to leave Romania there was a presidential election with twelve candidates and politicians being accused of corruption. The country has seen many upheavals during the last century and as I left it was in an economic downturn and political crisis. But they have seen worse times, notably in the 1980s, and remain positive about the future.

A year ago I was having second thoughts about participating on this project, but looking back on the year I worked and lived in Romania I have a sense of achievement. It had proved to be as challenging as I imagined. I didn't always find the Romanians easy to work with. They can be hot tempered and lack decision-making skills and this sometimes led to delays in the project, particularly the tendering process. When decisions are taken, those who have no involvement will argue that it's the wrong one and it's likely to be changed over and over again. But I liked their informality and relaxed nature, always ready to sit down to drink coffee, exchange family news, not afraid to speak their mind and have fun. I admire their disregard for rules, whilst hoping they would enforce the law passed by the government in 2009, which banned smoking in restaurants, cafes, pubs bars and clubs. My British reserve and strong work ethic was often at odds with the Romanian hot and quick temper, but this is outweighed by many good things about this country: generous, warm and friendly people who are always ready to relax; families having fun in the park on Sunday; shops that close on Sunday; the way parents always seem to be nice to their children.

I had begun my foray into Eastern Europe in 1970 when I first came to Romania as a newlywed young woman and the country was in the yoke of communism. In 2009 I found Romania to be a liberal and open society, its citizens warm and friendly, eager to be part of this new Europe. I had come full circle.

Olivia Manning, novelist and a close observer of life, said 'I write out of experience'. I have tried to do the same, inventing nothing but simply recording facts, conversations, people and places.

I would not have missed the experience and look upon the work in Romania among the best I have done. Having a generous budget for a public awareness campaign does help of course.

CHAPTER TWENTY-EIGHT

Reflections of a Traveller

Two roads diverged in a wood and I,
I took the one less traveled by,
And that has made all the difference
               (From 'The Road Not Taken' by Robert Frost)

MAKING THE DECISION TO leave a safe job in Trading Standards for the unknown territory of managing a project in Eastern Europe is probably one of the hardest I have had to make. I had faced a similar challenge in the late Sixties when as a naïve nineteen-year-old I relocated to Newcastle-upon-Tyne. For a long time I thought of the northeast as 'Life on Mars' (David Bowie's song being popular at the time). The easy thing would have been to stay in Nottingham, then a vibrant city with plenty of job opportunities. The easy way is safe but uninteresting; sometimes we must choose to do the hard things in life. Looking back I can't help noticing that every piece of work I have done, every project, has challenged me to acquire new knowledge and skills and temporarily leads to a feeling of being out of my comfort zone. Working overseas I have had to overcome problems and I can't say it has been straightforward or easy, but I wouldn't change a thing. The hard things in life shape you and offer personal satisfaction, and frontiers must continually be challenged. When George Mallory was asked why he wanted to climb Mountain Everest, he replied: *'Because it's there'*. I wish I had climbed more mountains.

Most journeys have an obvious starting point and a distinct end. Mine had begun with a holiday to Eastern Europe in 1970, when Romania was under a strict communist regime. After a hiatus of more than three decades I returned and continue to be invited to work in countries aspiring to be part of New Europe. More Balkan countries (Serbia, Bosnia, and Montenegro) have signalled an interest in membership of the European Union and capacity building projects are being awarded to non-European countries such as Armenia and Egypt who want to follow the European model of consumer protection, so it's too early to talk of retirement. In the countries of New Europe, where consumers and suppliers may feel separated by distance, language and tradition, nurturing confidence is an essential ingredient for the Single Market to survive and flourish. Through my work I have met and worked with people of different nationalities and have many friends and acquaintances beyond these shores – people I feel I have a lot in common with, who make me feel at home. But nothing compares to coming back to my English garden, admiring the first daffodils, eating roast beef and Yorkshire puddings, spending time with my family, relaxing with friends whose first language is English and I don't have to think so carefully about the words to use.

My travels as a consumer adviser must, I suppose, come to an end soon, but as yet I have not called time on my career. When I do, it will be with some reluctance, as this voyage has been full of discoveries, of me as much as the places I have visited.

End Notes

The Working Week of a Resident Twinning Adviser

IT'S ALWAYS DIFFICULT trying to describe the nature of my work, particularly when working on long-term projects, as the job encompasses a wide range of tasks. In 2008, whilst living and working in Riga, I wrote an article titled My Working Week, which was published in *Help and Advice*, a bi-monthly newsletter published by the Institute of Consumer Affairs. In it I describe a typical working week of a Resident Twinning Adviser.

On Monday I'm usually awake by 6.30 a.m. and the first thing I do is make a mug of lemon tea (I'm not keen on the local milk). After catching up with the news headlines on BBC World I walk across the park to the Albert Hotel to meet new Short-Term Experts (STE) who will have arrived from Britain the previous evening. Sometimes they are still having breakfast and I join them for coffee as we chat about the work they will be doing over the next five days. We take the trolleybus or tram to the office, a short ride from the centre. I have already purchased their bus tickets since they are unlikely to have small change. Looking after experts is part of the job, especially if it is their first visit. We are fortunate to have an excellent project office, which is modern, spacious and light. Laura, my Latvian assistant, will already have the coffee on and answers any of their questions, offers local information and takes them through our computer systems. Prior to their visit I have sent terms of reference for the work they will be doing and a Welcome Pack giving all the information they need about Latvia and Riga. We have a meeting to plan the week and make appointments with people or organizations they may need to visit. This will usually include a meeting at the Consumer Rights Protection Centre, a short distance away, which has a staff of a hundred, whose duties are similar to that of our Office of Fair Trading and Trading Standards. It is important that we ask CRPC to state their exact requirements and current needs so we can deliver outputs relative to Latvia, not assume that the UK model will work here. I remind experts throughout the week that on Friday they must submit a detailed Report and leave any training material they have prepared so that it can be sent for translation.

THE WORKING WEEK OF A RESIDENT TWINNING ADVISER

Most weeks I have training courses running, requiring a lot of organization and planning before the trainer arrives. UK experts come out to train on a variety of EU Directives: recreational craft, gas appliances, pressure vessels, machinery, child articles and E-commerce. I include a field trip into the training so that local inspectors are given practical skills to supplement the theory – they always want to know how we enforce market surveillance in the UK, not just the legislation. This started when Nick Riordan, a Trading Standards Officer from Hampshire County Council, came out to train Latvian counterparts on the Recreational Craft Directive. On an initial visit he had meetings with CRPC staff and boat sellers to prepare training material and we agreed that he would train for one day and the next take the group to visit a boatyard for an on-site inspection where they would check compliance with the Directive. They return to the training room for a workshop to discuss the results and complete a short test, marked by the trainer. We make it clear that it is not an automatic pass; it tests their understanding of the subject and encourages them to listen and participate fully in the training in order to pass. The format works well and we have followed it for all technical training courses.

The job of Resident Twinning Adviser is an unusual one in that it encompasses project management, planning, responsibility for delivering the objectives, not just to the satisfaction of the European Commission, but also to various Ministries in Riga who scrutinize the work. You need good planning and organizational skills, as well as an interest in people, to do this job. Fortunately it is not necessary to be fluent in Latvian as the project assistant is also my translator and we have a generous budget for interpretation at training seminars - simultaneous or consecutive.

On Tuesday I meet the Director of CRPC and our working group. I may also have a meeting with a trade organization as we are writing guidelines for entrepreneurs, or at an NGO. Every quarter we have Project Steering Committee, attended by senior staff from various Ministries, and Jim Spinks, our Project Leader, presents a detailed report about the work carried out during the previous three months and submits budget expenditure. It is a bureaucratic procedure but right that there should be proper accounting of EU money.

Most evenings I walk home after work, usually accompanied by the experts. Although an hour's walk for me (less for them) I prefer this to the tram as traffic becomes gridlocked from 4.30 p.m. and the journey can take just as long. Also if I have not left the building during the day the exercise and fresh air is welcome. I live in Old Riga, which is popular with tourists and it can be noisy during the summer (especially when invaded by British stag parties!) but my apartment is located in a quiet area facing the river Daugava. Sometimes I join the experts for a meal or go to the opera to see a performance of *Swan Lake* or *Tosca*, performed in a beautiful old opera house. If I've had a tiring day I might just sit on my window seat and watch the sunset. The lights reflect off the river at night and it looks really beautiful; often there are fireworks from the Radisson Hotel on the other side.

Despite daily reminders, on Friday there always seems to be a last minute panic when experts realize they have not completed their report and occasionally I agree they can send it from home. The final task is to make sure they sign a timesheet, which Laura prepares, so that they can be paid for the work. They enjoy the experience so much they often forget they are being paid! It has become a tradition to end the week with a visit to the Skybar. It is the highest point in Riga, on the 26th floor of the Reval Hotel, accessed by an outside glass lift – not good if you suffer from vertigo but the view is great and a glass of Riga sparkling wine or beer goes down well after an intensive week. Some experts are able to fly home on Friday evening, others will return on Saturday morning or stay longer at their own expense to look around the city. I always feel sad when they leave because we have worked closely together during the week – and of course they are returning to their home whilst I remain in Riga.

On Saturday I visit the farmers market and after browsing the stalls I call in at Emihls Gustavs, a famous chocolate shop, for a latte. On Sunday I walk in one of the many parks by the canal or river; in the summer I go out to the beach or countryside and always fit in an opera, ballet or a concert if possible. I make a lot of phone calls on Sunday and rely on Skype to keep me in touch with family and friends via the computer. Weekends at not always solitary - Riga has become a popular weekend destination, thanks to budget airlines flying from several UK airports, and I often have friends and family to visit. I enjoy showing them parts of Riga that ordinary tourists may miss.

I may watch a little TV on Sunday evening – BBC World News or there may be a documentary, classic comedy or costume drama on BBC Prime, but I am usually too tired to concentrate and retire to bed early on Sunday evening, ready to greet new experts the next day and begin a fresh week. I enjoy my job and feel fortunate to have been given the opportunity to work in interesting countries, but the 'ex-pat' life is not for everyone.

In 2006 the European Union celebrated its 50th anniversary. As I travelled around Poland that year I wrote the following A – Z, again published in *Help & Advice*.

A. Aims of the European Union -Peace, prosperity and freedom for its 501 million citizens in a fairer, safer world.

B. BEUC - the European consumers' organization which makes the consumers' voice heard. It defends and promotes the interests of consumers in the EU policy process, contributing expertise on issues that have direct economic or legal consequences for consumers' health, safety and environment.

C. Cross Border Shopping – the single market brings competition and choice; unified laws on Internet shopping protect consumers.

D. Directives – the source of new law. EU Directives are 'directly effective', prescribing policy but not the particular manner of their enforcement in national law.

E. European Commission – the Executive body and civil service of the EU. Proposes legislation to the Council of Ministers and the European Parliament. There are currently twenty-seven Commissioners.

F. Four Freedoms –the free movement of people, goods, services and money.

G. General Product Safety Regulations – producers must ensure that all products intended or likely to be used by consumers are safe.

H. Human Rights – protection of human rights is a general principle of EU law.

I. International protection – the new Consumer Protection Co-operation Regulation gives Consumer Protection authorities new powers to deal with rogue traders in the country where they are based. Each Member State must designate a 'Competent Authority' to enforce cross border infringements of EU laws.

J. Jobs - it is now easy to work in another European country.

K. Kosovo – one of the biggest challenges for the EU is to steer this province to independence.

L. London – said to be Europe's pre-eminent financial centre.

M. Member States – currently standing at 27.

N. Nationalism – many countries feel they have lost this. Member States must give up some of their sovereign powers and cannot unilaterally introduce conflicting law.

O. Openness –EU treaties state any European country can apply to join

if it meets certain conditions.
P. Population of the EU – as of January 2010 it was 501 million.
Q. Queuing – a feature of the communist system, now Eastern Europeans don't have to do it quite so much.
R. RAPEX - the rapid alert system for non-food products. Weekly reports from Rapex ensure that information about dangerous products that have been identified on the market is quickly shared between EU countries.
S. Schuman Declaration - On the 8th of May 1950, Robert Schuman presented his proposal on the creation of an organized Europe to maintain peaceful relations. The 8th May is now designated as Europe Day.
T. Timeshare – the Timeshare Directive brought in additional protection for consumers, for example the prohibition of advance payments before the cooling off period has expired.
U. Unfair Commercial Practices Directive – a new European law that replaced the Trade Descriptions Act.
V. VAT – private individuals in the EU only pay VAT once, in the country where the purchase is made. You don't need to make a customs declaration at the border if it is for your own needs and not for re-sale.
X. Xenophobia – hopefully there will be less of it once national prejudices start to break down.
Y. Yard – the imperial unit of measurement. The European Commission has agreed that Britain can advertise goods in both imperial and metric.
Z. Zagreb - capital of Croatia, likely to be the next country to join the EU.

TEN CONSUMER ADVICE TIPS

1. Shop around and compare prices before you buy – it will save you money.
2. Keep all receipts – just in case you have to return the goods.
3. If goods are defective, return them to the seller and ask for a refund.
4. Read contracts before you sign – there may be hidden clauses.
5. Ignore notices in shops that say 'No refunds in any circumstances'. You still have rights if the goods are faulty or not as described.
6. Be wary of letting doorstep salesmen into your home – and always ask for ID.
7. If you do sign a contract at home (or away from trade premises) you have a short time to cancel if you change your mind.
8. Consider paying for goods from a trader costing over £100 in value by credit card – both creditor and seller have responsibility for any faults or misrepresentations.
9. When shopping on the Internet, mail order or by telephone you have seven days to cancel.
10. Beware of scams – fraudsters have many ways of parting you from your money. Common scams are foreign lotteries that ask you to pay a fee to claim a prize; miracle health cures that have not been tested.

TEN TRAVEL TIPS

1. Make sure you have a valid signed passport.
2. Pay with a credit card – it gives extra protection if the airline or travel company collapses.
3. Travel with a photocopy of your passport.
4. Keep some emergency cash in your suitcase.
5. Don't have any fruit in your bag before arrival at a foreign airport.
6. Buy overseas medical insurance – the European health card only gives you the treatment received free by nationals of European countries. It won't fly you home!
7. Take care when using spinning suitcases.
8. If you buy a 'packaged' holiday that includes transport, accommodation and tourist services you will be protected by the Package Travel Regulations if anything goes wrong.
9. Don't be a target of crime by wearing conspicuous jewellery or clothing.
10. Carry ID (passport, driving licence card) particularly if you are over sixty – in some countries it will give you free travel and admission to museums. Age limits and concessions vary between countries.